As A City Upon A Hill

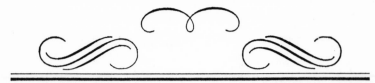

As A City Upon A Hill

The Town in American History

PAGE SMITH

The MIT Press
Cambridge, Massachusetts, and London, England

First published in 1966 by Alfred A. Knopf, Inc., New York

Copyright © 1966 by Page Smith

All rights reserved under International and
Pan-American Copyright Conventions.

First MIT Press paperback edition, June 1973
Manufactured in the United States of America

Library of Congress Cataloging in Publication Data

Smith, Page.
    As a city upon a hill.

    Reprint of the 1966 ed.
    Bibliography: p.
    1. United States—Social conditions.   2. City and
town life.   I. Title.
[HN57.S54   1973]   301.36′0973   73-1956
ISBN 0-262-69042-X

T O

Samuel Eliot Morison

INTRODUCTION

THIS BOOK BEGAN, AS I SUSPECT MANY BOOKS DO, IN A conversation; or a series of conversations. The conversations were with John H. Holmes, now in his ninety-ninth year. Mr. Holmes was born in the town of Mastersville, Ohio, and spent the greater part of his life in the towns of the Middle West. He is a wise and thoughtful man and his reflections upon the role and the meaning of the town in American history first drew my attention to the subject. Mr. Holmes's grandfather fought in the American Revolution and his half brother in the Civil War. He himself has lived through half of our history as a nation, and may thus be taken as a kind of compendium of American history. Although he resides in California and, prior to moving West, lived in many towns from Ohio to South Dakota, he still subscribes to the Mastersville (now Cannotton) newspaper and recently presented me with a copy of the Liberator which had been carefully preserved in the family since the 1850's. In dozens of conversations Mr. Holmes gave me a more vivid and immediate sense of the life of the American town, or that species of it with which he was familiar, than I could have gotten from any number of scholarly volumes on the subject.

As A City Upon A Hill is based on one self-evident proposition—namely, that if we except the family and the church, the basic form of social organization experienced by the vast majority of Americans up to the early decades of the twentieth century was the small town. In the words of Thorstein Veblen: "The country town is one of the great American institutions; perhaps the greatest, in the sense that it has and had and continues to have a greater part than any other in shaping public sentiment and giving character to American culture." * Following from this proposition—that town life affected the outlook and attitudes of most Americans prior to 1910—are a number of what I suppose might best be called at this stage in our investigation of the subject, conjectures and hypotheses. It is only indeed on the self-evident proposition that I am inclined to be dogmatic. And if this proposition can be taken to be true, a corollary would seem to follow: historians have given far too little attention to the role of the town in our history.

Since the historical study of the town (as opposed to particular town histories) is in its infancy (indeed this book presumes to bring it to birth), it naturally follows that there is no attempt here to be, as historians are so fond of saying, definitive. In the first place, I have been highly selective in the towns that I have discussed. I have concentrated on two types of towns, which I have chosen to call "colonized" and "cumulative," and in describing their respective characters I have perhaps stressed what seemed to me their differences, particularly in origin, more than their equally notable similarities. I have paid very little attention to the Southern town, in part because the presence of a large number of Negroes in Southern communities makes them to a degree unique. Beyond that, the secondary materials in the form of histories of Southern towns (as distinguished from sociological studies) are notably scarce.

I have moreover said relatively little about the towns of the Far West. The mining towns that sprang into existence to exploit some extractive mineral—gold or silver or lead— were for the most part too ephemeral to leave any enduring mark in our history. Colorful and dramatic, their importance was peripheral to the story of the town. The same

* "The Country Town," *The Portable Veblen*, Max Lerner, ed. (New York: Viking Press; 1961), p. 407.

could be said for most cattle and lumbering towns, although there are of course important exceptions.

I mention these omissions not to disarm criticism (although, of course, I should be very glad to do that) but to make clear how preliminary an excursion this is and how tentative are most of its conclusions. I suppose it could properly be said that I have tried in the pages that follow to develop a language and a series of concepts in terms of which the role of the town in American history can be more fruitfully investigated and discussed.

I wish to thank those who over a good many years now have read and criticized this manuscript in one or the other of several versions. My first debt, as I have indicated, is to John H. Holmes. My friend Joseph Botond-Blazek, as my graduate research assistant, helped very materially to give this work whatever shape it may have. Leo and Ida Gershoy read the manuscript and made invariably discerning criticisms. Among those who performed similar good services were Douglass Adair, Eugen Rosenstock-Huessy, Robert Winter, Sarah Hogan, and Elizabeth Calciano. I would like also to thank Dianne Norris, who guided the manuscript through final revisions and performed many tedious editorial chores with notable patience and skill.

PAGE SMITH

February 1966

CONTENTS

As A City Upon A Hill

I

The Covenanted Community

THE AMERICAN SMALL TOWN found its original and classic form in New England. From this seedbed a multitude of new communities spread out across the nation. By no means do all American towns bear the Puritan imprint; yet here was the archetype and, muted or modified as it might become in every particular re-creation, the earliest New England towns reveal themes which persist to the present day. At the heart of the Puritan community was the church covenant, forming it, binding it, making explicit its hopes and its assumptions.

On March 29, 1630, the ship *Arabella* sailed from Southampton, England, bearing a company of Puritans to the shores of New England. During the course of the voyage John Winthrop, "the Brave Leader and Famous Governor," wrote a tract for the soon-to-be-founded community. His "Modell of Christian Charity," was conceived as a guide for the Puritan adventurers.

The group of devout men and women on board the *Arabella* were undertaking the most extraordinary colonizing venture of modern times. A number of the company were Englishmen of substance and importance who had compacted to establish a "Bible Commonwealth." John Winthrop knew of at least some of the hazards that lay ahead of the little band. The group, despite its unity of purpose, was a heterogeneous one composed of Puritans from different communities and from different levels of English society. Indeed some were not Puritans at all but orthodox Anglicans unaffected by Puritan ideals.

There were few historic precedents for what the Puritans of the Massachusetts Bay Company were attempting to do. They wished to form a new kind of community dedicated to certain common articles of faith. This in itself was revolutionary. The communities of western Europe had had long growth through the centuries, springing up around episcopal sees, fortress towns, market centers, or trading junctures. Since the last decade of the fifteenth century the Old World powers had been establishing colonies in the New World, and these settlements were in a sense communities. But they were communities much like those of the Old World, extensions of the consciousness and the trading interests of the homeland. They were collectives, groups of traders, merchants, adventurers, administrators, colonists—a conglomeration of individuals who would in time develop communities of a kind, taking on form in response to external pressures, to environment, to their function within an imperial system.

Virginia had been settled in 1607, and after years of appalling hardship the colony had put down roots. The Jamestown enterprise had scarcely been a flourishing one at first, but it endured and slowly grew. Human material had been poured in with incredible prodigality and society had begun to develop a tentative form—a plantation economy based on servile labor.

In 1620 the Pilgrims had founded their Separatist colony at Plymouth, a different type of community from Jamestown—close-knit, devout, its settlers sharing the same ideals, the same theology, working out the colony's destiny with transcendent courage, resourcefulness, and determination. But Plymouth's significance was symbolic rather than practical.

In comparison with the previous colonies the Puritan venture differed radically. Far more ambitious, more self-conscious, representing another, higher stratum of English society, it presumed no less than to establish a *New* England in the wilds of the American continent. Winthrop was keenly aware of the novelty of the undertaking—that Massachusetts Bay sought to be a new community on a new scale. This was no miscellaneous collection of adventurers, craftsmen, farmers; it was a covenanted community, existing under a commission from God. So Winthrop turned his attention to the problems of such a community: how it was to be set up, how ruled, how shaped to God's purpose.

It was God's intention, he wrote, that "every man might have need of other, and from hence they might be all knit more nearly together in the bonds of brotherly affection."

Winthrop said further:

> In regard of the more near bond of marriage between Him and us, wherein He has taken us to be His after a most strict and peculiar manner, which will make Him the more jealous of our love and obedience. . . . When God gives a special commission He looks to have it strictly observed in every Article. . . . Thus stands the cause between God and us. We are entered into a covenant with Him for this work. We have taken out a commission, the Lord has given us leave to draw our own Arti-

cles . . . but if we shall neglect the observation of these Articles . . . and . . . shall fall to embrace this present world and prosecute our carnal intentions, seeking great things for ourselves and our posterity, the Lord will surely break out in wrath against us; be revenged of such a perjured people and make us know the price of a breach of such a covenant.

The only way to avoid this shipwreck, according to Governor Winthrop, was to follow the counsel of Micah,

To do justly, to love mercy, to walk humbly with our God. For this end, we must be knit together in this work as one man. . . . We must uphold a familiar commerce together in all meekness, gentleness, patience, and liberality. We must delight in each other, make others' conditions our own, rejoice together, always having before our eyes our commission and community in the work, our community as members of the same bond. . . . We shall find that the God of Israel is among us . . . when He shall make us a praise and glory that men shall say of succeeding plantations, "the Lord make it like that of NEW ENGLAND." For we must consider that we shall be as a city upon a hill. The eyes of all people are upon us, so that if we shall deal falsely with our God in this work we have undertaken, and so cause Him to withdraw His present help from us, we shall be made a story and a by-word through the world.

Such is the nature of the covenanted community. It is composed of individuals bound in a special compact with God and with each other. The ties extend vertically within the society, uniting the classes and the society to God. This community, so covenanted, was the unique creation of New England Puritanism. It found an ideal social form in the township, modeled on the English original. Adopted self-consciously by the Puritans, it became the matrix into which innumerable communities were poured.

Indeed, one of the most important attributes of the

covenanted community was that it could reproduce itself almost to infinity once its essential form had become fixed. Each new community was simply a congregation produced by fission from the old community. As such it stood in the same relation to God as did its parent community. There was no suggestion of subordination. It lay in the power of two or three faithful members to establish the nucleus of a new covenanted community.

The covenanted group understood intuitively that its life depended on preserving the delicate and complex structure of community life. It was only a common faith, a shared covenant, that held the community together, that preserved it from disintegration. Old World communities had been in existence for generations. They could be taken for granted by those who lived within them. Life was ordered and structured; towns had assumed a pattern that seemed as stable as nature itself, living in a symbiotic relationship with the surrounding country. But in New England everything around them reminded the settlers of the precarious, man-made, consciously fashioned character of their communities. There were no ancient walls suggesting continuity and stability midst flux; no marketsquare stones worn by countless feet to give a reassuring sense of permanence. Instead the insatiable wilderness encompassed the colonists, reaching westward beyond imagining, a fearsome, implacable menace. The physical dangers were ever present and the Puritans' belief in God's direct and continual intervention made them morbidly sensitive to the natural hazards of fire, pestilence, and storm.

But the external pressures, although they increased the strains and tensions within the covenanted communities, were not as severe as the psychological pressures. These came from a sense of vulnerability, from fear of English intervention, of disintegration, of failure to fulfill the terms of the covenant. The individual had to be concerned not only with his own behavior but with that of the total community. One's own sins imperiled the group; one could, by failing to observe the stern demands of the covenant, bring down God's wrath upon one's neighbors as well as oneself. In such a crucible was the spirit of the covenanted community forged, wracked by anxiety and yearning, tormented by self-doubt, exalted by hope, cemented by faith.

In Martin Buber's words, the true community is "a community of tribulation, and only because of that is it a community of spirit; it is a community of toil, and because of that is it a community of salvation. . . . They are communities only if they prepare the way to the promised land through the thickets of this pathless hour. . . . A community of faith truly exists when it is a community of work."

Such were the Puritan communities. Their members were from the first involved in a "society of expectation" that looked, not backward to an older tradition but ahead to the final establishment of a utopian Christian community. Living in a chronic state of crisis, particular communities needed a mechanism to relieve the anxieties created by the crisis situation and by individual and group failures to meet the standards that all professed. The covenant stated in explicit terms the expectations of the community; public confession and repentance provided an avenue of redemption for "delinquent saints," and at the same time served as a common reaffirmation of the covenant itself.

"The real essence of community," Buber has written, "is to be found in the fact, manifest or otherwise, that it has a center. The real beginning of a community is when its members have a common relation to the center overriding all other relations. . . ." [1] The covenant performed just such a function. It was not a vague theological formulation but a specific compact, signed by all communicant members of the church, stating their expectations as members of

[1] Will Herberg, ed.: *The Writings of Martin Buber* (New York: Meridian Books; 1956), p. 129.

a Christian community that was, indeed, hardly distinguishable from a utopian religious society.

The covenant of Braintree, Massachusetts, drawn up at
the time of settlement, was typical. In it the colonists
confessed themselves "poor unworthy creatures, who have
sometimes lived without Christ and without God in the
world . . ." With God's help they meant to "renounce the
devil, the wicked world, a sinful flesh, with all the covenants of Anti-Christian pollution wherein sometimes we
have walked, and all our former evil ways . . . and we
give up ourselves also to one and another by the will of
God . . . and we also manifest our joint consent herein
this day in presence of this assembly, by this present our
public profession, and by giving to one another the right
hand of fellowship." [2]

When the town of Hampton Falls, New Hampshire,
was founded early in the eighteenth century, its settlers
drew up a similar document stating:

> We whose Names are hereunto Subscribed, Appre-
> hending ourselves called of god to joyn Together in
> Chh. Communion: In humble dependence on free
> grace for Assistance & Acceptance, *We do this Day* In
> the presence of God, his Angels & This Assembly
> Avouch the Lord to be our god, and the God of our
> children wch we give unto him. . . . Promising y^t
> by the help of his Spirit & Grace to draw unto
> God . . . As our Choisest good, And to ye Lord
> Jesus X^t as our Prophet, Priest & King, by faith and
> Gospel obedience As becometh his Cov^t People for
> Ever *Making Att* all times, The holy word of God the
> rule of our faith and Practice.
>
> *We do also give* ourselves one unto another as a
> Chh. of X^t In all the ways of his worship, According
> to ye holy Rules of his word *promising* in Brotherly

---

[2] Charles Francis Adams: *Three Episodes of Massachusetts History*
(3 vols.; Boston and New York: Houghton; 1892), II, 749.

Love faithfully to watch over one Another's Souls, *And to Submit* our Selves unto the Decipline of X^t in ye Chh.[3]

A later and more literate covenant drawn up in 1772 by the congregation of Bluehill, Maine, affirmed that the signers did "covenant together in faith and love, and promise in love to watch over one another, and by all means in our power to promote the honor of Christ, and the peace and happiness of the whole Church." [4]

Though varied in phraseology and sometimes crudely and ungrammatically expressed, the covenant was thus a most positive contractual commitment between the members of the church, who, at least in the first century of New England history, made up the community itself. In addition to the public admonition, confession, and exculpation of sinners, many communities periodically renewed their covenants in ceremonies of extraordinary power and solemnity.

In 1861, long after such cities as Boston and Hartford had become centers of religious liberalism, the members of the Congregational Church of Hartford, Vermont, renewed their covenant, declaring: "We acknowledge to a great delinquency throughout this church in respect to Christian conduct and example, whereby the cause of Christ has been much dishonored." Gossip, dancing, and "a lack of Christian integrity in business engagements" were among the failings that members recognized and sought to purge themselves of.[5]

In the Western communities colonized by New England Congregationalists, Presbyterians, and Methodists, the

[3] Warren Brown: *History of the Town of Hampton Falls, New Hampshire* (Concord, N.H.: Rumford Printing Co.; 1900–18), p. 22.
[4] Mary Ellen Chase: *Jonathan Fisher, Maine Parson, 1768–1847* (New York: The Macmillan Company; 1948), p. 74.
[5] William Howard Tucker: *History of Hartford, Vermont* (Burlington, Vt.: Free Press Association; 1889), p. 230.

settlers, down almost to the end of the nineteenth century in some areas, drew up their own covenants imitating the forms they had followed in their native towns.

With the rise of competing sects in the New England settlements, the relation of the church covenant to the life of the community changed. Where a town contained Congregationalists, Baptists, Methodists and, as time went on, a number of smaller, radical offshoots, the covenant of a particular church, or of all the churches together, could not play the same role that it had when the town was religiously homogeneous. Yet the towns struggled ceaselessly to discover substitutes for the primitive covenant. They made determined and often desperate efforts to find a cause, an issue, an institution, or a social form to which they might adhere and which would give them a sense of unity and coherence amid a general chaos that was often physical (in the form of only partly subdued forests or prairies) and social (in the form of a society whose values and institutions were changing rapidly under the pressure of industrialization and the growing dominance of the cities).

What has hardly been understood in the American story is that although people could have been placed physically on the soil, in the absence of true communities we would have witnessed the re-creation of a system of European peasants and landlords. Every previous frontier had been subdued by some form of social organization representing a variation of the Roman mark: in England, the palatinates along the Scottish and Welsh borders; in colonial Spain, the encomienda; in New France, the habitant on his feudal allotment.

The frontiersman, and behind him the farmer, formed the advance guard of westward expansion, but the appropriation and organization of America's vast interior space was accomplished primarily through the small town, appearing in its archetypal form as the covenanted community, and re-enacting that covenant with the establishment of every new town.

The original colonists had to overcome two formidable obstacles. The first was an alien wilderness that threatened to reduce them to little more than features of the natural landscape, warped from their human shape by the struggle for bare survival; the other, more subtle, less tangible hazard was the temptation to adopt forms of common life that would be essentially static and protective. The covenanted community proved to be the ideal form. It was intensely communal in that it turned inward toward the interior spiritual life of the community; it was, however, remarkably dynamic, creating surpluses of human energy that were discharged unceasingly against an intractable environment.

What has been said of the covenanted community applies of course most specifically to New England and, to a lesser degree, to the Middle Colonies. The covenanted community also appeared in the Southern colonies but usually in the form of enclaves, of isolated communities, often the offspring of the covenanted communities of New England.

The Virginia colony, for instance, offers an instructive contrast to its neighbors to the north. We can find much evidence to suggest that individual Virginians were often quite as pious as individual Puritans. Early Virginia laws were as ruthless as those of New England in dealing with heretics, blasphemers, and dissenters. The real difference between the two groups of settlers was that the Virginians never formed a covenanted community. The Virginia colonists constituted a collective in the early years of the settlement, and they achieved the form of a general community as the result of adaptation to environment and of imitation of the model of English country life. In this the Virginians had their own remarkable success. If it can be assumed that every group of individuals finds a way to form itself into a pattern of community life, it would seem that politics and the county law courts constituted the nucleus of the Virginia community. But the Virginia enterprise, remarkable as its political achievements were, lacked the extraordinary fecundity of its northern neighbors. It could export individuals but not communities; by the early decades of the nineteenth century it had exhausted its creativity and no longer played a vital role in the life of the nation.

The remarkable productivity of New England was evident, however, for another seventy-five years in towns spread across the country from Ohio to the Pacific Coast.

The covenanted community of New England represented the most intense community experience of modern times. Perhaps it was only in the primitive Christian communities of the second and third centuries or in the kibbutzim of present-day Israel that individuals have lived under such severe and awesome imperatives. The men and women whose characters were formed in these towns and villages passed on to their children and grandchildren their own obdurate and intractable Puritanism, their own fervent sense of the "holy" nature of community life. The secularization of the town's religious values gave American liberal reformism much of its impetus and vitality; the town preserved, despite the weakening of its ancient faith, its emphasis on personal responsibility, on education as an avenue to salvation, on the "common good." It preserved also its utopian expectations of an earthly paradise that, if no longer religious, was nonetheless devoutly anticipated. Moreover the covenant manifested itself on two levels, one local, the other national.

At the time of the American Revolution the communities of the thirteen British colonies were united in a national covenant. Men who had been members of true communities had the strength of will to speak for the greater community. But without the earlier steps by which communities had been created, cemented, proliferated, without losing their initial vitality, the delegates to Continental Congress would have had no voices, could have touched no common chord and aroused no certain response. The slow conquest of political rights, the hardening of colonial temper under pressure from Great Britain, the growing rivalry of mercantile systems—none of these things, alone or together, could have produced the American Revolution. Without the construction of self-conscious, articulate communities that rose far above the organic communal life of most European towns and villages, the colonists would never have developed the power of common action. In a brief hundred and fifty years, and in the face of extraordinary mobility of movement, communities that were unique in history had grown up, and the psychology of a people had taken from them a peculiar and distinctive stamp. All resources had been mustered to bring into existence this delicate form and to protect it against erosion. Without the matrix of the covenanted community the colonists would simply have formed collectives; that is, they would have divided up into units of individuals, grouped within certain physical areas, directed by external powers and shaped largely by circumstances and by environment. In Martin Buber's words, the healthy nation is not built up "out of individuals, but only of small and even smaller communities: a nation is a community to the degree that it is a community of communities." [6]

This "secondary community," the nation, is a superstructure of ideas and ideals, of common aspirations sustained by "the mystic chords of memory" which bind the primary communities into a larger national community. The symbols of the secondary community are crude and highly simplified summaries of those of the primary communities, for the life of the primary community is concrete while that of the secondary community is abstract; it is from the primary communities that the secondary communities draw their life and meaning. In America the primary covenanted community was expressed concretely in particular small towns; the secondary covenanted community abstractly in the federal Constitution.

[6] Herberg, ed.: *Writings*, p. 130.

The Covenanted Community

Certainly all national entities are composed of primary and secondary communities, but the American experience is nonetheless unique. Other modern nations, almost without exception, have taken form over a long period of time during which their primary communities have had a slow, organic growth. In America the self-conscious creation of the complex social form of the true community was made possible by the covenant and its later substitutes.

The framers of the Constitution were engaged in drafting a secular covenant, and the indispensable prelude to this covenant was a common spirit, a unity of interest and affection greater than any apparent divisions. The secondary community was embodied in a formal covenant that took on the character of holy writ. There have of course been other written constitutions in modern times, but it seems safe to say that none has been the object of general worship to such a degree. The federal Constitution put the seal on the greater community and every assault on the Constitution was at once interpreted as a blow at the life of the community. The sensitivity of the secondary community to attacks on the Constitution was the counterpart to the sensitivity of the primary community to attacks on is "covenant," since the fabric of the Constitution was just as fragile as the existence of the covenanted community itself. Because everyone sensed that the Constitution was in a way miraculous, a kind of political trompe l'oeil, the nation reacted promptly, and often violently, to dangers which seemed to threaten it. If it had been dissolved by the acid of skepticism, the primary communities, with the passage of time less and less closely bound by the covenant, would themselves perhaps have disintegrated.

The aura of sanctity that surrounded the Constitution lasted until the attacks of Charles A. Beard and his followers, who, smashing the ark of the covenant, revealed it as after all a human document. Historians of the Beard school, scornful of the excessive claims made for the Constitution and its framers, have argued that the Articles of Confederation were quite adequate for the purposes of government since what mattered was not so much a particular governmental form but rather the existence of certain common ideals and aims in the country as a whole. These apologists for the Articles rightly perceive that there was no magic in the Constitution that could have brought into being the unanimity vital to its success. But they go too far in their reaction to the Constitution as national myth. The Articles of Confederation *were* inadequate; the federal Constitution was far superior as an instrument of government. It could, to be sure, only ratify a consensus that already existed, but it could and did allow for the development of new potentialities within American society, while preserving order and maintaining a certain level of common justice.

The secondary covenanted community, having survived the terrible test of the Civil War, has endured relatively unshaken down to the present day. But over the last seventy-five years we have witnessed the steady decay of the primary covenanted communities—the small towns —which have nourished and been subsequently overshadowed by the great metropolitan centers of the United States.

It is this drama—the rise and decline of the small town in America—that will be the subject of the chapters to follow.

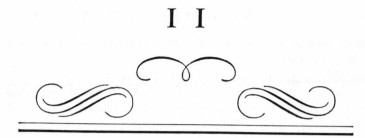

I I

Types of Towns

T HE COMMUNITY patterned on the New England town was perhaps the most important, but certainly not the only, type of town. There were for instance many communities not of New England origin that arose around a covenant of one kind or another, and there were others that developed without the "common core" represented by some form of the covenant.

In terms of their initial settlement, American towns can be divided into two general categories: those that were colonized as towns by relatively homogeneous ethnic and religious groups, and those, not the result of any prior plan, whose growth was cumulative and often fortuitous.

In this chapter we are concerned primarily with colonized towns. Long neglected by historians, who have been inclined to assume that American towns have had exclusively economic origins, the colonized towns have been far more numerous and far more important than historians have recognized.

Although all were founded upon some version of the covenant, there were four or five major types of colonized towns. First, there were those colonized from a home town or county. This was the origin of most colonies that emigrated from New England, New York, Pennsylvania, Maryland, and Virginia in the late eighteenth and the early nineteenth century. Another type of colonized town drew its members from scattered communities in many states and asked only that they subscribe to a common faith or a common ideal. Springdale, Iowa, a Quaker town, was such a community, settled by emigrants from a dozen states. Salem, Iowa, and Newport, Indiana, were other Quaker towns whose inhabitants came from many different towns.

A variation on towns colonized by a religious group is found in the story of "Aton," Indiana. This community was established by a company of Spiritualists from western New York State who believed in democracy, spiritualism, and free love. Newell Sims, in his study "Aton," estimated that as late as 1865 "nine-tenths of the population were Spiritualists and given to free-love." The town acquired a lurid reputation in the state as a "hot-bed of infidelity and vice." Preachers of various denominations were repeatedly driven from the town until a hardy Methodist minister finally established a toehold there. Mass conversions followed, and when Sims made his study in 1910 the church had become "the most dominant social force in Aton, leading reforms, promoting improvements, and directing pleasure." The town was the most rigidly orthodox in Indiana with three fifths of its citizens estimated to be in regular attendance at church. Of the community's original trinity of spiritualism, democracy, and free love, only the devotion to democracy remained. Aton, in reversing the usual progress of the colonized town from strict orthodoxy to liberalism, offers an engaging example of a secular covenant which became, in time, intensely religious.

But religion, or some aberrant form of it such as spiritualism, was not the only selective factor in determining the character of the town. Politics was almost as important, and although politics generally operated in conjunction with religion, there were significant variations. Pioneers from Rutland County, Vermont, who settled in Illinois in the 1830's were staunch Congregationalists and Whigs (later Republicans), while a nearby town, largely populated by emigrants from Addison County, Vermont, preserved its Democratic affiliations.

By the 1830's antislavery sentiment became another selective factor of importance. Indeed as early as 1794 a Presbyterian minister from Bourbon, Kentucky, attempted to secure a portion of the Virginia Military Tract with the hope of settling on it two of his congregations who wished to be free of slavery. A number of Midwestern communities were founded by Southern Presbyterians, Quakers, and Methodists who were anxious to avoid the incubus of Negro servitude.[1]

Another type of colonized town was the foreign community. A typical town was that of Zeeland, Michigan, settled by emigrants from the Dutch island of Zuid Beveland, who, involved in a schism in the Reformed Church, signed articles of association, agreeing to move en masse to America.[2] Great numbers of Swedes, Germans, and Dutch followed such a course, and Bohemians, Poles, and Russians came in lesser numbers to similar communities.[3]

Still another type of town established according to a

[1] James Bradley Finley: *Autobiography of Reverend James Bradley Finley, or Pioneer Life in the West*, W. P. Strickland, ed. (Cincinnati; 1858), p. 100.

[2] Henry S. Lucas: "A Document Relating to the Founding of Zeeland, Michigan, in 1847," *Michigan History Magazine*, XII (1928), pp. 99–107.

[3] Rudolph Leopold Biesele: *The History of the German Settlements in Texas, 1831–1861* (Austin, Tex.: von Boeckmann-Jones Press; 1930); Robert Ingersoll Kutak: *Story of a Bohemian-American Village* (Louisville, Ky.: Standard Printing Co.; 1933).

preconceived plan were the colonies sponsored by railroad companies seeking to turn their state or federal land grants into hard cash. The railroads frequently recruited foreign settlers to take up townsites along their right-of-way and, in addition, beat the bushes for native-born American settlers, who although they came less frequently as coherent groups established many towns under the aegis of the railroads or their land companies.[4] John H. Holmes, who worked as agent for an Iowa railroad at the end of the nineteenth century, recalled that the best prospects for settlers were middle-class, middle-aged men who had enjoyed moderate success in their own communities. If a substantial man could be lured from an existing community, "then the agent went back and worked that community and you built a new community around this man. There were many communities that were really a transplanting of former communities." [5] When the Illinois Central began its colonizing activities along the Chicago branch in 1850 there were ten settlements in the vicinity of its route, but twenty years later forty-seven towns had sprung up, of which a number had been established by the agents of the railroad.[6]

Perhaps the most dramatic of the colonized towns were those designed as experiments in communal living. In many of these some form of millennial religious expectation was the center of the community's life and the reason for its existence. Immigrant groups, often coming directly from the homeland, established a number of such communities.

The secular communist communities, of which the Fourierist phalanxes were most typical, were founded for the most part by middle-class American intellectuals re-

[4] Paul Wallace Gates: *Illinois Central Railroad and its Colonization Work* (Cambridge, Mass.: Harvard University Press; 1934), pp. 170, 188.

[5] Tape-recorded interview with John H. Holmes. Henceforth referred to as J. H. Holmes.

[6] Gates: *Illinois Central.*

volted at the waste, crassness, and greed of the industrial age.

The degree of communism attained by religious and secular groups varied from community to community as did the groups' longevity. Some lasted a few months, others for more than a hundred years. With few exceptions the secular experiments were short-lived, the most tenacious phalanx lasting but fifteen years while the average life of some twenty communities was little over a year. The religious groups are of special interest because they show in extreme form many of the characteristics of the covenanted community. Their ability to survive suggests that there was a direct relation between the community's persistence and the degree of its original commitment to some form of the covenant. The communities which practiced religious communism had, like the covenanted communities of New England, a compact to which they bound themselves, and, with very few exceptions, they made use of public confession, repentance, and forgiveness.

One of the earliest of such groups was Ephrata Community, started in 1728 by Dunker (German Baptist Brethren) schismatics. The Shakers who landed in America in 1774 believed in "Virgin Purity, Christian Communism, Confession of Sin, and Separation from the World." Their covenant declared that "whatever is contrary to the pure Christ spirit or virgin character must be brought to the light, and confession made thereof to God in the presence of a confidential witness." Despite its requirement of celibacy, the sect showed remarkable tenacity. In its heyday it included twenty-seven communities numbering over five thousand members and some groups survived well into the present century.

The Harmony Society was started in Württemberg in 1757. In 1803 a group of Rappites, named for their leader, George Rapp, established themselves at Harmony, Pennsylvania, where they thrived. A traveler, revisiting the colony, reported its progress in the following words:

We were struck with surprise and admiration at the astonishing progress in improvements and the establishment of manufactories which this little republic has made in the period of five years. . . . And this arises from their unity and brotherly love, added to their uniform and persevering industry. They know no mercenary view, no self-interest, except that which adds to the interest and happiness of the whole Community. All are equally industrious, for an idler has no companion. If any should fall into bad practices of idleness or intoxication he is kindly admonished by the head of the Family, backed by the countenance and wishes of all the rest; but if he is found incorrigible he is excluded from the Society; so that there is no opening for the practice of vice and immorality.[7]

The Rappites believed in the imminent second coming of Christ, acknowledged no creed but the Bible, and believed in the final restoration of this earth to the condition of paradise. Among their tenets was the belief that sexual intercourse, even in marriage, was wrong and that those who abstained would have the greatest happiness in the hereafter.

The Owenite communities, inspired by the English reformer Robert Dale Owen, enjoyed a brief but remarkable vogue in the 1820's. Owen's own colony at New Harmony, Indiana, which was purchased from the Rappites, attracted over 900 settlers in a few months. In the next two years secular communistic societies, tracing their origin directly or indirectly to Owen, were founded at Allegheny, Pennsylvania; Blue Springs and Forestville, Indiana; Coxsackie, Haverstraw, and Franklin, New York; Nashoba, Tennessee; Kendal and Yellow Springs, Ohio, and a half dozen other spots, but all were defunct within a few years of their establishment.

[7] William Alfred Hinds: *American Communities and Co-operative Colonies* (Chicago: C. H. Kerr & Company; 1908), p. 39.

A more enduring enterprise was that launched by John Humphrey Noyes of Putney, Vermont. Noyes's followers established themselves in two principal commnuities at Oneida, New York, and Wallingford, Connecticut. They believed "that the Second Coming of Christ is a past event, and hence that his true disciples are living in a dispensation of grace, in which personal, spiritual communication with him and his risen church is possible." From this it followed that man was capable of earthly perfection.

The life of the communities centered around "mutual criticism," a form of public confession and repentance. One observer wrote:

> The weekly meetings for criticism were conducted in the spirit of deep sincerity and faithfulness, and though none shrank from the ordeal all felt that "judgment was laid to the line and righteousness to the plummet." The general character was subjected to close scrutiny, and habits, manners and the spiritual and social state passed under crucial analysis. A good margin was always left for praise, and the kind, impersonal way in which criticisms were given caused but temporary soreness.[8]

The so-called Hopedale Community was formed in 1841 by some thirty individuals from various parts of Massachusetts. Its creed was "supreme love to God and man—that love which 'worketh no ill' to friend or foe." Hopedale aimed to be a miniature "Christian republic," and was in this sense a revival of the earlier covenanted community. Its founder, Adin Ballou, saw in it "the seedling of the true democratic and social republic, wherein neither caste, color, sex nor age, stands proscribed, but every human being shares justly in 'liberty, equality, and fraternity.'" Hopedale was, to Ballou, "a missionary society,

[8] Ibid., p. 74.

for the promulgation of New Testament Christianity, the reformation of the nominal church, and the conversion of the world." "Here," he wrote, "property is pre-eminently safe, useful and beneficent. It is Christianized." Soon Ballou added to the community life "monthly convocations . . . designed to consider and take action upon such instances of more or less reprehensible conduct on the part of the members as might have been made public, to correct existing abuses, to allay strife and bitterness, to reconcile alienated feeling, to restore harmony when broken or disturbed, and to apply the proper remedy to all known offenses and misdemeanors." The sessions were designed as "fraternal tribunals for obtaining judgment upon overt acts of folly and wrong, and at the same time schools for mutual discipline and culture in the things that pertain to the Kingdom of God." The covenant of Hopedale Community was a mid-nineteenth-century version of the expectations of the Bible Commonwealth; the town's recruits were the sons and daughters of the Puritans.[9]

Amana, "the Community of True Inspiration," was colonized by German Pietists who, after a brief period in New York State, established themselves in Iowa in 1855 as a communistic society, stressing plain living and withdrawal from the world. The *Untersuchung*, a general examination of the spiritual condition of all the inhabitants, was a regular aspect of the community. Members were called on periodically for "personal confessions of faults and sins" and exonerated or cast out by their fellows.[1] Amana, like many such religious communities of foreign born, showed a remarkable capacity to survive, but like its counterparts it did so at the cost of all contacts with the outside world. It remained isolated and exclusive, rejecting

[9] Ibid., pp. 176, 190, 234–5, 238–9.
[1] Berta Maud Shambaugh: *Amana That Was and Amana That Is* (Iowa City, Iowa: State Historical Society of Iowa; 1932), pp. 47–50.

any but the most elementary education for its members and renouncing all desire to reform the world.

Various communities of Old Order Amish showed a similar tenacity in clinging to the traditional ways of a self- and world-denying pietistic religion based on communal life. Where a foreign tongue and foreign birth and customs were supplemented by religious exclusiveness and determined other worldliness, the communist community had the best chance of survival.[2]

The most famous secular communist communities were the Fourierist phalanxes, which adopted as their motto, "Unity of man with man in true society, unity of man with God in true religion, unity of man with nature in creative art and industry." While most of the religious groups were composed of foreign peasants or the lower strata of agricultural workers, the phalanxes attracted middle and lower middle-class supporters. Beginning in 1842 they multiplied with remarkable speed. Six were founded in Ohio, seven in New York, six in Pennsylvania, two in Wisconsin, and one in Indiana. In a few years some thirty had been established in various parts of the country. Of these Brook Farm was the most famous and the North American Phalanx at Red Bank, New Jersey, was the most enduring. The Northampton Association, while only indirectly connected with Fourierism, was typical of the movement in its avowed purpose of getting rid of "omnipresent and oppressive" competition for money and material success.

The Wisconsin Phalanx got its start with a Lyceum lecture at Southport, Wisconsin, and by 1846 it had attracted 180 members, among them a former member of both branches of the state legislature, two members of the state senate, a delegate to two state constitutional conventions, and a candidate for governor.

[2] Walter Martin Kollmorgen: *Culture of a Contemporary Rural Community* (Washington, D.C.: U.S. Department of Agriculture; 1942), *passim.*

John Collins, a dedicated antislavery leader, founded the Skaneateles Community, the bases of which were common ownership of property, a vegetable and fruit diet, mental purity and social happiness, abstinence from all narcotics and stimulants, and the rejection of all government, human or divine. His object was to establish a society "that would ultimately work a perfect regeneration of the race, by bringing man into harmony with the physical, moral and intellectual laws of his being." [3]

If the religious communities are of interest because they offer case studies of the most extreme form of the covenanted community, the secular enterprises are of perhaps even greater significance because they demonstrate dramatically the yearning of the middle-class small-town American for the classic community that would be both the means of social redemption for the individual and a "model" for the redemption of mankind. Each venture saw itself as "a city set upon a hill"; each was obsessed with its version of the utopian dream that two hundred years before had carried the Puritans to the New England coast. Most members of the secular communities were the offspring of parents raised in communities of the true covenant, refugees from towns where the dream had been soiled by rampaging industrialism.

There was, in fact, the narrowest of margins between members of the older covenanted communities who pushed westward to found new towns that would be free of the strife, corruption, and greed which had corroded the old covenant and those zealots who, like Noyes and Ballou, became involved in more or less private fantasies. The hundreds of communist communities, religious or secular, that were founded and filled by native-born Americans were aberrant forms of the covenanted community and, as such, important indices of the American spirit. The emphasis in all such towns on the absence of "competition" indicates small-town America's hostility to the rise of

[3] Hinds: *American Communities*, pp. 248, 293-4.

business and the appearance of "individualism." Individualism and business competition (not business enterprise) were serpents in the Garden.

Few communities based on the older forms of the religious covenant were established after the Civil War; perhaps the most widespread substitute for the religious covenant was the temperance covenant. From 1865 to the later decades of the century dozens of temperance communities were formed, the most famous of which was the Union Colony at Greeley, Colorado. Horace Greeley, the crusading editor of the New York *Tribune*, was the town's sponsor and Nathan C. Meeker, a member of the *Tribune*'s staff, launched the enterprise by running an advertisement on December 4, 1869, which outlined his plan for a Western colony. "The persons with whom I would be willing to associate," Meeker wrote, "must be temperance men, and ambitious to establish good society, and among as many as fifty, ten should have as much as $10,000 each, or twenty $5,000 each, while others may have $200 to $1,000, and upward." The object of the colony in Meeker's words was "to exhibit all that is best in modern civilization. In particular should moral and religious sentiments prevail; for without these qualities man is nothing."

The advertisement evoked an immediate response. Within a few weeks twelve hundred letters had been received and over four hundred individuals had paid in various sums to the treasurer as warrant of their seriousness. The vast majority of applicants were from small towns of the Northeast and Middle West. Only twelve applied from five Southern states, and three of these lived in New Iberia, Louisiana. New York State provided almost a hundred, of whom three fourths were from small towns. Of ninety-two from New England, only five were from cities and the rest from towns. Of Iowa's sixteen applicants, one was a city dweller; Illinois had forty, five of whom lived in Chicago; Ohio contributed approximately fifty, with but one from a city. The Midwest as a whole contributed a total of one hundred and sixty-two, the highest for any region, the vast majority town dwellers. Of those who showed serious interest by making initial payments only a hundred and thirty-four actually reached Greeley, and of these sixteen were from cities and the rest from towns.

One pattern that emerges clearly is that groups of from three to six persons (representing individual family units, though often related) came from the same small towns. For example, Hoosick Falls, New York, contributed five; Ridgway, Michigan, three; Albion, Michigan, six; six from Fredonia, New York; five from Ripon, Wisconsin; five from New Lisbon, Ohio; six from Titusville, Pennsylvania.

The dominant attitudes of those who populated Greeley can perhaps best be gauged by the editorials that appeared in the pages of the Greeley *Tribune*. The editor never tired of proclaiming the virtue, morality, and enlightenment of the town. Before it had been founded, its citizens had to mix

> . . . with drunkards and tiplers, who swarmed in every rank of society and met us at every turn. . . . New York, with its wealth and immense business; Boston, with its high culture and its prohibitory law; and Philadelphia with brotherly love, are equally cursed with rum; and in western towns, Chicago, Davenport, St. Louis, St. Paul, & Omaha, are the Germans with their lager beer, and sonorous songs, and Sunday picnics. Even in small country towns, were the lager beer saloons, and ragged hangers-on—on all railroads were the Irishmen with their whiskey and shellahas, and everywhere young men of promise were growing red and bloated. All these are left behind. We have been emancipated, and we breathe freer. The day of Jubilee has come.

The statement is classically American and classically small town. The dream has been soiled by the cities, by the aliens —the Germans and Irish—and above all by rum, but the new day has dawned, the pure and uncorruptible community has been established and the covenant subscribed to; salvation is to be achieved by teetotalism and middle-class morality.

The Greeley citizen moreover was not only abstemious and moral, he (or she) combined "literary culture with everyday industry." A majority of the married women of the town had been schoolteachers, a fact which in the opinion of the editor of the *Tribune* contributed to the high cultural and moral tone of the community. "It is to be said," he wrote, "that both the men and women of this colony are select, for they were alike receptive of the aims and objects, of education, of refined society, of temperance, and of elegant suburban homes. . . ." [4]

At the same time that Greeley was being established, the Chicago–Colorado Colony founded the town of Longmont. Lacking perhaps some of its rival's zeal, Longmont was, nonetheless, dedicated to equally high ideals. Its charter (or covenant) declared:

> No man [is] integral within himself. We are all parts of one grand community, and it behooves every man to know what his neighbor is about. Hence we unite, for mutual benefit, large corporate interests to economize the movement of people by colonies, and immediately secure to members thereof all the home institutions, social and material. . . . Communities made up of miscellaneous settlers from all sections and nationalities, require years to become homogeneous socially, and prosperous in their industries.
>
> Industry, Temperance, and Morality are the watch-words of the Chicago–Colorado Colony. . . . The requirement that ardent spirits shall neither be sold or manufactured on the Colony grounds, brings together an organized and select body, the moral part of mankind, who hitherto have always lived disasso-

[4] Colin B. Goodykoontz and James F. Willard, eds.: *Union Colony at Greeley* (Boulder, Colo.: University of Colorado; 1918), pp. 1, 3, 321, 311.

ciated . . . a new class of men, stronger by reason of accumulated intellect . . . come together and clasp hands.[5]

Greeley and Longmont were churchgoing communities, but their theology was liberal and relaxed, more a symbol of moral rigor and God-fearing piety than of profound conviction or deep personal need. Nonetheless the towns were the spiritual descendants of the early Puritan communities. They had the same belief in a transcendent mission. Temperance, to them, was not simply a desirable social reform but a means of universal salvation. Their citizens believed that they were the elect, the heralds of a new day, the saints dwelling among strangers. For Puritan grace and salvation they read temperance and culture. Their claims were as extensive, their expectations as utopian, as those of their New England forebears; the defeat of earlier hopes had not destroyed the capacity to hope.

The towns whose growth was primarily cumulative displayed less variation than the colonized communities. The cumulative town was one that, without plan, or with no more than a townsite plot, grew by the gradual accretion of individuals, or, sometimes by rapid but disorderly accumulations of fortune seekers. Morris Birkbeck, an English traveler, describes such a community, established "on any spot where a few settlers cluster together." Here

some enterprising proprietor finds in his section what he deems a good site for a town [and] has it surveyed and laid out in lots, which he sells, or offers for sale by auction. The new town then assumes the name of its founder:—a storekeeper builds a little framed store, and sends for a few cases of goods; and then a tavern

[5] James F. Willard and Colin B. Goodykoontz, eds.: *Experiments in Colorado Colonization, 1869–1872* (Boulder, Colo.: University of Colorado; 1926), pp. 143, 148, 266, 391.

starts up, which becomes the residence of a doctor and a lawyer, and the boarding-house of the store-keeper, as well as the resort of the weary traveller: soon follow a blacksmith and other handicraftsmen in useful succession to this rising community. Thus the town proceeds, if it proceeds at all, with accumulating force until it becomes the metropolis of the neighborhood.[6]

In many instances a townsite was laid out on a river, or a trading juncture and such towns likewise grew, often very rapidly, by the accumulation of miscellaneous individuals whose common interest was wholly material. Timothy Dwight, the New Haven divine, commented on such towns as "mere collections of houses and stores, clustered around a landing; where nothing but mercantile and mechanical business is done; where the inhabitants appear to form no connections, or habits, beside those, which naturally grow out of bargain and sales; where the position of store determines that of the house; and that of the wharf often commands both; where beauty of the situation is disregarded, and every convenience, except that of trade is fogotten." With these towns, Dwight contrasts those colonized communities established "for the reception of men . . . not merely to acquire property; but to sustain the relations, perform the duties, and contribute to the enjoyments of life." [7]

Most towns that were started as economic ventures developed according to a common pattern. Often such communities were in their early years chaotic and lawless, unless, as sometimes happened, a "father-authority" figure emerged who took the lead in developing the religious and social aspects of the towns. Many cumulative towns were notably lacking in community structure. The ruling groups were "little more than leaderless gangs with neither a

[6] Morris Birkbeck: *Notes on a Journey in America* (London: Severn & Company, for Ridgway & Sons; 1818), p. 103.
[7] Timothy Dwight: *Travels in New England* (2 vols.; New Haven, Conn.; 1821–2), II, 334.

dominant interest nor a common tradition. Knowing no law, written or unwritten, and far from old ties and customs, their inhabitants tended naturally to disorder and strife." [8] Hackneyed in a hundred movies, the situation of law-abiding citizens striving to make the frontier town "a God-fearing place, fit for decent men and women to live," had many counterparts in American history from the middle of the eighteenth century on.

Those towns whose origin was wholly economic and which grew by the accumulation of heterogeneous individuals eventually acquired the social and institutional forms of the typical town. Here, indeed, time developed the "psychological fabric of a good community" [9] but the price was high, for the town meanwhile had to go through an inchoate and formless period that often left permanent scars, while towns that were colonized *as* towns showed, from the first, the characteristics of developed communities. Moreover most towns continued to show evidence of the manner of their origin. The town that placed the nobler aspects of the ethic ahead of material growth and expansion often remained modest in size and predominantly agrarian. John H. Holmes recalls that his boyhood town of Mastersville, Ohio, had no ambition to grow and made no effort to attract industries. The town, rather, took "great pride in its morality. The proper living, the right attitude on life—that was their main concern." [1]

[8] Carle Clark Zimmerman: *The Changing Community* (New York and London: Harper & Brothers; 1938), p. 117. Zimmerman is here speaking of two twentieth-century communities, Resettlement and Rayshell, but his words are applicable to many nineteenth-century frontier communities.

[9] Ibid., p. 119. In discussing the disorganization of Resettlement, Zimmerman states that "*time* is necessary to develop the psychological fabric of a good community with adequate organization." But time was what the small town did not have. The founders of American towns could not wait for time to work a slow process of social integration.

[1] J. H. Holmes.

Types of Towns

Since these towns, with few exceptions, were settled by farmers and were designed to serve primarily as religious and social centers for the farm community, it was natural that business and industrial development should be slighted. The town that wished to be a city, if it did not choke on its ambition, might become one. Most towns that by the middle of the twentieth century had grown to be cities or urban centers of 30,000 or more inhabitants were cumulative towns where the economic motive was paramount and where geographical and practical conditions were highly favorable to growth. Such towns, oriented toward commercial values, were unhampered by the essentially conservative, rural, anti-urban values of the typical colonized town. Lacking religious, social, or ethnic unity, and unhampered by community restraints, they gave free rein to "rugged individualism," to the often recklessly acquisitive instincts of their citizens.

While some towns grew into cities and others remained stable, thousands have simply vanished from the map; fields and forests have reclaimed their sites. Some indeed were hardly more than feverish gleams in the eyes of land speculators; others had brief existences measured in months or a few years, while still others lasted decades or even generations and then, seemingly assured of permanence, dwindled to crossroad hamlets.

By actual count Iowa alone has 2,205 abandoned places —towns, villages, and country post offices. Most of the towns established in Missouri during the period from 1818 to 1820 have vanished from the map. Chariton, Thornsburg, Monticello, Washington, Houstonville, Nashville, Rectorville, Missouriton, Osage, Belfast, Bainbridge, Bluffton, Alexander, Winchester, and Franklin are a few of the lost towns whose names have been preserved.

In state after state the story was the same. New Madrid in Ohio was an important town at the end of the eighteenth century, but by 1804 the population had begun to shrink and within ten years the town had disappeared. A gazetteer of 1881 dismissed Huron, Dakota, with a few lines, but devoted thirty to describing Jamesville in Yankton County. In a few years Huron had become an important town while Jamesville was soon to vanish.

In 1837 a group of New York and Philadelphia speculators formed a joint stock company with the intention of establishing a city in western Michigan. In six months fifteen substantial buildings had been built on the shore of Lake Michigan. Sixty thousand dollars was spent on a luxurious hotel, roads were built, a sawmill and a large general store erected. A hundred and forty-two blocks were laid out with twenty-four lots to the block, seven of which were reserved for churches, and four for a railroad depot which was to be a handsome structure built along Grecian lines. The depression of 1837 killed the enterprise and within a few years the site was abandoned.[2] Such

[2] "An Account of the Rapid Rise and Sudden Fall of Port Sheldon," *Michigan Pioneer Historical Collections*, XXVIII, pp. 527–33, quotes from the Detroit *Free Press* (September 13, 1891). See also Zimmerman: *The Changing Community*, pp. 248, 363, 372, 445, *passim*, for other "types" of towns. Zimmerman speaks of the "personality" of certain New England Communities which, in his view, show generalized traits such as "belligerency," "good nature," "stability," and so on. He has gone so far as to give towns included in his study of "the changing community" such names as "Lonely," "Utopia," "Hamlet" (the indecisive town), "Nudeal," "Babbitt," "Mayflower," and "Yankeeville."

Babbitt was a covenanted community which, although industrialized, has preserved its ancient values and ideals. The town contains a high proportion of native stock, which has provided continuous and aggressive leadership. The old families have been "sufficiently strong to preserve their entity, and to assimilate within their own culture the influx of foreign immigrants. . . . To their strong and paternalistic leadership," in Zimmerman's opinion, "is due the absence of conflicts which arise in an unintegrated community held together solely by contractual relations." The town has, moreover, preserved an interest in education and in cultural things that dates back to its founding. It sends an unusually high proportion of its young men and women to college, supports

episodes were commonplace in Western town building.

The manner in which American towns have been founded and the purposes behind their establishment have varied widely. In most instances the circumstances of settlement have determined the character and future development of the town. To say this is to say no more than that ideas, when they are translated into concrete human situations, have consequences, and that the forms of today have been conditioned by the events of yesterday.

While many towns preserved the dominant characteristics and ideals of their founders, others of course did not develop along the lines suggested by their early settlement. Towns, whatever their origins, grew more and more alike, not because of any logic inherent in the towns themselves but because they came increasingly under the influence of urban culture and urban values. Even so there is in the town, as Carle Zimmerman suggests, an often remarkable persistence of traits that have been present from the beginning. Most communities, despite the great changes that have taken place, are marked by circumstances of their origin; they contain residues that however muted or transmuted give to each of them a certain character.

The principal distinction made here is between colonized and cumulative towns. Where attention has been given to the development of towns, it has generally been assumed that the vast majority of American towns have been cumulative in origin. In 1918 James F. Willard wrote in the introduction to *The Union Colony at Greeley, Colorado, 1869–1871*:

> In the development of the agricultural regions of the West, group migration has ever held a prominent place. This is true whether the Piedmont region, the

---

a strong library and five "socio-literary and study clubs." The religious life of the community has remained consistently strong and to this fact Zimmerman attributes the preservation of "at least some of the vestiges of the stern Puritan morality of the founders."

basin of the Mississippi, the Southwest, or the lands of the Pacific slope be under consideration. One phase of the settlement of each of these districts has been that by more or less well-organized groups, companies or colonies.[3]

However, when Willard came to edit *Experiments in Colorado Colonization* with Colin Goodykoontz in 1926, he had capitulated to the general Turnerist view of frontier settlement, for he or Goodykoontz wrote: "The majority of those who went West at this time, as at all times in the nineteenth century, went as individuals, or in family groups, or as temporary members of a loosely organized band."[4]

It is impossible to say what proportion of new towns should be credited to colonized or cumulative settlement. But it is clear that colonized settlement was far more common than has been realized. The fact is that this type of community played an enormously important role in American town building. Almost invariably organized around some form of covenant, it showed remarkable qualities of persistence, energy, and stability.

[3] P. ix.
[4] P. xiv.

I I I

The Expansion of New England

"THE EXPANSION OF NEW ENGLAND" was the title chosen by Lois Kimball Mathews for her turn-of-the-century study of the spread of New England settlement and institutions to the Mississippi. Miss Mathews's book, published in 1909, marks a kind of watershed in American historiography. Most of the prominent historians of nineteenth-century America were New Englanders, bred and trained in a tradition-bound society and dedicated to the proposition that Old England had given birth to the greater part of what was estimable in the world and that New England had brought it to fruition.

The phrase "Anglo-Saxon" was often on the tongues of these historians, and through their genial monopoly of American history they spread the impression across the country that the finest flowers of our society had been nurtured in New England soil. There was, moreover, a good deal of evidence to back them up, and if they were sometimes inclined to bear heavily on the evidence in order to prove, for instance, that the Puritans were the fathers of American democracy, they were nonetheless high-minded, scholarly, and industrious gentlemen who contributed greatly to, if they did not in fact make up, American historiography in their century.

In the last decades of the nineteenth century a number of young historians rose to challenge what might be called the Anglo-New England interpretation of our past. Frederick Jackson Turner was the most effective spokesman of the thesis that it was to uniquely American factors, rather than to our English heritage, that the United States owed its remarkable development. Turner's brilliant essay on the role of the frontier in American history had symbolic as well as scholarly significance. It was received, not as proven fact—it was, as it turned out, not provable—but as revelation. The response that it evoked in the historical profession showed how inadequate the Anglo-New England version of our past had become in a world awakened to new intellectual currents. The hinterland could not forever be brought to worship at a temple whose high priests were Yankee historians. The Turner thesis was, perhaps primarily, the Midwest's declaration of intellectual and moral independence from the East. But there was more to it than that. The social and political attitudes of the older generation of historians had been thoroughly conservative. Their emphasis was on the persistence of tradition and the continuity of institutions; by dwelling on the Old World roots of American culture, they ensured New England's eminence as its preserver and transmitter.

It was hardly to be expected that these claims would go forever undisputed. If a Weaver, a Bryan, or a La Follette appeared to challenge the political hegemony of the Northeast, there must be a Turner to provide the historical rationale for the new claims. But if it was the West that saw in Turner the prophet of intellectual and cultural equality, the East was also ready to embrace him. He preached a national doctrine. The younger generation of historians had been deeply affected by those currents of reform that manifest themselves in Progressivism. Turner became the preceptor of a generation of historians many of whom came, like their master, from the Middle West and most of whom were passionate crusaders for a wider social democracy. Turner taught them to look skeptically on the old gods and to examine their credentials with a ruthless disregard of the accepted pieties. The study and writing of American history profited enormously thereby. But the new schools inevitably produced their own distortions.

Lois Kimball Mathews stood between the two traditions—that of George Bancroft on the one hand and that of Turner on the other. She gave her scholarly allegiance without question to the exciting new spokesman of the West, but she had strong emotional ties with the Anglo-New England school. As a result the subject on which she chose to write her doctoral dissertation—the expansion of New England—was perfectly suited to elaborate the new dogma while propitiating the old gods. Her book professed to show how important New England had been in the settlement of the West; but at the same time it acknowledged the Turner doctrine by stressing the degree to which the frontier modified the ideas and institutions of the pioneers, and it accepted as a basic tenet that, in every New England town, it was the "radical," "progressive," and "independent" spirits who migrated westward.

Although a product of the new scholarship, Miss Mathews could not free herself of all vestiges of the older tradition. Thus we find frequent references to the marvelous properties of "Anglo-Saxon blood," the same blood that Miss Mathews's predecessors had exalted as having unique propensities for freedom—in the classic phrase "liberty-loving Anglo-Saxon blood"—blood whose individual corpuscles were imbued with zeal for civil rights and popular government. For Miss Mathews, it was also blood containing a "wanderlust" that helped to explain the migratory impulses of those through whose veins it flowed. The mysterious properties of this blood, which it may be feared will continue to evade chemical analysis, was the favorite *deus ex machina* of the earlier New England historians. Whatever was otherwise elusive and inexplicable might at last be traced to this magic fluid.

In Miss Mathews we might therefore discern a historian of New England, ready to join the new champions of the frontier, but on terms which enabled her to preserve a good measure of glory for the auld sod. The story of the frontier, she wrote, in the best Turner tradition, was "a study of institutions transplanted and transformed, the old ones influencing the new ones, the new ones reacting upon the old, making the latter broader and more flexible." Cramped by the conservatism of the New England towns "the more radical spirits began to chafe, and turn to newer sections where they might be unhampered by either tradition or habit." In this way "the spirit of radicalism so conspicuous among the pioneer's motives" had contributed "immeasurably" to the development of the country, since the frontier showed thereby a "tendency to radicalism in all matters."

"The conservative element," by Miss Mathews's reading, remained in the "settled portions of the country" making those sections increasingly stodgy with each passing decade. The forces that influenced the pioneer to start on his westward trek were his "radicalism," his "sometimes excessive individualism," "the desire for greater material prosperity" and, of course, his wandering Anglo-Saxon blood. The classic pioneer was "a New Englander grown more independent and probably more tolerant under his new environment."

The pioneers were in the terms of the new dogma individuals who longed "for the open, for the free life of an unorganized community." But the fact was that the frontier town settled by New Englanders, far from being "a community where people might do as they pleased," was if anything more highly organized, more rigid and repressive than its parent community, while the forces of change, sparked by an expanding ocean commerce with its attendant prosperity, appeared first, as Carl Bridenbaugh has shown, in the large seacoast towns and cities. If there were any Puritans who founded communities "where people might do as they pleased" they have escaped this historian's notice.

The propositions about the migrating New Englander that are stated so confidently, Miss Mathews does not attempt to prove. They were part of the new dispensation, taken by her and by many of her contemporaries as articles of faith. Yet Miss Mathews, aware that theory is not entirely consistent with fact, reveals her own uneasiness when she notes of the pioneers that "curiously enough . . . when the malcontents found themselves in the majority instead of the minority (as they had been before their removal), they frequently became as intolerant as their comrades had been."[1] The key word in this passage is "curiously." That settlers on the frontier should be as intolerant as their cousins back home (or more so) was only "curious" if the historian saw the pioneer as the forerunner of Progressivism. The idea that the frontier was populated by individuals imbued with the ideals of twentieth-century liberal reform could be dismissed as simply naïve if it had not been accepted by so many historians. The myth of the "liberal" pioneer has been almost as enduring as the older image of the noble Anglo-Saxon, which it replaced.

The story of New England's expansion is far more complex than Miss Mathews suggests. The development of the American frontier has of course been continuous. From the earliest years of colonial settlement the older seacoast

[1] Lois Kimball Mathews: *The Expansion of New England* (Boston: Houghton Mifflin Company; 1909), pp. 4, 5, 6, 73, 72.

towns bred new communities deeper in the wilderness. The spectacular settlement of the West that took place in the nineteenth century had been preceded, and was indeed accompanied by the settlement of northern New England, New York, and Pennsylvania as well as the southern frontier of Kentucky and Tennessee. No radical change occurred in the motives of settlement from the colonial period through the early decades of the nineteenth century. The Puritans who had pushed out from the Massachusetts Bay area had had for the most part the same motives as their descendants who moved into Ohio, Illinois, and Michigan two hundred years later. One of the principal causes of such migration was religious controversy.

Robert East has pointed out that "a distinctive force in the expansion of the New England frontier in the seventeenth century *and later* [italics mine] . . . is a certain explosive character in Calvinistic Puritanism itself. The dynamic church principle inherent in the doctrine of every man his own priest was in constant disharmony with the severe external authority attempted in practice by the Puritan clergy and elders."

The result was the constant fragmenting of the parent communities, but the secessions were of a group, rather than an individual, type. True, the group generally formed about a person of unusual force of character, but it was as a group that the dissenters departed, not as separate individuals; and a new covenant was invariably the first order of business. Certainly some of "the rag-tag and bobtail element" fled from settled communities to the frontier, but as East states it, "the effective spearhead of expansion was generally in the religiously discontented."

With such a figure as Roger Williams in mind we are inclined to think of these dissenters as being somehow "liberal," but in reality they were often the most rigidly orthodox members of the community, individuals who were alarmed at the softening of Puritan dogmas and who withdrew to the wilderness to recover the purity of the ancient faith. It was often, at least in terms of theology, the liberal elements who achieved dominance in the older towns and cities, precipitating the exodus of the conservatives. In East's words, again, the farther west one traveled "the more 'orthodox' was the Puritanism at work; contrarily, the more liberal and enlightened (or corrupt and defiled, according to one's point of view) did Harvard and Boston appear. . . . The forward-looking, the liberal religious element of the eighteenth century was invariably found in the older settlements of the seaboard and the [Connecticut] valley." [2]

It was, after all, Cotton Mather, the high priest of Boston Puritanism, who favored private examination for church membership as opposed to the traditional examination by the congregation. It was in Boston, too, that the Half-Way Covenant got its strongest backing. The church at Branford, Connecticut, offended by the union of the colonies of New Haven and Connecticut and at the spread of the Half-Way Covenant, moved en masse to Newark, New Jersey; a similar dispute in Stratford led to the founding of Woodbury, Connecticut. Bennington, Vermont, was settled from Hardwick, Massachusetts, by Captain Samuel Robinson who took twenty-two people with him, all of them conservatives who wished to preserve the old faith.

The records of one New England town after another disclose bitter and often protracted disputes over theological doctrines and even over the personalities of particular ministers. Wethersfield, Connecticut, alone colonized a number of towns as the result of splittings off from the original church. It might be argued that quarreling was one of the principal causes of the expansion of New England. It was then, as it is today, difficult to repair the unity of the

[2] Robert A. East: "Puritanism and New England Settlement," *New England Quarterly*, XVII (June, 1944), pp. 255, 256–7, 263.

town once it was shattered; it was generally easier for the minority to withdraw, and it did so. The emigrants were, however, no more radical, tolerant, or independent than their less mobile neighbors.

In essence, the process was this: as the original community began to break down—sometimes because of theological wrangles, sometimes because of progressive economic and social differentiation, sometimes because of its own inner tensions—individuals within the community coalesced around aggressive leaders and then broke off to found their own communities, hoping thereby to recapture the classic unity of their common life.

An example of this is Worthington, Ohio, formed by settlers from Granby, Connecticut, who "drew up articles of association, among which was one limiting their number to forty, each of whom must be unanimously chosen by ballot, a single negative being sufficient to prevent an election." It would be difficult to discover in such action any yearning for independence or any desire to be free of the tyranny of the community.

Colonization by congregations and kinship groups, fiercely exclusive in many instances, refutes the argument that the pioneers were champions of "individualism." The settler who wished to go his own way, free from the scrutiny of his neighbors, stood a better chance in the older towns than in frontier communities, unless, of course, he was willing to live the precarious life of an isolated trapper and hunter. While it is true that the emigrants often left their home communities pronouncing an anathema on them as being sunk in vice, vain presumption, and worldliness, these strictures were not related to "radical" or liberal political theories, or indeed related, in most instances, to politics at all. They referred to the community's failure to live up to the covenant, and thus they have a better claim to the title of "conservative" than of "radical."

The New Englanders who colonized towns, far from

being conscious or unconscious innovators, sought to re-produce the institutions and values of their home communities. They wished in Norwalk, Ohio, to create a refined and purified version of Norwalk, Connecticut. A historian, discussing the founding of Hudson, Ohio, by colonists from New Haven, has written that while the town "might, in many ways, be more primitive and ruder than New Haven, yet, in another way, it was the Connecticut original in purer form, undiluted and undistracted by modern worldliness and the change encroaching on the east." [3]

It must be said that many communities did not have their origins in religious dissent and contention. The need for new land was undoubtedly the most persistent motive for emigration, and the strength of the ties between new town and old is suggested by the frequency with which the frontier settlement took the name of its parent community. Richmond, New Hampshire, was named after Richmond, Rhode Island. Lebanon, Lyme, and Plainfield of the Granite State were all offspring of Connecticut towns with the same names, and the list could be extended by the hundreds and indeed thousands. [4]

The settlement of Maine and Vermont was not halted by the Revolution. In 1780 nine new towns were founded in Maine and twelve in Vermont. Almost all the early settlers of Andover, Maine, migrated from Andover, Massachusetts, in protest of the relaxed theology of the Massachusetts town. New Vineyard was peopled from Martha's Vineyard, and Exeter, Maine, was settled from Exeter, New Hampshire. Vermont's Braintree was the offshoot of Massachusetts' Braintree, and Pittsfield and Groton were named after towns in the Bay State.

It was not, however, to northern New England that

---

[3] Richard Wohl: "Henry Day," in William Miller, ed.: *Men in Business* (Cambridge, Mass.: Harvard University Press; 1952), p. 164.
[4] Mathews: *Expansion*, p. 114.

emigrating Yankees went in largest numbers. New York, Pennsylvania, and Ohio claimed tens of thousands. A Congregational church organized in Poultney, Vermont, moved in a body to East Springfield, New York, and became like many others with similar origins, a model New England community. Wherever the settlers went they carried their politics with them as well as their religion. Luzerne County, New York, was a stronghold of New England Federalism and so it continued for more than a generation.

Hudson, New York, was settled in 1783 by thirty Quaker fishermen and their families from Martha's Vineyard; and from Plymouth, Massachusetts, to Plymouth, Connecticut, to Plymouth, Ohio, we can trace families, civil institutions, and church dogmas in an unbroken line; from Greenwich, Connecticut, to Greenwich, Ohio, and from the New England Deerfield to its western counterparts.

Religious revivals and "awakenings," perhaps more than any other single factor, were responsible for the establishment of colonized towns. The Great Awakening of the 1730's and 1740's led directly to the founding of a number of "New Light" communities and a half dozen colleges. The awakening which swept through Connecticut at the end of the eighteenth century scattered Connecticut towns through New York, Vermont, and Ohio. Hudson, Ohio, was just such a community; it was started by David Hudson, a native of Goshen, Connecticut, who, according to his own testimony, had been a Godless man and then was caught up in a revival, underwent a profound spiritual crisis and, pledging himself to God's service, vowed to found a community in the wilderness which would live according to God's ordinances. In the words of Richard Wohl: "From the very first he determined that his resolve should not be dissipated under the stress of a frontier life with its attendant hardships. He need not have feared. The isolation, the hard work done in common, sustained the original homogeneity of the group and served, indeed, to provide it with added vitality." Having established his covenanted community in the forest, Hudson went on to help found Western Reserve College.[5]

The story was a typical one. The older towns were like ripe seed pods which when heated by one of the periodic revivals would burst open and scatter seedlings wherever the winds of migration were blowing at the moment.

After the earlier period of migration, the increase in missionary activity—especially by the Congregationalists and Presbyterians—led to the settling of many new communities and to the gathering together of individual farm families into congregations.

When a group from Granville, Massachusetts, decided to move to the Ohio country, a 24-member Congregational church drew up a covenant and a constitution and transplanted pastor, deacons, and church members to Granville, Ohio. The emigrants numbered 176 and their first act upon reaching the new settlement was to hold a service of worship in the forest. One of the little band later wrote of how they wept when they heard their voices echoing among the lonely and forbidding trees; "they wept when they remembered Zion."

Oberlin, in Lorain County, was another classic example of the transplanted New England community. The colonists were asked to subscribe to a covenant which pledged them to "a life of simplicity, to special devotion to church and school, and to earnest labor in the missionary cause." [6]

Illinois and Indiana's earliest settlers were Southerners, many of them from North Carolina, Kentucky, and Ten-

[5] Wohl: "Henry Day," p. 162.
[6] Henry Howe: *Historical Collections of Ohio* (Cincinnati: Derby, Bradley & Co.; 1848), pp. 296, 297; James H. Fairchild: *Oberlin, the Colony and the College, 1833–1883* (Oberlin, Ohio: E. J. Goodrich; 1883), pp. 9–16.

nessee. The great influx of New Englanders into Indiana came in the 1830's and the decades that followed. In Elkhart County, 213 out of 255 settlers in the years between 1828 and 1840 came from New England. Grange, Noble, and La Porte counties were largely settled by families from Massachusetts, Connecticut, and Vermont. A Connecticut colony was established in 1834 at Rockwell, Illinois, and in 1836 three New England colonies were founded, one at Tremont in Tazewell County, one in Knox County, and one at Lyons near Varna. A company from Gilmanton, New Hampshire, settled Hanover in 1835 and settlers from Pittsfield, Massachusetts, established a purified version of their hometown in Pittsfield, Illinois.[7] Wethersfield was founded by a pastor and his congregation from Wethersfield, Connecticut, while a church colony from Benson, Vermont, moved as a group to Du Page County. From Rhode Island in 1836 came forty families, members of the Providence Farmers' and Mechanics' Emigrating Society, who had organized a church and school before their departure.

A colony from Northampton, Massachusetts, was adjacent to one from Norwich, Connecticut. The so-called Hampshire colony organized its own church and academy and planted a town in Bureau County. By 1840 Illinois could count at least twenty-two colonies in northern or central Illinois, all of which had their origin in New England or New York. There was, to be sure, a great number of people who came at random into the state and who either joined established towns or formed loosely knit rural communities. But the colonized towns played a role in the history of the state that was out of all proportion to their numbers. In a few years these centers came to dominate the social and political life of Illinois. As a former governor wrote, the Yankee was "the most liberal in contributing to whatever is for the public benefit. Is a schoolhouse, a

[7] Theodore Calvin Pease: *The Frontier State, 1818–1848* (Springfield, Ill.: Illinois Centennial Commission; 1918), pp. 178–9.

bridge, or a church to be built, a road to be made, a school or minister to be maintained, or taxes to be paid for the honor or support of the government, the northern man is never found wanting." [8]

The Southerners on the other hand, while more picturesque, were notoriously indolent, a vice which led to many others. "On a bright day," a traveler wrote, "they mount their horses and throng the little towns in the vicinity of their homes, drinking and trading horses until late in the evening." Toward education the Southerner had a humorous hostility. "He 'reckons' they should know how to write their names, and 'allows it's a right smart thing to be able to read when you want to'. . . but he don't 'calculate' that books and the sciences will do as much good for a man in these matters as a handy use of the rifle. . . . As for teaching 'that's one thing he allows the Yankees are just fit for'; he does not hesitate to confess that they are a 'power smarter' at that than the western boys. But they can't hold a rifle nor ride at wolf hunt with 'em; and he reckons, after all, these are the great tests of merit." [9]

Sixty New Englanders came to Romeo, Michigan, in 1827 and gave that town a thoroughly Yankee character. By 1850 almost half of Michigan's population had come from New England by way of New York, and as much as a third or a quarter came directly from New England.

The Union Colony got its start in Poultney and Bennington, Vermont, where the Reverend Sylvester Coch-

[8] Thomas Ford: *A History of Illinois* (New York: Iverson & Phinney; 1854), p. 281; Albert Shaw: *Local Government in Illinois* (Baltimore: Johns Hopkins University; 1838), p. 11; Charles A. Church: *History of Rockford, Illinois, and Winnebago County* (Rockford, Ill.: W. P. Lamb; 1900), pp. 160 ff.; William V. Pooley: "The Settlement of Illinois from 1830 to 1850," *Bulletin* of the University of Wisconsin, no. 220 (1908).
[9] Clyde E. Buckingham: "Early Settlers of the Rock River Valley," *Journal of the Illinois State Historical Society*, XXXV (September, 1942), pp. 242, 241 quoting Eliza W. Farnham: *Life in Prairie Land* (New York: Harper & Brothers; 1846).

rane recruited ten families, adding three more from Benson and Bellevue, Michigan. Before the Vermonters left home they signed a covenant which began:

> *Whereas*, The enjoyment of the ordinances . . . of the Gospel is in a great measure unknown in . . . the western country, and
>
> *Whereas*, We believe that a pious and devoted emigration is . . . one of the most efficient means, in the hands of God, in removing the moral darkness which hangs over a great portion of the valley of the Mississippi; and
>
> *Whereas*, We believe that a removal to the West may be a means of promoting our temporal interest, and we trust [may] be made subservient to the advancement of Christ's kingdom;
>
> *We do therefore*, form ourselves into . . . a colony with the design of removing into some parts of the western country which shall hereafter be designated, and agree to bind ourselves to . . . the following rules. . . .

The rules covered codes of behavior and, since the town wished to preserve equality among its members, the rules for the distribution of land. No settler was to be allowed to take more than "one farm lot of 160 acres, and one village lot of 10 acres, within the limits of the settlement."

A final injunction to the colonists of Vermontville, as the community came to be called, carried overtones of John Winthrop's "Modell of Christian Charity." "As we must necessarily endure many of those trials and privations which are incident to a settlement in a new country," the statement read, "we agree we will do all in our power to befriend each other; we will esteem it not only a duty, but a privilege to sympathize with each other under all our trials, to do good and lend, hoping for nothing again, and to assist each other on all necessary occasions." [1]

While the tide of colonizing by the purer type of covenanted religious community declined as the nineteenth century wore on, there continued to be many such towns founded. And those such as the temperance and antislavery towns that were established on some substitute version of the covenant were generally deeply imbued with religious feeling.

After the passage of the Kansas-Nebraska Bill in March, 1854, New England emigrants poured into Kansas. New Haven sent a band of seventy settlers known as the Connecticut Colony, a group which included tradesmen, teachers of music, tutors in Yale College, politicians, farmers, and ministers. The community, the forerunner of a number of future colonies, settled on the Wabaunsee River, armed with twenty-five rifles and twenty-five Bibles, gifts from Henry Ward Beecher's Brooklyn congregation.

Amenia, North Dakota, was founded by pioneers from Sharon, Connecticut, who planted their church at once and prided themselves on never having "sought from Eastern sources a single dollar in its support." Down to the end of the century, the Yale Divinity School dispatched its famous "Bands" of young ministers to the Far West and Northwest, and many New Englanders followed them to California, Oregon, and Washington. Moreover town building went on in the unclaimed regions of the older Midwestern states as well as on the frontier, and New England contributed generously to such communities.[2]

[1] Edward W. Barber: "The Vermontville Colony: Its Genesis and History," *Michigan Pioneer and Historical Collections*, XXVIII (1900); J. Harold Stevens: "The Influence of New England in Michigan," *Michigan Historical Magazine*, XIX (autumn, 1935), pp. 321–53.

[2] Lois Kimball Mathews Rosenberry: "Migrations from Connecticut after 1800," *Tercentenary Commission of the State of Connecticut*, LIV (New Haven: Yale University Press; 1936), pp. 18, 19, 20, 29.

As for the Turner-Mathews thesis, while it is undoubtedly true that much individual migration was motivated by a desire to escape from the restraints of organized society, myth has vastly exaggerated their number and importance. Such emigrants were certainly not town builders, though they became in many instances the nucleus for towns. They were the cutting edge of the westward movement (Timothy Dwight called them "foresters"), whose function it was "to cut down trees, build log-houses, lay open forested grounds to cultivation, and prepare the way for those who come after them. These men," Dwight wrote, "cannot live in regular society. They are too idle; too talkative; too passionate; too prodigal; and too shiftless; to acquire either property or character. They are impatient of the restraints of law, religion, and morality; grumble about the taxes, by which Rulers, Ministers, and Schoolmasters are supported; and complain incessantly, as well as bitterly, of the extortions of mechanics, farmers, merchants, and physicians; to whom they are always indebted." [3]

This is, to be sure, a somewhat jaundiced view of the classic pioneer figure. Nevertheless we know from many other accounts that the description is not far wide of the mark. Such individuals were the restless, the discontent, the psychologically and economically marginal portions of older communities. Yet the myth has associated them with a dream of romantic freedom. We might well recall the words of D. H. Lawrence: "Men are free when they are in a living homeland, not when they are straying and breaking away. Men are free when they are obeying some deep, inward voice of religious belief. Obeying from within. Men are free when they belong to a living, organic, *believing* community, active in fulfilling some unfulfilled, perhaps unrealized purpose." [4]

The lonely, wide-ranging frontiersmen bulk large in

[3] Dwight: *Travels*, II, 459.
[4] D. H. Lawrence: *Studies in Classic American Literature* (London: M. Secker; 1933), p. 12.

historical fiction and in the popular mind, but they counted for little in comparison with the town builders of the covenant.

If New England placed the stamp of its own spirit on the Middle West, it did so by dispatching what were by any reasonable standards its most conservative sons and daughters to fill up the vast empty spaces. The colonized communities of Puritans who occupied the frontier states were composed neither of "radicals," nor "independents," nor "lovers of freedom" as an abstract principle. Far from being "tolerant," they were highly intolerant of cities, of the big business of the day, of alien races and faiths, of drinking, of Sabbath-breaking, and indeed of a host of things. Those who remained in the Eastern towns and cities learned to live with the Irish, the French-Canadians, the Poles, the Italians, "the offscourings of the earth," and often to make profits from them. They learned to tolerate what they could not well evade. But in the iron soul of the Puritan town builder there was little tolerance for those who sood outside of the covenant of grace. These builders were the true believers, nerved by their faith to subdue the heartland of a continent in the name of a Jehovah who, if he was terrible in his wrath, was also wonderfully forgiving.

The transplanting of Eastern "culture" froze rather than liberated it. The new town "clung to traditional institutional forms and social practices; and it hungered after intellectual and social contact and parity with the East. A large part of western opportunity was the opportunity to imitate an older society." Before the West could claim parity, it had to prove that it could successfully emulate its supercilious parent. The frontier towns were thus an enormously conservative force since they clung tenaciously to "forms" and "practices" that were a generation old by city standards.

"Much has been said, and foolishly said, of Western character," wrote the Reverend Rufus Babcock. "Most people in the West formed their characters before they emigrated thither; and they have been slightly or not at all modified by their change of residence." [5] The great majority of those who came to the frontier were conservative to begin with. Their situation on a frontier where they felt that the forms and order of civilized life were threatened made them far more resolute in resisting change than their urban cousins.

[5] Earl Pomeroy: "Towards a Reorientation of Western History," *Mississippi Valley Historical Review*, XLI (March, 1955), pp. 597, 593.

Religion in
the Town

I F PROTESTANTISM GAVE the American town its initial
form and continued to exert the strongest of influences on it, the town has in turn left its indelible imprint on American Protestantism.

Earlier chapters have dealt with the character of the
covenant and its effect on the development of the town; its
relation to the extraordinary proliferation of towns; and its
function as the preserver of the inherited order of community life. Through the covenant the precious essence of a
civilized life was maintained in the midst of a wilderness
that always threatened to extinguish the spark of humane-
ness. Through the covenant the community was kept in
good faith and order, and almost daily redeemed from the
anxieties that were a part of the natural and savage world;
through the covenant the community was protected from

the severe social tensions that were an inevitable accompaniment of the lives of highly self-conscious and articulate people living in remote isolation. What remains is a closer examination of the role of religion in the day-to-day existence of the inhabitants of the small town.

Roger Galer's recollections of a Midwestern town in the late nineteenth century would apply equally well to a Puritan community in the early seventeenth century. In such a town

> there was no doubt that God really existed and that he exercised a fatherly care over his children. In all the history of the community through a period of perhaps sixty years there was but one known atheist. He was a good man but he was regarded as decidedly odd—it did not occur to any one to inquire into his reasons or to argue with him. How any one could deliberately doubt God's existence was beyond conception.

> Every event of your life was determined by the direct will of God. It was God who sent you children, made the potatoes turn out well, put the blight on the orchard trees, and caused the roan mare to sicken and die. Likewise if one of the family was sick it was not because some physical law had been violated, it was a dispensation of Providence. . . . People followed literally the text of the Bible which they considered inspired and they supplemented their beliefs with all the odd notions gathered from pagan rites and superstitions. . . . [People] must feel the human touch or the divine touch made personal in order to brave the ordeals through which they must pass. Given this personal contact with the Divine they could endure earthly trials, assured that beneath them was a mighty arm which would ultimately rescue them out of all their troubles.[1]

In the earlier ages of the town there was no line drawn

[1] Roger B. Galer: "Recollections of Busy Years," *Iowa Journal of History and Politics*, XLII (January, 1944), pp. 17–19.

between God's province and that of the world. Everything one did and thought—one's craft, one's crops, one's family life—were under the direct eye and the constant superintendence of the Almighty. The terms of the covenant committed its signers to an exemplary Christian life. Already among the saints of God, predestined for salvation and heavenly glory (though there were always doubts), the pioneer settlers gave, by the covenant, assurance to God and to each other that they would follow in his way "and do all such things as the Lord required of them."

But the flesh was lamentably weak. We know from their remarkable diaries the agonies that engulfed the stoutest of the saints. The most devout might find himself mired in sin, or terribly tempted. Cotton Mather despaired over the fact that in his preaching he often sought to display his "gifts" in "an abominably proud Fishing for popular Applause," and he bewailed his "many Miscarriages, for which the terrible justice of God, might righteously and easily, make mee loathsome among all His people."

Mather recorded elsewhere in his diary that he cast himself "prostrate on my Study-floor, with my sinful Mouth, in the Dust before the Lord." After the death of his wife he was strongly attracted to "a young Gentlewoman of incomparable Accomplishments," whose reputation had been "under some Disadvantage." "Was ever a man more tempted," he wrote, "than the miserable *Mather*. Should I tell, in how many Forms the Divel has assaulted me, and with what Subtilty and Energy, his Assaults have been carried on, it would strike my Friends with Horrour.

"Sometimes, Temptation to *Impurities;* and sometimes to Blasphemy, and Atheism, and the Abandonment of all Religion, as a meer Delusion; and sometimes, to self-Destruction itself." [2]

The chief saints were not the only ones to suffer doubts

[2] Cotton Mather: "Diary," *Massachusetts Historical Society Collections*, LXVII, Part 1, pp. 93, 338, 340, 457–8, 475.

and to engage in constant self-examination. John Marshall was a typical New England artisan. Born in Boston in 1664, he was a mason, carpenter, constable, and noncommissioned officer in the Braintree militia. On the first of October, 1704, he wrote in his diary:

> To-morrow is my birthday. I am now forty years old, and cannot but be ashamed to look back and consider how I have spent my lost time; being at a great losse whether any true grace be wrought in my soul or no: corruption in me is very powerful; grace (if any) is very weak and languid. I have reason to pray as the spous, awake o north wind, and come thou south wind and blow upon my garden, to stir up myself to take hold of God, to engage my cry to the Lord and my whole man in his service, which the Lord enable me to doe.[3]

If the most devout saints could suffer such temptations and such misgivings, it was hardly surprising that lesser Puritans frequently fell into sin. These were not cold, hard, emotionless men, convinced of their own righteousness; rather they acknowledged themselves "very great sinners," only to be endured at all by a God who gave freely of His grace.

Whatever might be the professions of the covenant, the towns of New England were filled with men and women of more than ordinary passion and energy. Emotions lay close to the surface in these rural communities, and the intimacy of town life, if it meant close scrutiny by one's fellows, meant sharper temptations of the flesh. Sentimental pictures of the country town as a haven of rustic simplicity and purity have no correspondence with the reality that the Puritan villager knew. If the town lacked some of the ingenuous temptations of the city, it had a considerable range of its own. The New Englanders knew this very

[3] Charles Francis Adams: *Three Episodes of Massachusetts History* (Boston and New York: Houghton; 1892), II, 718.

well; they knew that the covenant embodied an ideal somewhere beyond the limits of human attainment, but they knew that it was the hard way that God had ordained —Pilgrim's way to the Holy City.

It followed that if one acknowledged the covenant, there was no sin, however black, that the congregation would not forgive. By repentance and forgiveness the sinner could be brought back into full fellowship, and the authority of the community reasserted; the ritual of confession and forgiveness lay at the heart of the New England community.

In the souls of the saints the warfare between God and the Devil was unremitting. The ways in which the sinners might fall were indeed many—from malicious gossip to murder and incest. A sampling from the records of the Congregational Church of Bluehills, Maine, shows some of the more common sins for which members might be called to account. Included were sinful anger, extreme intemperance, falsehoods, abuse of wives by husbands and of husbands by wives, flagrant neglect of family worship, betting on horse racing, dishonest business dealings, desecration of the Sabbath, profanity, propagation of scandal, adultery, lewd behavior, and fornication.

For those who were not in the original covenant, admission to full membership in the church was in itself an ordeal. The candidate for admission had to offer himself, or herself, "individually and under conviction, and this conviction was to be avowed." A conference with the minister followed and if the minister was satisfied that the candidate had indeed gone through a genuine experience of conversion, he was "propounded" before the whole congregation for admission into the inner circle of the covenant, at which time any member of the congregation might ask the most embarrassing questions about the candidate's past life. The next step was for the candidate to rise from his seat when called upon by the pastor and, before the full congregation, give an oral or written account of his religious experience.

More demanding of course were the public confessions of sin. The Braintree records tell of Temperance Bondish who, confessing that she had fallen into error, was

> called forth in the open Congregation, and pre-
> sented a paper containing a full acknowledgement of
> her great sin and wickedness [in which she] publickly
> bewayled her disobedience to parents, pride, unprofita-
> bleness under the means of grace, as the cause that
> might provoke God to punish her with sin . . . beg-
> ging the church's prayers, that God would humble her,
> and give a sound repentance. . . . Which confession
> being read, after some debate, the brethren did gener-
> ally if not unanimously judge that she ought to be
> admonished; and accordingly she was solemnly ad-
> monished of her great sin . . . and charged to search
> out her own heart wayes and to make thorough work
> in her Repentance. . . .

While most of the members bore the discipline of their church, there were occasional rebels such as Samuel Tompson, "a prodigie of pride, malice and arrogance." Tompson was called before the church to answer for his absence from "Publike Worshipe," but instead of showing a disposition to repent proved "proud and insolent, reviling and vilifying [the] Pastor, at a horrible rate, and stileing him their priest, and them a nest of wasps." Faced with such recalcitrance the church unanimously voted to admonish him; his "sin and wickedness" was thus "laid open by divers Scriptures for his conviction," and he was warned to repent.[4]

The member who would not confess his sin and express repentance was generally admonished and suspended from communion. If he remained obdurate he was then excommunicated, but the truly penitent had to be restored, no matter how grievous his sin, and this restoration had to be extended without limit of time. The door was never closed

[4] Ibid., II, 152-3, 754-5.

to the penitent. Excommunicated, he could, upon confession, be received again a communicant in good standing.

Excommuncation was itself a terrible sentence. Although the expelled member was still required to attend church in the hope that he might thereby gain a better understanding of his errors and be brought to repentance, the Cambridge Platform directed that he be deprived of "all familiar communion . . . farther than the necessity of natural, of domestical, or civil relations do require. . . ." [5]

Lydia Foster of Haverford, Massachusetts, was suspended by the church on the birth of her second illegitimate child. With the arrival of number three, she made "a very penitent" confession, but the congregation, skeptical, refused to lift her suspension, and after she had a fourth bastard, the congregation excommunicated her. When, at last, the frail sister married, her confession was accepted and "Lydia Dowe" (lately Foster) "was restored to the fellowship of the church." [6]

Censure might be applied to the farmer who worked in his garden or traveled on the Sabbath, and refusal to confess such a sin could bring excommunication as readily as failure to confess incest or adultery. One man accused of deliberately singing off key in order to interfere with orderly worship was excommunicated for impenitence. Ebenezer Parker of Cambridge who tried to stab his wife was, upon public confession, restored to full communion in his church, while Goodwife Shelley was excommunicated when she refused to express repentance for her malicious slander. [7]

Negro slaves and bond servants might be members in full communion with their masters and mistresses and, like them, were called on for public confession and repentance when they erred. In Deerfield, Massachusetts, in a period of six years two Negroes made five confessions which each

[5] Emil Oberholtzer, Jr.: *Delinquent Saints* (New York: Columbia University Press; 1956), pp. 30, 39.
[6] Ibid., pp. 61–6, 137.   [7] Ibid., pp. 135, 61, 67.

time included theft. In addition, Peter and Adam, acknowledging fornication and drunkenness, were restored after confession. Peter made two subsequent confessions of the same offenses and was, each time, taken back into the flock. Pompey, a Negro in Westfield who had confessed to fornication, attempted assault on his mistress, and disrespectful language to his master, was restored to full communion, although later excommunicated for impenitence on other charges.[8]

Two of the most frequent breaches of church discipline were fornication and adultery. As early as 1668 the General Court of Massachusetts was deploring the large number of bastards in the colony, and the church records of all New England towns contain many instances of married couples who confessed to having had sexual relations before marriage. Sometimes such confessions were voluntary but more often they were forced by the early birth of a child. The general rule was that any child born less than seven months after the marriage of its parents was presumed to have been conceived out of wedlock and the parents were expected to confess and to express their penitence. In Westfield, Massachusetts, a town of some eight hundred persons, twenty-five men and women were accused of fornication between the years of 1750 and 1759. Dedham recorded twenty-five such cases in twenty-five years, and the Groton church records show that of two hundred persons owning the baptismal covenant in that town between 1761 and 1775, no less than sixty-six confessed to fornication before marriage. From 1789 to 1791 sixteen couples, of whom nine confessed to fornication, were admitted to full communion.

The majority of fornicators made their confessions willingly, and there seems to have been little stigma attached to such falls. Indeed, in some communities the Seventh Commandment was broken with such regularity

[8] Oberholtzer: *Delinquent Saints*, p. 199.

that sinners were provided with a set form for their confessions. That of Bluehills, Maine, read:

> We, the subscribers, trusting that by the Grace of God we have been brought to see the evil of sin in general and especially of the sins we have committed, do now humbly, we hope, and penitently confess the sin of fornication of which we have been guilty, and this we do from a conviction that it is reasonable to bear public and marked testimony against scandalous offenses whereby we have been instrumental in weakening the bonds of society and injuring the cause of religion. . . .[9]

The congregations were doubtless on occasion cruel, and the system itself put fearful strains on the delinquent saints as well as on their judges. But the records are impressive evidence of the fidelity with which most congregations observed the scriptural injunctions to charity. Within a harsh system they frequently showed great patience and forbearance with the sinners who appeared before them. If their church was a community of justice, it was also a community of mercy, surrogate for a Christ who had spoken of God's forgiveness as inexhaustible.

By any reasonable standard there was a great deal of illicit sex activity in the Puritan small town of New England and the Middle West. The stereotype of the Puritan shows him as full of sexual inhibitions, prudery, and repressions. These supposed aspects of his character are not much in evidence in the towns we have examined. Rather there is a country realism about sex that is in sharp contrast to late nineteenth-century sexual attitudes.

The publicity that attended sexual irregularities in the small town and the general tolerance with which they were regarded was an encouragement to potential sinners. The fact is that other breaches of the covenant, such as malicious gossip and theft, which threatened the integrity of the

[9] Chase: *Jonathan Fisher*, p. 83.

community, were viewed more seriously than sexual lapses. Industry, thrift, honesty, neighborliness, and piety were rated more highly than strict observance of the sexual code. Of course at the same time it was true that the community had no intention of relaxing its control over matters involving sexual morality. It would not condone "lasciviousness," vulgarity, or deviations from sexual normality, for such offenses imperiled the good order of the common life. As long as sexual activity outside of marriage culminated in wedlock and the production of offspring, or did not destroy the unity of the family, it was regarded with astonishing tolerance.

The inhibitions and pruderies about sex that we generally associate with the Puritans did not originate either with them or in their towns. Kinsey's studies of twentieth-century American sexual behavior suggest what a good deal of other evidence confirms—that sexual "Puritanism" is a product of the urban middle class, and that it was only with the development of a clearly defined middle class in the towns that the attitudes which we identify as "Puritan" made their appearance, copied, for the most part, from the middle-class mores of the city.

While public examination for admission to the covenant and public confession of sin declined in the older towns with the advent of liberal theology and the stratification of the community along class lines, they continued in many small towns of the West down to the end of the nineteenth century. The most careful student of New England church discipline has pointed out that disciplinary action for such lapses as absence from church and misuse of the Sabbath "was considerably intensified [in the West], at a time when the churches in the seaboard area became increasingly lax in disciplinary matters." [1]

The proliferation of denominations and sects meant wide variations in the form of the confession, but as late as 1900 Sims notes in his study of Aton that "cases of

[1] Oberholtzer: *Delinquent Saints*, p. 48.

infraction of the sexual code coming under the authority of the church are dealt with publicly. The discipline is kindly, but those proving incorrigible are dismissed publicly from fellowship." [2]

In Vermontville, Michigan, "citations and trials for unbrotherly remarks and conduct were of frequent occurrence." Many church commissions were appointed to heal breaches between various members of the church, and during the first twenty years of its history "scarcely a male member" of the church escaped censure. The public confession was, moreover, reinforced by the yearly revival, which "would often bring discordant members together again, after the confession of some wrong and asking pardon of each other."

Vermontville continued to resist the liberal currents of theology long after they had captured the New England homeland. It was not until the 1860's that the church, prodded by a liberal minister from Oberlin, "gave indications of breaking away from its earlier Calvinistic moorings and traditions," but the breakaway was resisted by the older members of the congregation "with their fixed New England notions," and half a dozen liberal ministers were broken on the rock of the town's orthodoxy. [3]

It is also possible to trace the breakdown of the redemptive machinery of the town. In its early years the community redeemed the great majority of sinners, but with the growth of rival denominations and the increasing emphasis on morality rather than piety, the sinner was more often expelled than reformed. When the church congregation was no longer coterminous with the population of the community, the pressures on the individual to accept the judgments of his fellows on his behavior were relaxed. Both church and member hardened in their attitudes—the church as it felt itself on the defensive, the individual as he

[2] Newell L. Sims: *A Hoosier Village* (New York: Columbia University Press; 1912), p. 106.
[3] Barber: "The Vermontville Colony," pp. 256, 258, 254.

discovered that expulsion from the church did not mean complete social ostracism and that he could avail himself of alternate choices in the form of rival denominations.

The way in which religion was carried westward by the covenanted community has already been discussed. There were many communities on the frontier, however, which had little or no religious life. "Normally the frontiersman was unreligious." Sunday in many Western towns was a day of riot and disorder, and if one may believe the testimony of many frontier preachers deism and atheists flourished in the Western states in the first half of the nineteenth century. When the Reverend H. D. Fisher arrived in Olathe, Kansas, he found that "rum had a stronghold and infidelity and spirtualism were thoroughly intrenched." [4]

The same conditions existed in many of the cumulative towns on the Vermont frontier that were demoralized by the Revolution and the disintegration of the covenanted community. Manchester, Vermont, in the early years of the nineteenth century was known as an "immoral place" where "drinking, gambling and whoring were common." In Clarendon, a traveler reported "vice predominant and irreligion almost epidemical Sabbath disregarded profanity debauchery drunkenness, quareling by words and blows & parting with broken heads and bloody noses. . . ." [5]

The missionary who landed in such a town concentrated his energies on converting the convertible and driving out the irredeemable. The Reverend Fisher found the struggle a bitter one in Olathe, "but by a combined effort upon the part of all Christian churches in lyceum and

---

[4] Theodore C. Pease: *The Frontier State, 1818–1848* (Springfield, Ill.: Illinois Centennial Commission; 1918), p. 23; Hugh D. Fisher: *The Gun and the Gospel* (Chicago: Kenwood Press; 1896), p. 225.
[5] David M. Ludlum: *Social Ferment in Vermont* (New York: Columbia University Press; 1939), p. 19; Ludlum quotes John Pettibone: "History of Manchester," *Proceedings of the Vermont Historical Society* (December, 1930), p. 156.

pulpit the enemy was routed, horse, foot and dragoon. The infidel club was broken up, the spirtualists were put to flight . . . and the rum power, though in city ordinances backed by the common council and mayor, was undone. . . ." [6]

The circuit rider is one of the most familiar figures on the frontier. Romantic and appealing types, their heyday came in the years prior to the Civil War when they rounded up tens of thousands of settlers, most of them for the Methodist fold. Many of these itinerant preachers were highly articulate. They wrote numerous accounts of their experiences which captured the imaginations of prosperous Easterners who were charmed by this picture of Protestantism winning the West. [7]

If missionaries and itinerant preachers were the agents of the Christian faith in frontier communities, revivals were the principal means by which they accomplished their aim of bringing religion to the newly settled areas of the West. Revivalism was the most important religious phenomenon in nineteenth-century American towns. Revival experiences were, to be sure, as old as the towns themselves, but the first "epidemic" of revivals, which bears the name of the Great Awakening, began in the 1730's and 1740's. After the American Revolution they became an institutionalized part of American Protestantism. The revivals were useful in providing a substitute for the fragmented covenant, and by asserting the community's common faith and common hope they provided an effective substitute for the earlier unity. In addition they offered an essential emotional outlet for people living in the midst of severe

---

[6] Fisher: *Gun and Gospel*, p. 225.
[7] Pomeroy, in *Mississippi Valley Historical Review*, XLI (March, 1955), p. 592. Mr. Pomeroy says "Until recently the image of crudity has persisted especially in pictures of western religion, although religion was a major factor in acculturation . . . the circuit riders now appear as a hard-working and relatively literate group."

tensions and anxieties. Most of the churches that participated in the revivals were "covenanted" churches. The tendency of rival denominations and sects to fragment the social and religious life of the community was balanced, in large part, by the fact that the revivals drew all church groups together for a week or more of prayer and preaching which almost invariably resulted in recruiting new strength for all groups. An itinerant Congregational minister wrote:

> I was by no means particular under what denominational auspices I held these [revivals]. Thus often I preached through a revival meeting with Baptists, then with Presbyterians and Methodists. Indeed, my own denomination complained much that I helped other denominations more than my own; but . . . I believed I had a special mission to bring all these churches a little nearer together, and to show to outsiders the essential unity of the whole household of faith.[8]

That the towns were usually ready for an "awakening" is suggested by the reflections of the minister of Windham, Connecticut, in 1790:

> The present day is peculiar for men's throwing off the fear of the Lord. Declensions in religion have been increasing for about thirty years past, such as profaneness, disregard of the Sabbath, neglect of family religion, unrighteousness, intemperance, imbibing of modern errors and heresies and the crying error of infidelity against the clearest of light.

By 1790 twenty churches in Connecticut had experienced revivals, and within four or five years a hundred and fifty more had joined the ranks. The great revivals of 1800, 1831, and 1858 were parts of nationwide movements, but the pattern of revivals varied from church to church

[8] Sherlock Bristol: *The Pioneer Preacher* (Chicago and New York: Fleming Revell Company; 1887), p. 209.

throughout New England. Often the revival was triggered by some local event—an epidemic or a disastrous fire; sometimes it was set in motion by word of a freshening of the spirit in a neighboring community, sometimes at the prompting of the ministers themselves.

In 1815 Connecticut experienced a wave of revivals. One reporter noted that "in Winchester, Norfolk, New Marlborough, Sandisfield, Goshen, Cornwall, and Salisbury, sinners hastened to Christ as clouds, as doves fly to their windows. From the most correct information received, I conclude that seven hundred were born again in these towns, in the course of the revival." [9]

As Protestantism moved westward the revival moved with it, adopting as its own the camp meeting, which had first made its appearance during the Great Awakening of the 1740's; the "pragmatic" frontier lived in fact in an orgy of emotionalism, mysticism, and fanaticism.

We have a classic description of a revival at Austinburg, Ohio, in 1803. A number of the participants experienced "bodily exercises," such as "the *Falling* exercise, *Jerking Rolling* exercise, *Running, Dancing, Barking* and *Visions & Trances*." The jerk was a series of

> very quick and sudden [movements] . . . followed with short intervals. . . . the convulsive motion was not confined to the arms; it extended in many instances to other parts of the body. When the joint of the neck was affected, the head was thrown backward and forward with a celerity frightful to behold, and which was impossible to be imitated by persons who were not under the same stimulus. The bosom heaved, the countenance was disgustingly distorted, and the spectators were alarmed lest the neck should be broken.

[9] Mary H. Mitchell: "The Great Awakening and Other Revivals in the Religious Life of Connecticut," *Tercentenary Commission of the State of Connecticut*, Committee on Historical Publications, pamphlet no. 26 (New Haven: Yale University Press; 1934), pp. 22, 40.

When the hair was long, it was shaken with such quickness, backward and forward, as to crack and snap like the lash of a whip. Sometimes the muscles of the back were affected, and the patient was thrown down on the ground, when his contortions for some time resembled those of a live fish cast from its native element on the land.

It was apparent that "the more anyone labored to stay himself and be sober, the more he staggered and the more his twitches increased. He must necessarily go as he was inclined, whether with a violent dash on the ground and bounce from place to place like a foot ball, or hop around, with head, limbs, and trunk twitching, and jolting in every direction, as if they must inevitably fly asunder. And how such could escape without injury was no small wonder among spectators." [1]

The impact of the revival experience on the individual was often profound and lasting. James Finley, one of the most famous of the circuit riders, lived in his youth in such a mire of sin that he finally contemplated suicide. Despairing of his soul he "would crawl, feet foremost, into a hollow log, and there read, and weep, and pray." After one such session in the log, he went to a Methodist "class meeting," a gathering at which members of the group gave testimony as to their spiritual state and their "Christian experience."

Finley's description of his own conversion is a typical account of such awakenings. Leaving the class he felt the promptings of the Holy Spirit "in such a manner, and in such a measure, that I fell, my whole length, in the snow, and shouted, and praised God so loud, that I was heard over the neighborhood. . . . For an hour I could do nothing but praise the Lord." For several days Finley was in a state of religious ecstasy and during this time he decided to become a Methodist minister. His Cross Creek circuit

[1] Howe: *Historical Collections*, p. 46.

"included the towns of Steubenville, Cadiz, Mount Pleasant, Smithfield, and several other villages, embracing all the country in Jefferson, part of Harrison and Belmont counties. It took four full weeks to travel round it, with an appointment for every day and two for the Sabbath."

The area included a church membership of some one thousand and Finley preached thirty-two times and met fifty classes on every circuit.[2] The classes were, with the love feasts, the center of the Methodist life in the West. The class was educational, disciplinary, and redemptive. We have a description of such a session from the pen of a skeptical observer:

> The company being assembled and seated, the one acting as leader, rose from his seat, which was a signal for others to do the same. A sort of circle . . . was then immediately formed by the whole assembly taking hold of hands, and capering about the house surprisingly. Their gesture could not be called dancing, and yet no term that I can employ describes it better. This done, worship commenced with extempore prayer, not indeed in language or style the best selected. . . . The following part of the service was exceedingly exceptionable. All the persons present being again seated, an individual started from his seat, exclaiming in a loud and frantic shriek, "I feel it," meaning what is commonly termed among them the power of God. His motions, which appeared half convulsive, were observed with animated joy by the rest, till he fell apparently stiff upon the floor, where he lay unmolested a short time, and then resumed his seat. Others were affected in a similar manner, only in some instances the power of speech was not suspended, as in this, by the vehemence of enthusiasm.[3]

[2] James B. Finley: *Autobiography* . . . , W. P. Strickland, ed. (Cincinnati; 1858) pp. 177, 179–80, 268.
[3] Rebecca Burlend: *A True Picture of Emigration*, Milo M. Quaife, ed. (Chicago: R. R. Donnelley & Sons; 1936), pp. 144–5.

In his autobiography Fisher describes a typical conversion at a revival meeting. An "infidel and scoffer" came to a service one morning to sneer at the worship. Fisher asked the congregation to pray for his soul.

> The spirit of prayer continued to rise in fervor about him. As I stood with my hand on him I prayed God to have mercy and enlighten him and save him. Presently he cried aloud as though pierced with a dart, and fell in the aisle as one slain in a battle. There he lay until midnight, stiff and stark, as though indeed dead. . . . About midnight the sweet, low subdued singing began to penetrate to his soul and he showed signs of returning animation. A heavenly smile came over his face, his lips moved, some of the brethren near by stooped to listen to his whispers; his words became more distinct as he repeated with indescribable sweetness, "Glory, Glory, Jesus saves me! Glory, Glory, to His name!" [4]

As the century wore on the religious life of the towns took on a common pattern. The principal Protestant denominations were represented in most communities, supplemented by a number of sects. The dominant church was often that of the first settlers, although in some cases, when this denomination was and remained on the "fringe" of orthodox Protestantism, another sect—frequently the Methodists—replaced it as the leading church of the community. Conspicuous exceptions were the foreign communities where faith and language reinforced the racial homogeneity of the town and raised a barrier against alien intrusions. The German Lutheran communities of the Middle West were in this category. [5]

As the towns aged and grew, enjoying at least a limited prosperity, the social attitudes of the churches changed, but the change, arrested by the frequency of revivals and

[4] Fisher: *Gun and Gospel*, p. 91.
[5] Heinrich H. Maurer: "Studies in the Sociology of Religion," *American Journal of Sociology*, XXX (November, 1924), p. 276.

freshenings of the spirit, was glacial in its slowness. As the intensity of religious experience diminished the churches, clinging to their negative injunctions, became increasingly repressive. "Thou shalt not," without the counterpoise of love and saving grace, was often harsh and life-denying. As secular society developed alternatives to the narrow social life of the churches the churches fought stubbornly to preserve their control over the towns. Many of them stuck to a rigid fundamentalism which made the literal interpretation of the Bible the principal test of faith. They attempted to maintain an ethic of asceticism and self-denial in the midst of an increasingly sensate and consumption-oriented society with results that were often equally disastrous for the church and for the individual who experienced his religion primarily as a pressure for social conformity.

It might be said of the churches in this period that the ethic must correspond to the general mode of life if it is to be fruitful. This does not mean relaxing ethical restraints, but rather returning to the center of faith and letting the new ethical imperatives emerge from that, through the modes of life which in turn are to raise them to their highest potential. Otherwise it is left to secular society to find acceptable alternatives that are supported only by existing mores or by current fashions. And this is indeed what happened to large segments of American society in the twentieth century.

The social development of the town can be traced through the changes in the character of the churches themselves. The simple democracy of the churches in their early days gave way gradually to distinctions based on material success. Prosperity awakened social aspirations that brought noticeable differences between members of the covenant. The more affluent members pre-empted the better locations for pews within the church, and as communities became more sharply differentiated in terms of worldly possessions, the poorer people of the town, feeling themselves at a disadvantage with their brothers, often turned to rival denominations and sects. Moreover the well-to-do, if they were inclined to political conservatism, gave disturbing evidences of liberalism in theology.

As a town developed social stratification individuals sought churches which offered them a covenanted relationship with others of similar status and outlook. If denominations or sects did not exist to provide such refuges, it was no great matter to create them. Thus one of the most conspicuous features of small-town religious experience in the nineteenth century was the constant splitting off of new sects from the older churches. Some of these divisions undoubtedly arose over genuine doctrinal issues, but many more were social or political in origin. The crisis over slavery produced numerous realignments within the older denominations and gave birth to such groups as the Wesleyan Methodists. The development of new sects was further encouraged by the fact that the new communities were often made up of individuals who had belonged to half a dozen or more different churches. Such persons would sooner join a new sect than a rival denomination, especially when they were assured that the new sect, or the new covenant, was the most democratic and the most universal—that it was the New Church, the heir of primitive Christianity, and the enemy of dogmatic sectarianism. Thus joining the church meant affirming the solidarity of the community and striking a blow for Christian unity. The growth of sectarianism was also aided by the ease with which a minority group could, by emigrating to a new area, turn itself into a majority and often grow rapidly by adding to its membership those who came in later waves.[6]

The fragmentation was at least in part the result of bitter strife within the denominations. Anton Boisen gives an example in "Blankton" of such fragmentation in the Presbyterian Church. The town contained a "New Side

[6] H. Richard Niebuhr: *The Social Sources of Denominationalism* (New York: Henry Holt & Company; 1929).

Reformed Presbyterian Church," a "Psalms of David Presbyterian Church," which in turn split into a New School
and an Old School, an Associate Reformed Presbyterian
Church, an Associate Presbyterian, and an Old Side and a
New Side Presbyterian Church. Thus with a population of
scarcely twelve hundred, the town had six Presbyterian
churches.[7]

In the drive to "socialize" the churches, less and less
attention was paid to the doctrinal and theological side of
the churches' life and more and more to "activities." There
was a growing emphasis on music and on the liturgical
aspects of church services. Sermons became, in many
instances, tepid moralizings. The minister who had been the
father-authority figure, the model of self-denial and unworldliness, was replaced by the affable "mixer"—a kind of
ecclesiastical social director—"a handsome, well-dressed
sociable man . . . who had traveled and read widely" and
was thus able to stimulate the cultural life of the community, since it seemed that salvation was to be obtained
through culture rather than through faith. With the stratification of the community the churches became part of the
social hierarchy. A man's place in the community was
often indicated by the church to which he belonged and
the churches began less to impose their imperatives on the
community and more to enforce the authority of the
town's elite. Since the ministers of all but the most extreme
sectarian groups were included in or attached to the town's
elite, all congregations were accessible to the social and
business leaders of the community who encouraged the
emphasis on personal morality.

An Old Home Week picnic held in Waterbury, New
York, in 1902, demonstrated the degree of social stratification represented in the churches. All church members in
the community were invited but only seventy-eight came,
and of these forty-nine were Presbyterians, twenty Episco-

[7] Anton T. Boisen: *Religion in Crisis and Custom* (New York:
Harper & Brothers; 1955), p. 11.

palians, four Methodists, and two Baptists. The picnickers grouped themselves by denomination (which was also by class) and though one elderly speaker recalled nostalgically the absence of caste in the town in its early history, he got no response from his predominantly middle-class audience.[8]

In many small towns churchgoing declined sharply after the turn of the century. Where churches have maintained their congregations they have often done so by playing down religion and playing up social activities. Church attendance has held up best in the prosperous middle classes which feel an obligation to support the church "as a good thing." James West, for example, found that although the people of Plainville were "non-religious" they were ready to support the church on the basis of "good citizenship," and one informant added the revealing comment that "if it wasn't for the churches and schools, land here wouldn't be worth ten cents an acre." [9]

It is clear that Protestantism in the American small town has from the beginning imposed both a social order and a remarkably coherent set of values on the community. The covenanted community was an extraordinary invention through which the town was "governed by a supernatural principle of socialization." The religion that it professed gave meaning to the life of the individual, "ennobling it by dedicating it to God's larger purposes; it interpreted for him his relationships to the groups around him—his family, his town, the commonwealth. . . . It set the social pattern of his group and determined its function." [1] Against all the disintegrative forces of a hostile environment, of a phenom-

---

[8] James M. Williams: *An American Town* (New York: The J. Kempster Printing Company; 1906), pp. 26–7.
[9] James West: "Plainville, U.S.A.," in Abram Kardiner, ed.: *Psychological Frontiers of Society* (New York: Columbia University; 1945), p. 309.
[1] Liston Pope: "Religion and the Class Structure," in Reinhard Bendix and Seymour Lipset, eds.: *Class, Status and Power* (Glencoe, Ill.: The Free Press; 1953), p. 321.

enally expanding society, the covenant, in its various forms, held fast. Like the cement that binds living cells while allowing them to multiply, it knit individuals together in a unique alliance and armored them against physical and psychological hazards that would have daunted a prizefighter and dismayed a saint.

The covenant and its companion and successor, the revival meeting, both emphasizing redemption, were perfectly adapted to the needs of frontier towns. Such towns whether in the Plymouth Plantation or in Iowa were faced with the problem of making the best use of their human resources. Among the inhabitants of the typical town were undoubtedly a high proportion of social misfits—psychotics, psychoneurotics, the difficult, distressed, and ne'er-do-wells.

Anton Boisen estimates that in one modern Midwestern town which he studied during the depression of the 1930's, such individuals constituted as much as one third of the community. If we assume that most pioneer communities, in the very nature of things, had a relatively high proportion of such persons, we can understand the importance of the covenant, with its public confession and repentance, with its absolution by the community, and its constant affirmation of common ideals; and the covenant's later corollary, the revival, operated to much the same effect. These were, from one perspective, mechanisms by which the community, maintaining its control over individuals, could draw them back, time after time, into useful lives within the group. A town of a few hundred inhabitants could not jail those who deviated from its code. The petty thieves, the liars, the compulsive quarrelers, the sex deviates, the licentious, the intemperate could neither be locked up, placed in institutions, left undisturbed to poison the life of the group, nor driven out. They had to be accepted by the community; as long as they could guide a plow or lift a rifle they were precious to the town. As long as they would accept admonishment or come in penitence to the mourner's bench, they could be rehabilitated as useful citizens. Even the outcast who had destroyed his standing in the community by years of idleness and dissipation could, by public profession of repentance, be restored to the full life of his town. James West noted this same fact among the Holiness sects of Plainville: "A man who has been considered worthless as a worker, sexually immoral, or dishonest financially can through salvation gain social acceptance by the religious sector of his own class." [2]

Much emphasis has been put on the harmful effects suffered by the sensitive person as the result of the grim ideas often associated with evangelical Protestantism—hellfire, eternal damnation, predestination, Divine Wrath, and public confession; but it has been less often noted that the revival experience, in its widest meaning, permitted the externalizing of individual and group anxieties. There is evidence that after the dissolution of the initial covenant revivals prevented a large-scale breakdown in many communities. The town that was established in the wilderness or on the prairie was built on the exaggerated hopes of those who wished for a religious utopia or who saw in their towns the seeds of flourishing cities. Between such expectations and reality lay a gap wide enough to swallow up the hardiest spirit. The disappointments and frustrations of actual settlement could be evaded by moving on to the next utopia beyond the western hills, by accommodating oneself to the harsh but real state of things (which often meant defeat and despair), or by keeping a tight hold on the vision until the situation lost its grimmer aspects.

Boisen has noted that in towns where the "church of custom"—the formal, institutionalized church—prevailed, there was apt to be a far higher incidence of mental breakdown than in the communities that were dominated by evangelistic and "Holiness" sects. "Where the old-line church serves as the custodian of the ancient faith and of

[2] "Plainville," p. 314.

the standards on which the personal and social organization is built," he writes, "we find . . . an enormous amount of mental illness, explainable in large part by the inner conflicts which these same standards produce."

In other words, where the old demands remain, reinforced by the sanctions of the community, but where at the same time "the channels of redemption" are closed, the individual suffers far greater psychic stress than he did in the days when profound emotional fervor distinguished the religion of the community. This is the repressive community that we find etched with such bitterness by many novelists of the small town who, growing up in a period of their town's maturity, suffered severely from its negative injunctions.

"Springville," a town of about five hundred inhabitants, was dominated by "churches of custom." Boisen classified sixteen percent of the community as the "faithful," those who were unselfishly dedicated to the church as an expression of their desire to serve the community. The greater portion of the churchgoers were simply the complacent who used the churches but had little genuine commitment to anything beyond their own well-being. Nine percent of the community Boisen characterized as "pagan" individuals who were failures in terms of the standards of the community and who had acquiesced to the judgment of the town. In a community dominated by "churches of custom" there was for these people no recourse from the judgments of their neighbors. They had become the victims of the image that the community had of them. The avenues of redemption were largely closed. But in towns where the revival was still an institution, the community was obligated to restore the repentant sinner to its good graces, even if earlier backslidings and reformations had raised doubts about the permanence of his reform.

Twenty-five percent of the inhabitants of Springville were judged by Boisen to be "more or less ill mentally. That is, they had more or less serious maladjustments, and instead of defying the community judgments or socializing their inferiorities among the poolroom and barber shop habitués, they subjected themselves to self-blame and self-punishment, or resorted to various concealment devices, or took refuge in drink or daydreaming." [3] It is these individuals who suffered most from the absence of revivals, testimonies, public confession, and experiences of conversion. They had not accepted the level of adjustment of the "pagans," but were tormented by feelings of guilt and inadequacy. Formerly these types were refreshed and rehabilitated by the revival experience.

The mentally ill, as described by Boisen, include a gallery of familiar figures who have appeared in many fictional portraits of the town. We have the hypochondriac, the malicious gossip, the chronically irritable and suspicious. The town itself bred many of the abnormalities represented among such mentally ill persons, but any number of these marginal types were excellent human material and frequently the best subjects for conversion. To know despair, "unspeakable worry," torment, and mental anguish is to become open to true conversion. One comes to feel from reading many accounts of conversion experiences that these were people who, once they had been touched by a sense of God's redeeming power and love, became engines of reform and witnesses to the efficacy of God's grace.

If the "churches of custom" in Springville offered little hope or help for the third of the community which was socially, economically, or emotionally "marginal," the story was quite different in "Blankton," where the Pentecostal or Holiness sects predominated and afforded the community much-needed emotional outlets. While the Great Depression shook Springville to its foundations, Blankton experienced little breakdown; instead the Holiness and Pentecostal churches underwent a remarkable

[3] Boisen: *Religion in Crisis,* pp. 4–5, 28.

growth and were able, without a doubt, to channel off much anxiety and emotional stress.

It is the Holiness churches which today most effectively reproduce the religion of the "frontier." These sects are distinguished by their intense emotionalism and their religion-centered lives. "All their social life," James West noted in his study of Plainville, "is permeated by religious conversation and prayer; theirs is the only congregation practicing material charity for their poor; and their mutual helpfulness in every day life exceeds that of all other Plainvillers." [4] They thus reproduce, alongside of the formal faith of the urbanized middle class, many of the characteristics of historic small-town Protestantism.

But it is important to make one clear distinction between the members of present-day Holiness sects and their Puritan predecessors. While the internal functioning of both types of Christianity shows certain striking similarities, the contemporary Holiness sects are made up of socially marginal groups whose sense of rejection has turned their churches into fortresses the primary function of which is to reassure their members that as individuals they stand outside the judgments of society. The ethic of work and the sacredness of calling are not strong elements in the Holiness churches. Members belong to these churches primarily because they have failed in terms of the most insistently publicized values of our society. Obsessed by a feeling of social helplessness, they have turned toward religious groups that place their emphasis on salvation and the life hereafter. Such sects grew in importance in the town as the feeling diminished that the individual or the community could affect the course of events or modify the forms of institutional life. The ideals of the Puritans, on the other hand, were the dominant values of our society for over two centuries, and the Puritan, as a classic type, was an aggressive, outreaching individual who had little reason

[4] "Plainville," p. 311.

to doubt the ultimate triumph of his values. He wished, while worshipping God, to remake the world according to Divine injunctions. The Pietist asked only to be left alone; the Puritan insisted on his authority to reform the world in the image of his own covenanted community.

If the Puritan covenant gave the community its essential form, the character type created in that crucible could not be contained within it. For the Puritan, time was continuous; the walls were demolished between earthly time and eternal time, and time-serving was thus made impossible because every moment contained the possibility of grace. The Calvinist, moreover, enjoyed a remarkable mobility. "The effective calling of Calvin," Heinrich Maurer wrote, "is not one of place stewardship. On the contrary, the saint of Calvinism has a roving commission, entailing unlimited liabilities and risks before God, responsibilities unlimited in time and space." [5]

The result was that by involving the ordinary details of everyday existence in the drama of salvation, an extraordinary tension was created which, carried to new towns and to the cities, gave nineteenth-century America much of its dynamism. To live always under God's eye is to live dangerously and at the peak of awareness. It was not the rationalistic and historical theology of the eighteenth and the nineteenth century that produced community builders. It was, rather, the simpler, more rigorous faith of earlier generations that was manifested in the establishment of new towns spreading westward.

The covenanted community created a character type that endured through successive transplantings and through successive transformations. That the type was being transformed in the more liberal centers was, to some extent, balanced by the fact that in its transplantings from town to

[5] Maurer: "Studies in the Sociology of Religion," p. 276; Leslie Fiedler: *An End to Innocence* (Boston: Beacon Press; 1955), p. 142.

town across the country it preserved almost intact the imperatives of the original covenants.

Here was the paradox: the covenanted community, remarkably stable and unshakably conservative produced outwardly propelled, inner-directed individuals capable of the most startling innovation and the most revolutionary change, carried through in the name of the ancient values of the town.

The religious varieties of the covenant are no longer a mortar capable of binding together the life of the community. The Protestant churches of the town (except perhaps in the South) are hardly distinguishable from those of the city. Liberal in theology and "social" in polity, they are less concerned with producing saints than good citizens. The search for peace of mind has replaced the fervent evangelizing of an earlier generation. The small-town congregation no longer expects to be the instrument of universal Christian reformation; its aims are more modest; it wishes to stay solvent, to be included in the national TV network, and to be given periodic assurance of its own righteousness. Its members are encouraged to seek in the church "a partnership with God," which, they are told, will help business, remove anxiety, lower blood pressure, and make America strong; the church offers them "a life with meaning," but, it is to be feared, one without the deeper commitment of faith and without moral grandeur.

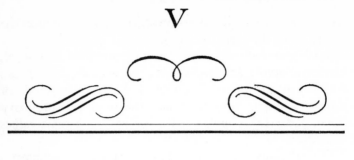

V

The Economic Life of the Town

THE ECONOMIC LIFE OF THE TOWN was in its earliest period undifferentiated. In its classic form the New England village was made up of farmers who among themselves represented the skills needed to maintain the community. This pattern was repeated in the majority of rural towns throughout America down to the middle of the nineteenth century.

The diary of Mathew Patten of Bedford, New Hampshire, provides a remarkable picture of such a small-town economy. In August, 1755, Patten recorded:

> Paid Mrs. Wadal one pound for knitting a pair of barrd stockings for Benjⁿ Linkfield and went to Chester and Indented with Mr Jonathan Sanders to Come and make me a pair of Cart Wheels by the

middle of the weak after next and returned home again.

4ᵗʰ James Kennedy finished makeing a set of Cart Hoops and Charged me 2–10–0 and a pair of Beetle rings and Charged 3ˢ & Joˢ Thomas gave my wife 15 £ old Tenor for a deers Leather a buck skin and fawn skin.

5ᵗʰ Went to Alexʳ MacMurphys mill & got 2 bushels of rie and ¾ of a bushel of Turkey wheat Ground and went Adam Weirs and got the promise to fill 2 yds of Double Dimaty with Cotton and gave him 14 Cutts to do it with.

8ᵗʰ Got two pigs from John Quig and Got a striped jacout cut out by Hannah Barnet.

14ᵗʰ Had Hugh Macguines helping me reap rie on John Maclaughlins account and Kathrine Little & Isabell Mclaughlin helping me pull flax in the forenoon.

In February, 1757, Patten "got 2 bushell of Potatoes from Gawin Riddel and gave him 40s/."

The next day he "bought 8 bushels of Indian corn from John Holms and gave him for it 61 £ in mony and 3¾ yd of Checked woolen Cloath for a shirt and my wife made it up. . . ."[1]

In addition to farming, Patten trapped, hunted, and fished, worked as a carpenter, tanner, lawyer, judge, town selectman, surveyor, and businessman. Mary Ellen Chase gives us, from the journal of the Reverend Jonathan Fisher, the picture of a Maine parson with talents almost as diverse as Patten's. The Reverend Fisher painted, made butter molds, rose conserve, picture frames, a cure for the sore throat of "sweetened pine booze," and tooth powder compounded of "pulverized hardwood coal, rendered savory by a few drops of oil of lavendar." He made baskets from reeds, twigs, and grasses, and buttons from the bones

[1] Mathew Patten: *Diary of Mathew Patten, 1754 to 1788* (Concord, N.H.: Rumford Printing Co.; 1903), pp. 18–19, 33–5.

of slaughtered animals. He records setting window sashes, making chests and tables, decorating sleighs, and painting the names on ships and schooners. He built a horse trough for the village, turned out drumsticks at twenty-five cents a pair, and bound books for himself and his neighbors.[2]

The marvelous variety of skills represented by a Patten or a Fisher gave way increasingly to specialization of function, which came, in time, to mark off the town from the surrounding farms. Our picture of town industry in these years is of such small-scale ventures as tanning, cabinetmaking, shoemaking, the manufacture of plows or barrel staves—enterprises designed to meet the needs of the town and the adjacent farms and to provide a surplus for export to the nearest city. Such undertakings are generally represented as the golden age of the small-town economy. Independent artisans, skilled and loving practitioners of their crafts, worked and prospered without "bosses" or "unions," or assembly lines.

The industries of Manchester, Massachusetts, in the first half of the nineteenth century suggest such an ideal picture. The town produced shoes, reed organs, and fire engines. In 1837 the shoe factory, employing 15 workers, turned out 425 pairs of boots and 2,750 pairs of shoes. The tannery had 3 employees, a capital of $7,000, and tanned 2,000 hides with a value of $5,500. Twelve chair and cabinet factories employed 120 townspeople and did a gross business of $84,000. Three thousand palm-leaf hats were produced in the same year and in the shipyards four vessels that could transport a total burden of 190 tons were built.[3]

Stated thus, however, an important fact about small-town industry is obscured. At best such enterprises were highly precarious. From the early days of the new nation,

[2] Mary Ellen Chase: *Jonathan Fisher, Maine Parson, 1768–1847* (New York: The Macmillan Company; 1948), p. 129.
[3] Darius F. Lamson: *History of the Town of Manchester, Essex County, Massachusetts, 1645–1895* (published by the town; 1895), p. 161.

and indeed for a generation before the Revolution, local industries were apt to be extremely transitory. The relation of the town to a wider economy was so casual and uncoordinated that the town was defenseless against relatively minor shifts in the economic pattern. The tradition-bound workman of the pre-industrial age had little capacity to adapt himself to changing demands; he had no stable supply of labor; no efficient channels for marketing his products; no capital to speak of, and few credit resources. If he was a store or tavern keeper he was expected to extend credit without stint, and he could not, in bad times, dun his debtors for payment. He was thus excessively vulnerable and the enterprises that he launched failed with monotonous regularity.

The colonial towns struggled to maintain some degree of stability by securing the passage of statutes that aimed at regulating wages and prices. But not until the Revolution, when the problems of a national economy had to be faced by the Continental Congress, did anyone seriously suggest that price- and wage-fixing were not the proper way to control the economy; even then no one rose to argue that wage- and price-fixing infringed on the rights of the individual entrepreneur or worker. Established tradition placed the interests of the community clearly above those of the individual. It remained for the nineteenth century to discover "rugged individualism" and proclaim it, quite erroneously, as a classic American doctrine.[4]

---

[4] Richard B. Morris: "Labor and Mercantilism," in R. B. Morris, ed.: *Era of the American Revolution* (New York: Columbia University Press; 1939), pp. 83 ff. For colonial price-fixing policies, see R. B. Morris: "Price-fixing in Colonial America" in the same book, and for later developments see Louis Hartz: "Laissez-faire Thought in Pennsylvania, 1776–1860"; Frederick K. Heinrich: "The Development of American Laissez-faire in the Age of Washington"; and Oscar Handlin: "Laissez-faire Thought in Massachusetts, 1790–1880," in *Tasks of Economic History*, supplemental issue in the *Journal of Economic History*, III (December, 1943).

Another treasured part of the American myth is the image of the shrewd, hard-working individual who starts a small business, nurses it through lean years and economic adversity, and becomes at last a rich and famous industrialist (or, more modestly, a prosperous and respected businessman). In the first half of the nineteenth century the myth seldom coincided with reality.

The industrial story of Exeter, New Hampshire, can be taken as typical of hundreds of similar towns. The Pickpocket Mills, built soon after the end of the Revolution and backed largely by the townspeople of Exeter, contained 8,000 spindles. A large undertaking for Exeter, it was in fact a faltering, small-scale operation that limped along for some twenty years through a succession of managements, losing money almost continually. It burned, finally, and was rebuilt as a paper mill; as such it passed through four different hands in a period of less than ten years and was finally converted into a mill for the manufacture of wooden boxes which was no more successful than its predecessors.

An Exeter powder mill, started in 1776 to supply powder for the Continental Army, was turned into an iron furnace and slitting mill following the war. After ten limping years, land, mills, and water rights were sold to new investors. In 1814 the plant was converted into a cotton mill; it was sold a few years later, and then again in 1838 to Oliver Whipple, a Lowell merchant, who established a powder mill once more. Several serious explosions occurred, and in 1855 a new mill was constructed for the manufacture of hubs, spokes, and shingles; this venture failed within ten years.

A starch mill, founded in the town in 1824, was successful at once because its builder had discovered a cheap process for making starch. The factory lasted as long as the secret of the process was preserved, and after ten years went out of business. Pottery, cotton-duck, saddles, hats, wool, leather, and shoes were all products of Exeter during the first half of the nineteenth century. Neverthe-less, one enterprise after another collapsed, and while in time the town became thoroughly industrialized, it failed to grow, its dreamt-of prosperity was never achieved and its industries, rather than enriching the community, kept it impoverished and insecure.

Typical of the small-town entrepreneur was James Derby of Exeter, "an energetic machinist," a young man of the type who, if he were industrious, polite, thrifty, and pious, could not presumably avoid amassing "a comfortable estate." At one time or another, Derby established a printing plant to turn out Bible commentaries, the first machine shop in New England to manufacture gas pipes, and a plant to produce carriage fittings. All were disastrous failures.[5] Perhaps Derby, disheartened by successive finan-cial calamities, came to view the rags-to-riches saga with a jaundiced eye.

Hartford, Vermont, like Exeter, struggled to develop the industries that it was assumed would bring it fame and prosperity. In 1771 four local men sold a sawmill to an enterprising neighbor, Jonathan Burtch, for £86. Burtch added grist and fulling mills, and in 1778 sold the property to a businessman from Stephantown, New York. Between 1778 and 1824 the property changed hands some twelve times before the fulling mill was at last abandoned and a brick factory established in its place. The brick factory failed promptly, but the site and buildings were sold in 1826 to the Quechee Manufacturing Company for $12,000. This company failed in 1828 and the property was pur-chased by Boston interests who sent an agent to run the plant. The agent was no more successful than previous managers, and in 1836 the mills were sold to the Mallory Woolen Company for $27,914.34. Seven years later the company was foreclosed for a debt of $24,582.50 by a William Jarvis who, after struggling with the venture for

[5] Charles Henry Bell: *History of the Town of Exeter, New Hampshire* (Exeter, N.H.; 1888), pp. 326–30, 341.

fourteen years, disposed of the entire property for $8,500.

By 1857, then, the mill, located on a splendid natural site with an abundance of power and a large supply of cheap local labor, had failed innumerable times, costing hundreds of backers thousands of dollars and subjecting the community to a series of economic shocks. The Civil War brought only temporary surcease. A distillery in Hartford made potato whisky during the war and prospered, as did most of the other industries of the town, but peace brought the price of whisky down from $1.50 to 33¢ a gallon and the company folded. The same story was repeated with every other industry in Hartford—the tannery, the bed-spring factory, the dyeing and carding mills—all failed.

In the series of failures that marked the town's history several local capitalists defaulted, one committed suicide, several lost their minds, and at least two took to drink. If such failures were due to managerial incompetence, one must assume that the proverbial New England thrift and shrewdness were a fraud. It is hard to believe that among the several score of enterprising Yankees who directed these ventures there were none who were competent.

The fact that the Civil War put the mills on their feet for a few years and that by the 1880's certain plants had become highly successful operations reinforces the conviction that the earlier disasters were due less to human shortcomings than to "the system." Moreover when the story of an Exeter or a Hartford is repeated with monotonous regularity in one small "industrial" town after another it seems apparent that the conventional picture of American business enterprise, at least in regard to the small town, is quite erroneous.

Of course urban businesses failed in enormous numbers, but these failures were generally individual rather than community tragedies. When the small town had committed itself to being an industrial center, every business failure shook it to its foundations. It is indeed not hard to imagine the atmosphere created in a small town by such repeated catastrophes. Yet the town, generally speaking, demonstrated remarkable resilience. That repeated failures did not destroy the towns was due in a large measure to the fact that agriculture remained the real base of the economy. Most of the businessmen of the town had farms that they maintained with the help of hired men and seasonal labor. The working force was drawn, generally, from the unmarried or spinster daughters of farmers, or boys still in their teens. When a particular venture failed, the labor force and management alike returned to the farm, assured of subsistence. For most small towns in the first half of the nineteenth century local industry meant simply a supplement to agricultural income. This gave the towns their extraordinary capacity to survive repeated bankruptcies. Nobody got rich but very few ended up public wards. Moreover, once rooted in a town the "rags-to-riches" myth was so persistent that for each soldier fallen in the battle another true believer, armed with the maxims of Poor Richard, stood ready to replace him. The truth of failure and ruin had no force against the dream of success.

There were of course triumphs—few, but enough to give substance to the myth. All could not fail; and the successes were seized upon eagerly. One such success could efface the memory of a hundred defeats. Hartford, Vermont, in its dreary record of reversals, produced one figure who fulfilled the image. The life of Albert Gallatin Dewey, the son of impoverished parents, was a parable of the pious, industrious youth who made good. He had worked as a boy as a carpenter's apprentice, then in the Quechee Mills and in the mills at nearby Woodstock. In 1835, with carefully accumulated savings, he built a woolen mill on the Quechee River. At the end of two years he was $15,000 in debt. However, he continued to run the mill, laying hands off and taking them on in response to every fluctuation of the market. He was saved finally by a machine invented by a Woodstock mechanic which manufactured "shoddy," the cheapest kind of yarn made from woolen rags. By such expedients did this archetypal Yankee survive—by making inferior goods, by using a machine that he was lucky enough to come upon that was some years ahead of existing ones, by sweating his labor, and by carrying an enormous debt. Finally, the Civil War brought him fortune and established him as one of the leading industrialists of the state.

The story of Holyoke, Massachusetts, is one of a village which achieved the dream of industrial growth accompanied by results that were, at least in human terms, more disastrous than any failure. In the 1780's a gristmill, a sawmill, and a corn mill were built in Ireland Parish on the Connecticut River. A tannery was started along with a cider mill, a wagon shop, and a clock-making business. Bog iron was dug and a foundry operated fitfully. By 1827 the ironworks had given way to a cement factory, but the cement was of poor quality and the cement works were soon transformed into a straw paper mill. The base of the town's economy remained agricultural, supplemented by the shad runs that in the spring drew hundreds of farmers from the surrounding country. The industrial ambitions of the town, originally stimulated in 1795 by the construction of a two-and-a-half-mile canal which provided ideal factory sites, were dampened by the gradual realization that the town could not amass sufficient capital to launch and sustain sizable industries. It remained for Springfield capital to build the town's first successful large-scale business, a mill that produced an excellent grade of paper and that was soon joined by a rival company, which established itself nearby. The two plants together employed more than a hundred men and women at wages of 85¢ a day for men and 33¢ for women. But despite their initial success both companies went bankrupt in the depression and panic of 1837.

In 1832 the Hadley Falls Company was established to produce cotton cloth. For the first time a company was founded in the community whose stockholders were not local men. The change marked the beginning of a new era in the industrial development of the town. The company was capitalized at the almost unimaginable sum of $2,450,-000, and its stock was subscribed by over a hundred individuals and fifteen business concerns. The modest factories started by enterprising citizens of the town and destined, according to the "myth," to grow and prosper through the operation of that natural law which Americans had been assured must inevitably reward industry, thrift, and skill—all these had failed, repeatedly and dismally. What brought "success" to Holyoke, and to towns similarly blessed, was not patient industry, nor wise thrift, but the activities of the financial wizards of Boston and Lowell who had mastered the mysteries of stock issues, mergers, and corporate finance.

The new mill was five stories high—quite the grandest structure in Ireland Parish. Of the several hundred people employed, some hundred and twenty-five were natives of the town. Most of the rest were Irish immigrants brought in by the company to fill up the labor force. The farmers' daughters who had been willing to take jobs in the small-scale industries of the town were not inclined to work beside rough Irish laborers. The native workers were thus gradually replaced by immigrants. Holyoke, although it did not know the word, found itself with a new social class —the proletariat.

The Hadley Falls Company, as the chief agent of industrialization, helped to transform Holyoke in a decade from a pleasant rural town to a noisome pesthole vividly described in a report issued in 1856 by the town Board of Health. "Many families," the Board's inspectors found, "were huddled into low, damp and filthy cellars, and others in attics which were but little if any better, with scarcely a particle of what might be called air to sustain life." Twenty years later the town had "more and worse large tenement houses than any manufacturing town of textile fabrics in the state, and built in such a manner that there is very little means of escape in case of fire. The sanitary arrangements are very imperfect and in many cases there is no provision made for carrying the slops from the sinks, but they are allowed to run wherever they can make their way. Portions of the yards are covered with filth and green slime, and within twenty feet, people are living in basements of houses three feet below the level of the yard."

When the officers of the company, undoubtedly genuinely distressed over the ravages of smallpox in the town, offered free vaccinations for all employees, the local press hailed them as models of enlightened benevolence. The newspapers carried many accounts of surprise parties given for one overseer or another by his subordinates. Elaborate presents were accompanied by flowery but patently sincere addresses. When Isaac Berry, a popular fiddler, was shifted from the post of overseer in the weave shed of Number Two Mill to that of the Number One Mill, the weavers visited his house in the evening and presented him with an easy chair and a pipe, and his wife with silver forks and knives. Speeches were exchanged, and the Holyoke *Transcript* observed "that although Mr. Berry is of course exceedingly happy at receiving such generous keepsakes from his employees, he still does not feel any ways aristocratic. . . ."

The foremen and managers of such companies were keenly aware of their responsibilities in the community. They contributed generously to local churches, sponsored libraries, encouraged "workingmen's associations" designed to improve the laborer's mind and character, and helped to organize temperance societies. The impulse for such activities was religious and moral rather than social. The industrial manager who behaved so responded, not to the promptings of a "social conscience" nor to an abstract picture of the benevolent executive, but rather to the Protestant ethic, which instructed him that it was his duty to God and to his fellow man. And his employees, working long hours at low pay and living in the most sordid and unwholesome conditions, admired him as a Christian gentleman and sought to emulate him.

If the extreme dislocations produced in the town by the advent of large-scale industry caused anxieties and resentments these were directed, not against the executives of the Hadley Falls Company, but against the Irish laborers and their families that the company had brought to Holyoke. The town was quite ready to attribute the magnificence of the enterprise to the wisdom and piety of the entrepreneurs, even down to foremen, and to equip them, in their imagination, with the classic pedigree required by the myth —a humble childhood of hardship and privation, then, successively, industry, frugality, and piety, and finally riches, although not one in a dozen of the principal stockholders of the Hadley Falls Company had such a background.

A depression in 1857 brought an end to the company's enlightened regime. The Hadley Falls enterprise, along with its competitors, went bankrupt and paid its creditors $1.32 on each hundred-dollar share of stock. Its failure might be said to mark a second step in the development of American industrialism as it appeared in the town. The techniques of financing had been mastered, but managerial skill still lagged. Methods of distribution were primitive and the desire of stockholders for enormous initial profits prevented industries from establishing reserve funds that would enable them to survive stormy economic weather.

The company was reorganized a year later but conditions in the town grew steadily worse. In 1873 the Holyoke *Transcript*, launching a crusade to improve the health services of the community, described

> one pitiful and miserable sight which we have seen night after night in front of the fruit and vegetable stands, since green and ripe fruit came into the market. It is a drove of poverty-stricken children, often girls, clad only in one or two ragged and dirty garments, down on their hands and knees in the gutters, greedily

picking out of the mud and dirt and eating the bits of spoiled and decaying fruit which have been thrown out as worthless. . . . Nothing is so far gone, but some child will be found hungry enough to eat it. A day or two ago we watched some little girls who had lit upon a spot where a few mouldy berries had been thrown out. They clawed in the mud with their fingers, and wrangled over the possession of a berry as if it had been a lump of gold. . . . If driven away, they troop back like a flock of famished vultures to pick up refuse coated with dirt that a pig would reject.

Holyoke was a success. It had achieved what thousands of towns had yearned for: it had become a major industrial center; it had grown rapidly; it was "on the map." It was also true that the sewers of the town emptied into the canal that flowed through it; that the community was unable to provide for its paupers; that its disease and death rate had tripled. But only the enemies of progress grumbled—cantankerous farmers and chronic malcontents. The company itself exuded a conscious air of virtue and public spirit. All employees without families were required to live in a company boardinghouse where "respectable keepers" took note of their comings and goings, locked the doors at ten o'clock in the evening, and prevented "the inmates" from collecting "on the front steps or sidewalk in front of their tenements." [6] What had been initially accepted as thoughtful benevolence became, with the passage of years, increasingly harsh and oppressive. Callousness and lack of responsibility toward factory employees was bred by the fierce struggle for survival in which the company itself was engaged. If the rewards were great the risks were no less so.

The successful or relatively successful industrial ven-

[6] Constance McLaughlin Green: *Holyoke, Massachusetts, A Case History in the Industrial Revolution in America* (New Haven: Yale University Press; 1939), pp. 43, 116, 108, 125–6, 44.

ture was not generally speaking founded or owned by a son of the town. In Massachusetts, as in most other industrial states, a powerful financial oligarchy of families bound together by marriage controlled a large part of the financial and industrial life of the Commonwealth. The Cabots, Lowells, Lawrences, Higginsons, Lees, and Eliots made up an "institutionalized elite" whose "alliances and counter-alliances" dominated the "economic, political and social life" of the state prior to the Civil War. The number of "honest mechanics" or "ambitious sons of farmers" who mounted through industry, thrift, and piety to the top of the pile were few indeed.[7] The town which failed in the race for industry dwindled into gentle impotence; to succeed as Holyoke did meant to explode into some terrible and tormented form whose sickness was acclaimed true health; to neither succeed nor to fail meant to live from one hope to the next, finding in each just enough nourishment to keep dreams alive.

Starting as rural communities that were also business ventures, frequently of a wildly speculative nature, Midwestern towns progressed to the specialized functions of rural "trading centers." Loudly proclaiming the superior virtues of country life, they waged ruthless campaigns to attract railroads and industries while lusting for the forbidden riches that their spokesmen never tired of denouncing. And by and large they suffered the same frustrations and defeats as did their parent communities in the East. The Western towns gave homage to the ethic, but their settlement was often accompanied by the most exaggerated hopes of material success. Even the covenanted communities were not immune to the periodic fevers that ravaged counties and states.

[7] Robert K. Lamb: "The Entrepreneur and the Community," in William Miller, ed.: *Men in Business* (Cambridge, Mass.: Harvard University Press; 1952); and Dorothy Gregg: "John Stevens, General Entrepreneur, 1749–1830," in the same volume, p. 121.

James Finley, riding circuit on the Ohio frontier in the second decade of the nineteenth century, observed the

almost universal spirit of speculation which prevailed. . . . A money mania seemed to have seized, like an epidemic, the entire people. Every body went to banking. Within the bounds of our circuit there were no less than nine banking establishments, seven of them within the county of Jefferson, and one of them said to have been kept in a lady's chest. . . . But it did not stop here. Tavern-keepers, merchants, butchers, bakers—every body seemed to have become bankers. This fever not only raged in this vicinity, but throughout the entire west.[8]

In addition to such periodic fevers of speculation that swept through whole areas, individual towns had their peculiar frenzies—mining, oil, various industries. But most important of all was the railroad. Hundreds of towns were founded by optimists who were sure a railroad would come through their community and make it into a metropolis overnight. Rival towns fought for railroad lines like condottieri struggling for a dukedom. And the railroad, like a capricious god, made and broke towns, offered its favors to the highest bidder, and pillaged established communities to found new ones farther west. Occasionally, after a town had raised the required ransom, the railroad came and brought with it steady commercial growth and prosperity, but more often it brought nothing but disappointment for inflated hopes, and not infrequently it destroyed what precarious industrial life existed in the town by introducing more cheaply produced city products. John Holmes recalls that although Mastersville was so situated that the railroad could hardly have missed it, the people of the town raised the inevitable subsidy to attract it only to find that "it was more of detriment to the town than a help as far as growth was

---

[8] James B. Finley: *Autobiography* . . . , W. P. Strickland, ed. (Cincinnati; 1858), pp. 273–4.

concerned, because right away it shipped in goods that . . . the town was making." [9] The first casualty was a local broom factory.

Republic, Ohio, had big plans for growth but when the railroad was run through Seneca County, the town was left out in the cold. "Business went all to pieces, houses were deserted and the town soon assumed an air of general dilapidation. It remained in that condition until the making of the Baltimore & Ohio railroad. . . ." When finally the railroad passed through Republic, the town revived and enjoyed a few years of mild prosperity before it once more lapsed into rural somnolence.[1]

The railroad reached Hillsboro, Iowa, in 1882, producing the following effects described by Roger Galer:

> We began to be conscious of being a part of the great world outside. Heretofore we had been a little rural eddy. Now we were out in the stream, though still far from being in the rushing current of modern life. Soon daily newspapers began to arrive in small numbers. . . . A drugstore came to town. There were also furniture and undertaking establishments. . . . The two stores became five. A new, much larger, schoolhouse was erected. . . . A bank was organized. The churches were rebuilt. Gradually the tempo changed. . . . The new day had come.[2]

The story of the Western railroads has often been told, but never with specific reference to their effect on the towns. They doubtless have been too much abused for their exploitation of the farmer; by bringing in settlers and carrying away their products, they played a vital role in the settlement of the West. But to the town, an institution

[9] J. H. Holmes.
[1] William Lang: *The History of Seneca County* (Springfield, Ohio: Transcript Printing Co.; 1880), p. 588.
[2] Roger B. Galer: "Recollections of Busy Years," *Iowa Journal of History and Politics*, XLII (January, 1944), p. 16.

struggling for survival, the railroads represented a force that produced endless hope and anxiety, that was both a promise and a menace. In the towns that stretched themselves, that consciously entered the race for the golden prize, we find a familiar pattern of failure. Almost every one of these towns had a bank or more often a succession of them. In good times the banks lent money to all reputable applicants and in hard times they failed.

The Seneca County Bank in Seneca, Ohio, was founded in 1847 and failed the next year; was revived in 1851 and failed dramatically in 1857. In Tiffin, Ohio, Tomb, Huss & Company operated as a private bank until it was chartered as the First National Bank in 1865. Ten years later the bank failed and Huss, its president, shot himself. The Tiffin Savings Bank was started in 1873 and collapsed after four years.[3]

In the middle decades of the nineteenth century insurance companies took the small towns by storm. In Tiffin the Seneca County Mutual Fire Insurance Company was chartered in 1850. The manager appointed agents "who had no experience in insurance matters," and made up in "impudence and avarice" what they lacked in knowledge. The company issued 1,502 policies during its brief lifetime and after several crises collapsed in 1860. The story was repeated in hundreds of other towns.

Vermontville, Michigan, was settled by individuals who were models of New England thrift and prudence, but this did not spare the town its allotment of financial disasters. In 1853 two of Vermontville's most substantial citizens opened a store with a large and carefully chosen stock. It failed in a few years, was reopened with a new partner, failed again, was run for several years by another proprietor, and finally under new owners did a good business for ten years, thereby displaying an unusual tenacity. Another general store, started in 1854, had four different owners in

[3] Lang: *Seneca County*, pp. 337–9.

nine years. Nonetheless, the historian of Vermontville noted that "there have been fewer changes among the merchants than in most villages." [4]

Newell Sims, in his study of "Aton," Indiana, has given us a detailed picture of the economic life of a typical Midwestern community. Aton, started by Spiritualists from the burnt-over region of New York State, demonstrated most of the characteristics of small-town life once it had sloughed off its ideological eccentricities. Its citizens sought to lure a railroad with a $75,000 subsidy and the Aton *Republican* proclaimed:

> We can reasonably expect that a few years will put our town in the ranks with the most beautiful and prosperous in the State. . . . Every means must be used to induce the manufacturer, the merchant, men of science, mechanics, and good industrious people of all classes and nationalities to settle among us.

The railroad brought the hoped-for boom. In 1870 twelve business blocks, thirty-eight dwellings, and two churches were erected. The town hummed with activity and real-estate values doubled. The editor of the *Republican* announced triumphantly:

> No other town in northern Indiana has made as much progress within the past four years in wealth, population and permanent improvements as Aton. . . . We need, though, in the way of manufactories to make our town what it should be, a manufacturer of Cheese, Staves and Barrels, Furniture, Chairs, Hub and Spoke, and woolen factories. . . . Our capitalists are land-owners and their money is locked up in lands, but as soon as responsible men with available means settle here and purchase these lands, the proceeds will be expended in assisting in these enterprises.

With such exhortations, the people of Aton "made a

[4] Edward W. Barber: "The Vermontville Colony . . . ," *Michigan Pioneer and Historical Collections*, XXVIII, pp. 244–5.

real co-operative effort, poorly planned and impulsive though it was, to build up their town. Little came of it. . . . The boom 'busted' and the village became dormant again."

As other towns got other railroad spur lines which tapped the same agricultural area as Aton, the town declined as a market. In 1880 16 million pounds of agricultural produce were shipped from Aton; but thirty years later the amount had diminished to 13 million. Hope died slowly, however, and when, in 1906, the town had an opportunity to attract an East-West railroad, $50,000 was raised as bait and the "Aton Commercial Club" was organized for the purpose of "aiding and encouraging the location and operation of manufacturing and other industrial enterprises in Aton." Three hundred and fifty members joined and the *Republican* gleefully predicted that within a few years the population of Aton would soar to 15,000 (from 2,000). The watchword of the Commercial Club was "Boost for Aton" and when the club induced "a large refrigerator factory" to move its plant from a distant city to Aton, over 500 Atonites subscribed to $70,000 worth of stock. When the factory was ready to go into operation, it was dedicated with a "Big Booster Banquet" attended by 600 citizens. But it turned out, sadly, that the company which was to bring prosperity to Aton was bankrupt and the factory never opened. For some years boosterism was dead in Aton.

Sims adds that "the annals of the town are full of fruitless ventures of all sorts. Many companies for the manufacture of local inventions, such as perpetual motion machines, sewing machines, wind pumps, engines, signal boards, etc., have sprung up and speedily failed for want of reasonable consideration as to their practicability or failure to estimate the demand for their products." [5] In addition, the people of Aton put up incredible amounts for bogus oil

[5] Newell L. Sims: *A Hoosier Village* (New York: Columbia University Press; 1912), pp. 27–30, 30–1, 35, 40.

and mining stocks, and a fraudulent life insurance company wrote over $200,000 in policies in the town and then made off with the boodle.

No one had suggested to the citizens of this Indiana town that techniques of production, of management, and of distribution were perhaps more important than industry, thrift, piety, and inventiveness. Their constant evocation of the ethic brought nothing but defeat; their desperate plunges into speculation simply ended in more spectacular disaster.

Alma, Michigan, displayed many of the classic features of small-town economic development. Early in its history it became involved in a bitter struggle with the rival town of St. Louis for a railroad spur. St. Louis won the first round by raising $25,000 as a subsidy. Several rich men in Alma countered by raising funds to build a connecting line. This brought the T.A.A. & N.M. to Alma by a roundabout route. The railroad was "persuaded" (i.e., bribed) to straighten its line, leaving St. Louis connected only by the Alma spur. Alma then destroyed the spur and its neighbor was left without a railroad. St. Louis was out of pocket the $25,000 it had raised as subsidy, plus the inflated land values of the community produced by the arrival of the original line. However, the prosperity that Alma anticipated as the result of having outwitted her rival was slow to materialize. A "Business Man's Improvement Association," set up in 1886, did its best to encourage local enterprise and attract outside industries to the town, but the record of the failure of industrial ventures was, like that of Aton, a long and disheartening one. "Many concerns were promoted, operated for several years and then scrapped because they proved to be unprofitable." [6]

Another problem of small-town industrial life is illustrated by the case of Warsaw, Illinois. After putting forth "much effort and considerable expense" the citizens of

[6] Arthur Weimer: "Economic History of Alma Since 1900," *Michigan History Magazine*, XIX (winter, 1935), p. 289.

Warsaw had prevailed upon the Mirro Leather Goods Company of Chicago to settle in the town. Then to its horror Warsaw learned that the employees of the company planned to strike to win recognition of a union. The Factory Committee, composed of prominent Warsaw businessmen, urged the townspeople to put up with no such nonsense. The committee wrote:

> Unfortunately, agitation and intimidation is being attempted by paid organizers who care nothing for our community and who are schooled and trained in the art of creating unrest.
>
> The citizens of Warsaw are capable of handling any situation that may arise without the aid of outside paid agitators, who do not have the best interests of Warsaw and its people at heart. The local Factory Committee will be in constant contact with the situation for the mutual welfare of the Mirro Leather Goods Company and its employees.
>
> Let us stand behind the Mirro Leather Goods Company and give them a chance for our mutual success.[7]

Carle Zimmerman, in his study of industrial communities of the Northeast, has also noted the effect of attempts at unionization in the small town. With the interests of the whole community involved, the pressures against unionization are very strong, especially in the town with imported "foreign" labor. Zimmerman apparently felt that unions usually did more harm than good by destroying the feeling of confidence between employer and employee that was of special importance in the town. The local employer was apt to be sensitive to the good opinion of the community and was therefore inclined to benevolence as he understood it. The absentee corporation was something else again, and

[7] Dale Kramer: "What Price a Factory," *Survey Graphic*, XXIX (August, 1940), p. 441.

here the danger was great that the local labor force would be exploited quite mercilessly (for it was the prospect of such exploitation which had attracted many industries in the first place), while the townspeople, anxious at any cost to retain the factory as a prized source of revenue, brought severe and sometimes brutal pressures to bear to prevent any action that might imperil the dearly bought industry.

Such situations meant the further fragmentation of the community and the deepening of class antagonisms. And since the great majority of such enterprises ended in failure rifts were seldom healed. Lewis Atherton notes that "forty Wisconsin towns subsidized a total of 130 industrial plants between 1930 and 1945" with results that were very meager in comparison with the size of the subsidies.[8]

Yet the town once it had invested in a plant and created out of its own vitals or attracted from the outside a dependent labor force was under great pressure to continue its search for new industries to replace those which had collapsed. In Ed Howe's *Story of a Country Town* the hero observes that the people of Twin Mounds

> were always miserable by reason of predictions that, unless impossible amounts of money were given to certain enterprises, the town would be ruined, and although they always gave, no sooner was one fund exhausted than it became necessary to raise another.[9]

The small-town businessman had not only to face the hazards of local conditions—bad crops and unfortunate speculations—he was acutely vulnerable to national panics and recessions. He suffered from the blind and destructive force of a national economy incompatible with that of the town. Moreover, managerial success involved qualities not

[8] Lewis Atherton: *Main Street on the Middle Border* (Bloomington, Ind.: Indiana University Press; 1954), p. 343.
[9] Edgar Watson Howe: *Story of a Country Town* (Boston and New York: Houghton Mifflin Company, 1927), p. 27.

normally included in the inventory of the ethic. It is safe to assume that early to bed and early to rise made the small-town businessman nothing but healthy. Observing the town we find few instances where industry and patient accumulation resulted in riches. Large-scale entrepreneurial activity required very different attributes from those recognized and approved by the small town. Business and industrial tycoons came, generally, out of urban environments. They grew up in a milieu which could be said to have expended its greatest energies in breeding the entrepreneurial type. But the entrepreneur, the skilled and imaginative manipulator whose genius lay in the abstractions of higher finance, the mysteries of holding companies, mergers, and watered stock, never ceased to proclaim the myth. The small-town businessman heard and believed.

By the end of the century towns often managed to attract plants that were components of nationwide industries. The creamery at Alma, Michigan, was bought by Swift and Company in 1908, and the Alma Sugar Company was absorbed by the Michigan Sugar Company. Libby, McNeill and Libby set up a pickle plant, and in 1913 Republic Truck Company began operations, bringing money and skilled workers into the town. The businessmen of the community felt that their hopes had at last been realized: the town for a decade knew its greatest prosperity. However, Republic collapsed in 1923, and although reorganized, failed again in 1931. The next year, Libby, hit by the depression, shut down its pickle factory and Swift closed its creamery. Meanwhile land values declined from $200 an acre in 1919 to $75 an acre in 1933. The crash of 1929 killed the local Chamber of Commerce, which was replaced by a "Booster Club" that, after the financial shocks of the early thirties, turned back to agriculture as the mainstay of the town's economic life.

Some towns have of course succeeded in attracting national industries, which have brought with them an increased stability. But such successes have not been unalloyed blessings. The national corporations have placed their higher management personnel in the towns, and however kind and enlightened these satraps may be, they are in most instances urbanites without deep attachments or loyalties to the community. They are the instruments of an alien power which has reduced the classic dimensions of the town to that of a working force, and their power, however discreetly applied, is enormous. As the sociologists have put it, in their metallic language, "the local familistic-communal upper classes were absorbed in a new upper class which was increasingly extra-communal and associationally defined." [1]

The appearance in the towns of branches of nationwide industries coincided with the rise of the ubiquitous chain store, which, although much lamented by sentimental champions of individualism, brought a measure of stability to small-town merchandising.

While the tendency in recent years toward an increasing decentralization of industry offers many towns prospects for a brighter economic future, the experience of such communities as Alma, Michigan, suggests that these towns will continue to be excessively vulnerable in times of financial crisis. It seems indeed that the town that does not remain primarily an agricultural "trading center" is fated to become a type of industrial suburb. In the late fifties General Motors ran a series of ads in national magazines pointing out how its largesse, distributed to certain small communities, had given them a new lease on life. "How a little Wisconsin village gave itself a big boost with some help from General Motors," one such ad was headlined. There followed the story of a 105-year-old Wisconsin

[1] E. Digby Baltzell: " 'Who's Who in America' and 'The Social Register,' Elite and Upper Class Indexes in Metropolitan America," in R. Bendix and S. Lipset, eds.: *Class, Status and Power* (Glencoe, Ill.: The Free Press; 1953), p. 175.

town which had experienced a boom through the resourcefulness of a local citizen who had lured a General Motors subcontractor to St. Anna with such inducements as a factory, built largely by volunteer labor, a low tax rate, and a docile work force.

In West Virginia, Kentucky, and Ohio giant industries have taken over impoverished river towns and turned them into modern industrial communities. In 1956 the Kaiser Aluminum and Chemical Corporation built a 230-million-dollar aluminum smelter and mill at Ravenswood, West Virginia, a town with a population of some 2,000. The company planning its new empire felt that one of its biggest problems was "to prepare these people for something which is going to change the whole pattern of their lives." It therefore dispatched a squad of public relations men from the West Coast offices of the company for a seven-week tour through the hillside hamlets around Ravenswood. At each hamlet Kaiser's experts ran three movies (a cartoon, a Western, and a film of Kaiser Aluminum), served soft drinks and cakes (bought at two dollars each from local housewives), and explained the plans of the company. Ravenswood now has a residential district for 6,000 homes and a $350,000 elementary school built by the company.

Much the same process was followed in the adjacent states of the Ohio Valley. Olin Revere has established itself in Wilson, Ohio; Union Carbide has a plant at New Martinsville, West Virginia; and the American Rolling Mills has built a foundry at Ashland, Kentucky. Perhaps in time most of the smaller communities in America will become "company towns"—the beneficiaries of mammoth corporations which, however motivated by benevolence, must bit by bit come to dominate the life of these communities, prosperous, antiseptic, and uniform.

Certainly the shift from the unspecialized labor of a Mathew Patten to the General Motors assembly line produced profound dislocations in the economy and the psychology of the town.[2] While eventually a considerable number of small-town entrepreneurs became prosperous and in some cases wealthy, these were the exceptions. Such prosperity as the town enjoyed usually waited on the rationalization of the methods of production, distribution and management techniques. Towns founded at the end of the nineteenth century obviously enjoyed better prospects for moderate prosperity than those established prior, let us say, to the outbreak of the Civil War.

The Great Depression, as the Lynds' study of *Middletown in Transition* has shown, called into question most of the "verities" by which Muncie and towns like it had lived. But the depression of the 1930's was after all only the most cataclysmic of a series of financial crises that stretched back to the 1790's. The towns shared the periodic instability that was characteristic of the American economy as a whole. What is argued here is that the town, generally speaking, was the scene of chronic business failures throughout the greater part of its history. And these failures, persistent, incalculable, demoralizing, constantly imperiled the town's image of itself. The number of colonized towns, religious and secular, established during the course of the nineteenth century bore witness to the depths of that demoralization.

[2] Robert and Helen Lynd, in their classic study of Muncie, Indiana, *Middletown* (New York: Harcourt, Brace & Company; 1929), placed great stress on this transition from craft to industrial or assembly-line production, and this is also the theme of Sherwood Anderson's *Poor White* (see Chapter XIII). At the same time it must be kept in mind that this transition was not concentrated in the latter decades of the nineteenth century, as the Lynds' study suggests. It began early in the nineteenth century in the textile mills of New England. It received fresh impetus from Eli Whitney's pioneering work in interchangeable parts, and we have seen its effects in numerous New England and Midwestern communities of the mid-nineteenth century. See also Maurice R. Stein: *The Eclipse of Community* (Harper Torchbooks; New York: Harper & Row; 1964).

V I

Politics in
the Town

THE MOST FAMILIAR ASPECT of small-town political life is undoubtedly the New England town meeting. Orators have never tired of extolling it as the seed of American democracy, the most perfect expression of responsible citizenship. It was, in essence, the church congregation assembled to decide secular matters. In practice it was democratic, but it had no underpinning of democratic theory. Because the individuals who gathered for town meeting were of the same church, the same racial stock, and shared to an extraordinary degree the same ideals and values, the town meeting as a practical method of local government was remarkably successful. The men who met to decide community affairs had no concept of "the popular will," nor any intention of admitting to the franchise individuals who might be out of sympathy with the accepted communal values. This was true of American towns in general, whether in Massachusetts or Indiana. The modern concept of political democracy did not grow up in New England towns or in the Western frontier communities. It was city-born and city-bred. It was the city which created classes, which divided neighbors along social and economic lines, which destroyed the simple equality of community life, and which nourished the principles of political democracy. This is not, of course, to say that the city consciously pursued an ideal of democracy, but that, given the broader context of American life, the contradictions of an urban industrial society produced our modern concepts of democracy.

The town did have what it called democracy, but this democracy was in fact simply the elevation of social equality to the level of one of the community's principal values. It meant a lack of pretense, an absence initially of social distinctions, a spirit of neighborliness. Its tenets had been put forth in Winthrop's "Modell of Christian Charity." Humility, unworldliness, Christian equality—these were the ingredients of small-town "democracy." It provided no room for tolerance of other creeds, religious or political; it was not based on the assumption that government represented a consensus among disparate groups with different interests and different conceptions of the truth. For the town there was only one truth—its own. The town in its homogeneity, in its racial and cultural "purity" was for the most part able to avoid those conflicts between rival groups and interests out of which modern democratic practice and theory have developed. As soon as alien groups moved in town-meeting "democracy" began to break down. Nor were the towns "liberal." They did not produce liberal political ideas. They did not develop doctrines that were "radical" or "progressive" in the generally accepted meaning of those terms.

It has been argued that the frontier was primarily responsible for the development of liberal and radical ideals in American politics. This thesis, briefly stated, maintains that it was the "radical," the "freedom-loving," the "independent" individuals who were inclined to emigrate to the frontier, while the conservative and tradition-minded stayed behind. A corollary to this theory has been the argument that conditions on the frontier encouraged the growth of democracy and political liberalism. Some of the fallacies of this doctrine as it applied to New England emigration have already been discussed.

From the earliest days of Western settlement in the new nation "when the founders of the state of Franklin turned down a more democratic system in favor of the North Carolina constitution" down to the end of the nineteenth century when the West was in a ferment of social unrest, "pioneers held to the old laws, and to the more conservative laws." As Earl Pomeroy has pointed out, even the Ordinance of 1787 "figured as a channel in the large process of acculturation, transporting American ways from East to West. . . . The system of restraints—the authority of appointed governors, secretaries, and judges—brought with it eastern personnel and methods, and connections with eastern party systems." The history of the Federalist and Whig parties in the early period of the West has received little attention, perhaps as Pomeroy suggests "because the facts do not correspond satisfactorily to the environmental-radical interpretation. . . ." [1]

If we look at the political affiliations of the frontier communities, it is apparent that these were generally determined by the place of origin of the settlers. In Michigan in the 1830's those pioneers who came from eastern New York and New England were Whigs, while those from Vermont and western New York were generally Jackson men. By the end of the decade the conservative Democrats, many of them from New England, cap-

[1] Earl Pomeroy: "Towards a Reorientation . . . ," *Mississippi Valley Historical Review*, XLI (March, 1955), pp. 585, 583-4, 587.

tured the party. Of the conservative Democrats in the state constitutional convention, six were from New England and two from New York. The New York township system of local government was adopted by the convention, and although New York and five of the New England states had admitted free Negroes to the suffrage, they were excluded by the Michigan constitution. By insisting on a citizenship requirement conservatives defeated a movement to grant suffrage to all males over the age of twenty-one who had declared their intention of becoming citizens.

To one historian who has traced the transit of ideas to the frontier, it seemed obvious that those pioneers who were "radical" on the frontier were radical at home, and became in their new environment, if anything, more conservative. If initially there were certain "liberal" impulses, the wealthier land speculators and town builders soon took control of the political parties of the frontier and gave them a generally conservative tone.[2]

More than one observer of the frontier has noted the persistence of inherited political loyalties. Far from encouraging independence and dissent the frontier seemed to intensify partisanship. In Vermontville, Michigan, "it was expected as a matter of course that partisan politics would descend from sires to sons with unbroken regularity." Those settlers from Bennington County, Vermont, were Democrats; those from Rutland and Addison counties were conservative Whigs; so they remained, and so their sons were. The solitary dissenter in Vermontville was Willard

[2] Marcus L. Hansen: "Remarks," in Dixon Ryan Fox, ed.: *Sources of Culture in the Middle West* (New York and London: D. Appleton-Century Company, Inc.; 1934), pp. 103–10. Mr. Hansen says: "I believe that for every liberal (who emigrated to the West) there were ten conservatives. . . . They emigrated, in fact, because they were conservatives—conservatives being those that have something to conserve. They wanted to conserve their religion, or their property, or their standing in society." Hansen is speaking of European immigrants, but his comments could be applied equally well to native Americans.

Davis, an early abolitionist. Although he was "one of the best educated and best read men in the town he was a political outcast." [3]

Sims writes of politics in "Aton" that loyalty to party was placed very high. Any other behavior was considered "very dishonorable, almost immoral." A prominent citizen of Aton

> who from conviction left the Republican ranks thirty years ago, was bitterly hated by his fellows, charged with all manner of sinister motives, and even to-day is a "disreputable turncoat." Any sign of political independence is a mark of instability and an occasion for censure. Fathers take it as a matter of course that their sons will be loyal to their party. . . . Where coercion is necessary to keep the son in line, threats of disinheritance, and the withholding of financial assistance have been employed.[4]

John Holmes remembers, similarly, that Mastersville was almost solidly Republican in the 1870's, with only one or two families in the town who dared to dissent. Explaining the persistence of political attitudes Mr. Holmes recalls:

> My grandfather engaged all his life in some form of merchandising—trading. As a young man he started early in life speculating. [His brother] turned to a military life, but my grandfather never had any interest in the military. After the War of 1812 . . . the one that was a merchant was harassed with paper money. That was the Jackson period. Every time he got a piece of paper money he made the man sign a receipt, and that annoyed and harassed him. He turned against Jackson. . . . His brother . . . had no trade

---

[3] Edward W. Barber: "The Vermontville Colony . . . ," *Michigan Pioneer and Historical Collections*, XXVIII, p. 237.

[4] Newell L. Sims: *A Hoosier Village* (New York: Columbia University Press; 1912), p. 58.

after he left the service. The government gave him 640 acres of land and he just lived on that. And he associated all that with Jackson and the Democrats. And clear down on that side, every one of the boys and girls were Democrats. Still are. Over on my side because my grandfather started it with his opposition to Jackson's financial policy, they were all Republicans, clear down to the present.[5]

In the political history of Illinois, like that of Michigan, it is difficult to discover what might be called a "spirit of frontier democracy" at work in the period before the Civil War. As a historian of the state has expressed it: "The course of Illinois politics between the years 1818 and 1836 may stand as a warning to the superficial historian of the danger which attends an attempt to describe and classify political parties at different periods by the same terms or under the same categories"; [6] and, one might add, of characterizing certain developments in such terms as liberal or radical, or, indeed, "democratic." The danger is especially great when an effort is made to explain "state politics exclusively in terms of national issues and leaders. . . . State factions differed from period to period, not only in alignment and personnel but in degrees of unity and effectiveness." What sometimes appeared to the outsider as frontier democracy might simply be, as Illinois democracy was in the years following 1830, "individual cliques" which at first "used Jackson's name and then his measures . . . to embarrass their opponents." [7]

It was indeed Andrew Jackson's most illiberal acts, such as his policy of Indian removal, which won most support on the frontier. Tariff and internal improvements seem to have aroused little interest among the factions in Illinois or among the people in general. The response to Jackson was

[5] J. H. Holmes.
[6] Theodore Calvin Pease: *The Frontier State, 1818–1848* (Springfield, Ill.: Illinois Centennial Commission; 1918), p. 136.
[7] Ibid., p. 141.

personal rather than doctrinal. Jackson was against the aristocrats, against the cities, and the bankers and the businessmen. It was this which appealed to the West, not any abstract devotion to democratic principles. A small-town Illinois businessman, writing in the 1830's to a friend, assured him that "all of our solvent business men in Town are opposed to the Administration. We have but two solvent merchants in Town as exceptions; they are doing small business." [8]

It is significant that the Whigs—the party of conservatism—won their first great political victory on a purely sentimental appeal for a return to the political and moral purity of the past. William Henry Harrison, their candidate, was offered both as the paternalistic squire (for the voter with Southern roots), as the simple country boy from the log cabin (for the egalitarian farmer and small-town voter), and as "one of the last links to the days of the Revolutionary heroes for all who yearned after the simpler glories of the past. The atmosphere of sentiment and conservatism cloaked a party whose allegiance was frankly to the eastern business man." Within this general picture Yankee farmers voted Whig and Southern businessmen voted Democratic.

From the beginning Illinois had a savage "Black Code." Harboring runaway slaves was a felony. No Negro could appear as a witness against a white man, and a law passed in 1829 provided that "no black or mulatto, not a citizen of one of the United States, was to enter the state unless he gave bond of a thousand dollars and exhibited a certificate of freedom." Another act passed the same year prohibited marriage between the races under penalties of stripes, fine, and imprisonment. Indeed slavery itself was not pronounced legally at an end in Illinois until the 1850's. [9]

Such Draconian attitudes on the slavery question were the result of the fact that early immigration into Illinois

[8] Ibid., pp. 256–7.   [9] Ibid., pp. 46, 47–8.

came from the Southern states. The pioneers of the late twenties and the thirties who filled up the north and central portions of the state were New Englanders, New Yorkers, and Pennsylvanians deeply imbued with Calvinist morality. Yankees and Southerners fought for laws congenial to them, with the result that Illinois statutes were, in many instances, modeled after New England blue laws a century old, while the laws concerning Negro slavery were often more severe than those in the seacoast slave states. In Earl Pomeroy's words: "Frequently Westerners restricted the suffrage or the rights of Negroes by sizable majorities, while Easterners kept older restrictions only because the restrictions tended to perpetuate themselves in spite of majority opinion." [1]

What was true of Illinois was true, in varying degrees, of the other Midwestern states. Benjamin F. Wright, surveying frontier political institutions, has been unable to find evidence that those who framed the early Western constitutions wished "to introduce governmental forms different from those long well established in the East."

Ohio had a county-township system modeled after that of Pennsylvania. The same form was adopted by Indiana, while Michigan followed the township-county system of New York which was copied by Wisconsin. As Wright points out, the principle of separation of powers was followed in most of the constitutions drafted for the states of the old Northwest and in the matter of tenure of office there was no "genuine difference between the opinions of contemporaneous constitution makers, in the older and in the newer states."

As for the suffrage, the new Western states did help "to accelerate a process under way before they were settled . . . but . . . they did not attempt, or even desire, to carry that process beyond the goal previously attained in several of the older states." The Pennsylvania constitution

[1] Pomeroy: "Towards a Reorientation," p. 586.

had had no property qualifications (other than the payment of some tax) since 1776. South Carolina, New Hampshire, Georgia, and Delaware had by 1792 followed Pennsylvania's example. New Hampshire and Georgia abandoned even the tax qualification by 1798, but when Ohio entered the Union in 1802 her constitution contained the tax limitation already dropped by two of the Eastern states. Not until Indiana became a state in 1816 did any Western state go beyond the point which Pennsylvania had reached in 1776.

Popular election of state officers has often been taken as one of the watermarks of democracy. Mississippi in 1832 was the first state to elect most of its judicial and executive officers. When Michigan became a state in 1835 it did not follow this example, nor did Iowa eleven years later. It was left to Illinois and Wisconsin to abandon the older method of appointment in 1848.

Wright sums up the case: "In their choice of political institutions the men of [the Midwest] were imitative, not creative. . . . Their constitutional, like their domestic, architecture was patterned after that of the communities from which they had moved westward," and the pioneers who lived through the early days of settlement "were at least as desirous of establishing political and legal systems on the eastern model as they had been when they moved to the frontier." [2] If by "conservative" we mean the social and political attitudes that predominated along the Eastern seacoast, there is much evidence that members of frontier communities grew more conservative as time passed.

Western political parties were in Pomeroy's view

less often media for frontier revolt against other sections than arteries by which policies and personnel

[2] Benjamin F. Wright: "Political Institutions and the Frontier," in Dixon Ryan Fox, ed.: *Sources of Culture in the Middle West* (New York and London: D. Appleton-Century Company, Inc.; 1934), pp. 17, 22, 24, 28, 32.

moved westward. New and radical parties, unsupported by national patronage or unknown to Westerners when they were last in the East, usually took hold slowly. Beyond the Mississippi, Westerners were slow to join the Republicans, and when they did they often repudiated the radicalism of the middlewestern and eastern branches of the party.[3]

What relevance have these facts to the town? Simply that the focus of political activity in Midwestern communities was the town. It was the town which tempered any incipient radicalism among the farmers; it was the town which proved most receptive to urban influences. What has been said in general of the states can be said specifically of particular communities.

We have already remarked on the extraordinary persistence of party affiliations in the town. In election after election issues were ignored in favor of traditional political loyalties. As recently as the Presidential campaign of 1956 Samuel Lubell, the political analyst, questioned a woman in Los Angeles who turned out to be a native of Dyersville, Iowa, a town with whose political attitudes Lubell was familiar. The woman had left Iowa twenty years before; yet to every question concerning political issues which Lubell asked her replies were almost identical to responses he had received a few months earlier in Dyersville.[4]

Slavery was the only national issue capable of modifying traditional political alignments in the West. While it strengthened the hold of the Democrats on the slave states, it confronted the Whigs with a challenge that they were quite unable to meet or, indeed, understand.[5]

It was in the period after the Civil War that Western

[3] Pomeroy: "Towards a Reorientation," p. 586.
[4] "Analyst Lubell Picks Ike as Winner in California," Los Angeles *Mirror-News*, October 15, 1956, p. 18.
[5] Chester McArthur Destler: "Western Radicalism, 1865–1901: Concepts and Origins," *Mississippi Valley Historical Review*, XXXI (December, 1944), pp. 335–68.

radicalism is supposed to have manifested itself most clearly in the Populist party and the wave of agrarian radicalism which swept the West in the 1880's and 1890's. As has been pointed out, "the contention that Populism was an extension of frontier democracy" runs aground on the fact that Southern Populism, which could hardly have been affected by the "frontier spirit," was "at least as strong as the Western brand and contained the radical wing of the agrarian revolt of the nineties." Populism was not a "Western" movement; rather it was confined to the single crop areas: the South with its cotton, Kansas, Nebraska, and the Dakotas with their wheat.[6] Without ideological or philosophical basis, it was largely the product of economic and sociological processes at work in certain rural areas. It produced "a patchwork of remedial proposals" designed to restore the prosperity of a small business and rural economy.[7] Moreover, South or West, Populism was saturated with Protestant fundamentalism. It was, in effect, a throwback to an earlier tradition of hostility to business and to the cities. Its theoretical framework, where it had one, was drawn from Genesis and from the New Testament story of Christ driving the money changers from the Temple.

Nor was it a movement that was widespread through the Middle West. The attitude of many Midwestern towns toward Populism was expressed in William Allen White's "What's Wrong with Kansas"; but at the same time it was the towns which provided the leaders for the Populist movement. A large number of its most eloquent champions were farm boys who went to town, "made or failed to make a fortune there, and then in later life became leaders of rural reform." None of the seven founders of the

[6] Richard Hofstadter: *The Age of Reform* (New York: Alfred A. Knopf; 1955), p. 49.
[7] Chester McArthur Destler: "Western Radicalism, 1865–1901: Concepts and Origins," *Mississippi Valley Historical Review*, XXXI (December, 1944), p. 336. Destler's effort to establish the ideological provenance for Populism is unsuccessful.

Grange "was by occupation a farmer for more than a small portion of his life. Of the ten masters of the National Grange only two could be called practicing dirt farmers." As Paul Johnston notes, "agriculture has taken its political leadership from the town. . . ." In Iowa, out of a total of 419 congressmen elected between 1844 and 1938, only 15 were farmers. Three hundred and nine, however, were lawyers; 35 were bankers; 22 were editors, journalists, or publishers; 34 were businessmen (merchants, manufacturers, brokers, nurserymen, grain dealers, lumbermen); and 4 were of the learned professions.[8]

It should be noted that the towns of Iowa provided the great majority of these 404 non-farm congressmen. Thus it was the towns which undertook to represent the country, and generally speaking, it was the more conservative individuals of these communities who were sent to the state and national legislatures. Therefore, the leadership position of the town was crucial. From having accepted the role of spokesman for the farmer, it came to echo the ideals of an increasingly urban industrial society. The town thus tempered agrarian discontent while providing it with leadership. Whatever the farmer's problems and complaints, he had to express them largely through the town, and there he received more and more unsympathetic hearing.

With the rising tide of farm protest many towns came to resent their dependence on the farmer and, seeking to escape this yoke, pressed their efforts to develop an industrial life of their own. Further diluting and dissipating the pressures for agricultural reform was one of the most conspicuous features of small-town life—the personalizing of politics. A politician with strong personal appeal paid little attention to specific problems and even less to great national issues. He sought to impress voters with his friendliness and accessibility; if he was pressed for a

[8] Paul H. Johnston: "Old Ideals Versus New Ideas in Farm Life," *U.S. Department of Agriculture Yearbook* (Washington, D.C.; 1940), pp. 156–7.

statement of principles, he fell back on the grand abstractions of God, family, and flag, the Constitution and the Declaration of Independence, and called for a return to the purity of the early Republic, the ideals of the Founding Fathers, and government by the people.

In Waterbury, New York, sociologist James Williams noted that "town officials were chosen not for their ability to administer the affairs of their offices efficiently so much as for their personal impressiveness. The town officers most readily and favorably recalled by old residents have been 'great big men,' good natured, unassuming and holding their power in reserve, but able, on occasion, to display it to advantage, particularly on election day and town meeting day." [9]

Granville Hicks has remarked on the same attitudes in his study of a contemporary rural town in New York State. There, too, "politics is largely personalized," and there is still a premium on oratory as opposed to campaign literature. Hicks quotes a local politician's scornful reference to such material. "That's all printed matter, y'unnerstan' what I mean? All printed matter. That won't get you anything. You got to talk to 'em . . . in a body, or you got to go to their houses and talk to 'em separately. But you got to talk to 'em." [1]

Hicks found that campaigning in Granby

follows a peculiar ritual. In spite of the fact that Republicans are elected ninety-nine per cent of the time, Republican candidates usually worry about their chances, and there are always a few optimists in the Democratic camp who are sure they are going to win. Candidates for the more important offices go from house to house, each carrying a box of cigars and cigarettes and a box of candy bars. After every

[9] James M. Williams: *An American Town* (New York: The J. Kempster Printing Co.; 1906), p. 60.
[1] Granville Hicks: *Small Town* (New York: The Macmillan Company; 1946), p. 187.

member of a family has had his pick, the candidate sits down and talks, usually about the weather and other neutral topics. If his host makes any comment on political affairs, he deals with it to the best of his ability, and he may bring up a political issue on his own initiative, but more often than not he leaves without directly mentioning the campaign. As a rule it is considered unwise for a candidate to ask for a vote, and if he refers to his rival, it is good form for him to say that he has nothing against the man.[2]

On election day itself "there are more substantial inducements. One of the churches serves dinner and supper on that day, and the leaders of both parties distribute tickets to the voters. Moreover, it is general gossip that the Republicans always buy votes and that the Democrats do when they have the money." If the weather is good on election day "the politicians stand outside the town hall, joking with their rivals, handing cards to newcomers, sometimes capturing an individual and taking him aside for a final argument, financial or otherwise."[3]

Nevertheless the town exercises a good deal of restraint in regard to political discussions. As Hicks puts it:

> In so small and interrelated a community political controversy cannot be conducted in public without acrimony or even with candor, though there is a vast amount of whispered slander and adroit backstabbing. A man can make his views clear, however, even though he says nothing at which political opponents and their relatives can take offense, and if he is a man of influence, his views are repeated, probably without benefit of his qualifications, in many homes.[4]

The small-town politician had an obligation not to disrupt the harmony of community life. He was more concerned with healing than creating divisions, all of which served to obscure issues and emphasize personalities. Per-

[2] Ibid., p. 188.   [3] Ibid.   [4] Ibid., p. 122.

sonal greeting was of great importance. Visiting, being likable, having oratorical skill, and inspiring confidence— these were the qualities that were admired in a candidate. Perhaps above everything else the aspiring politician must put on no airs, must convince the electorate beyond question that he considered himself on an equal footing with them.[5]

Angie Debo describes the master politician of the Oklahoma territory in classic terms. He was a "slender, sprightly young Irishman with a pleasant voice and an eager, friendly manner." He was, by general agreement,

> the most effective campaigner, who ever ran for public office in Oklahoma. For four years he had gone out among the people, speaking in brush arbors, sod schoolhouses, country churches, on the street. . . . Once he had greeted a man with his quick, close handclasp, he was his friend forever. He treated the women with a deferential courtesy that made them forget shabby clothes and work-roughened hands. And it was no figure of speech to say he kissed the grubby tired babies; he not only kissed them but he learned their names and ages. . . . And he remembered.[6]

To say that the small-town politician's appeal was personal does not mean that it was superficial or meaningless. The citizens of the town were trained in the assessment of character. They were, of course, taken in on occasion by a bombastic orator or a genial fraud, but on the whole their assessments were remarkably good—if not in terms of the intellectual qualities of the candidate, then in terms of character and general intelligence. The classic small-town politician was Abraham Lincoln. He became a symbolic figure because he represented the human under-

[5] Albert Blumenthal: *A Sociological Study of a Small Town* (Chicago: University of Chicago Press; 1932), pp. 295–303.
[6] Angie Debo: *Prairie City* (New York: Alfred A. Knopf; 1944), p. 73.

standing, the humor, sympathy, and warmth of the local politician at his best. The home-grown politico was expected less to stand for issues than to embody the diverse interests and aspirations of his constituents. This generally meant a basic conservatism and tolerance. Although he was sometimes a manipulator of unusual shrewdness who played with calculated effect on the passions and anxieties of his audience, his tendency to exploit was generally kept in check by the diversity of those to whom he appealed for support. The small-town politician had to have the backing of the farmer as well as of the town banker; despite the homogeneity of a particular community, its neighbor might have very different racial stock and different expectations. The structure of American society in the non-urban areas made the politicians more anxious not to alienate particular groups of voters by taking explicit positions on specific issues than to provide aggressive leadership in the name of clearly stated objectives. Hence his fondness for the unifying abstraction, his evasiveness on particulars, his dependence on inflated rhetoric designed to reassure rather than inform his auditors.

Politics were simplified for the town by the constant evocation of certain symbols. Though the symbols changed, the emotional content remained unaltered. From the beginning the town had believed that the world was involved in

> some great but essentially very simple struggle . . . at the heart of which [lay] some single conspiratorial force, whether it be the force represented by the 'gold bugs,' the Catholic Church, big business, corrupt politicians, the liquor interests and the saloons, or the Communist Party, and that this evil is something that must be not merely limited, checked and controlled but rather extirpated root and branch at the earliest possible moment.[7]

Highly conservative politically, the town has been a

[7] Hofstadter: *Age of Reform*, p. 16.

balance to agrarian radicalism and ballast to the ship of state. Its emphasis on personal politics has profoundly affected American political attitudes; it has been the most effective agency for shaping our classic native type—the orator, the compromiser, the pragmatic politician.

The Presidential election of 1960 can be seen as, to a degree, a classic contest between the small town and the city. Richard Nixon was the prototype of the small-town boy, John F. Kennedy the model of the liberal urban intellectual. Kennedy's accent, his clothes, and his Choate and Harvard background dramatized the difference, a difference that was not missed by the small-town and rural voters of the West. Even in religious terms, Kennedy's Catholicism was identified with the big cities and with the Irish immigration of the nineteenth century. Nixon's mild Quakerism was typical of his small-town origin.

Many people acclaimed the debates between Kennedy and Nixon as a return via television to the face-to-face intimacy of the small-town political forum. In terms purely of debating "points" it is possible to argue that Nixon carried off the palm (this at least was the impression of many impartial listeners who heard the debates on the radio), but on television the story was just the opposite. Kennedy obviously came across much more effectively on the visual medium. A considerable number of people found Kennedy, quite apart from what he said, a more reassuring personality, a man of greater presence and power, and this counted far more than the points made by either speaker in the great "debate." The American people, through television, judged the Presidential candidates in much the same way that small-town citizens have judged political aspirants since the beginning of the Republic.

With President Kennedy's assassination the small town, defeated at the polls, asserted itself once more in the person of Lyndon Baines Johnson, whose Presidential "style" could hardly have been in more dramatic contrast to that of his predecessor.

VII

Law and the Lawyers

THE FIRST SETTLERS who came to the British colonies of North America brought with them the basic concepts of English common law. The seacoast towns, accessible to English influences, developed legal practices and forms much like those of the mother country although from the first there were important variations. Throughout the seventeenth and the early eighteenth century there was a deep suspicion of lawyers in all the Crown's colonies. This antagonism was undoubtedly based on the fact that the experiences of the average English settler with the law and with lawyers in his homeland had not always been happy ones. Even by the end of the sixteenth century English law had become as formalized as a minuet—and just as remote from the life of lower-class Englishmen. The lawyers, the "sons of Zernial," had also aroused middle-class opposition, and whatever it might mean to Sir Edward Coke the intricate structure of common law was baffling and often oppressive to the average Englishman.

As one writer has expressed it, English law "as a science was in so rigid condition that it failed to touch the popular life. . . . The people felt the restrictions it imposed, and knew little of the liberties it guaranteed." In the words of a sixteenth-century protester: "There was a Law before Lawyers; there was a time when the Common Customs of the land were sufficient to secure Meum and Tuum. What has made it since so difficult? Nothing but the Comments of Lawyers confounding the Text and writhing the Laws, like a Nose of Wax, to what Figure best serves their purposes." [1] The same view was expressed in tracts with such titles as: *The Downfall of Unjust Lawyers; Doomsday Drawing Near with Thunder and Lightning for Lawyers; A Rod for Lawyers Who are Hereby declared Robbers and Deceivers of the Nation.*

Equipped with a general concept of the function of law, the American colonists were quite ready to improvise. Among them only a few men had even the most rudimentary legal training, and most of these individuals established themselves in the commercial towns. The interior settlements were thus left to devise such law as they needed. In New England the Massachusetts Bay Colony attempted to transform Old Testament law into civil statutes with limited success. The larger urban centers, involved in trade with the mother country, rapidly adopted law and procedures modeled on those of England, but the small towns resisted the formalization of law.

Law in the small town was chiefly a lay affair. Sheriffs or justices of the peace dispensed justice by rule of thumb, depending on common sense rather than legal precedents. All the elaborate paraphernalia of pleadings and briefs were

[1] Charles Warren: *A History of the American Bar* (Boston: Little, Brown & Company; 1911), pp. 5, 6.

discarded. Every community had one or two individuals, a little better educated than their neighbors and perhaps equipped with Dalton's *Justice of the Peace,* who ran surveys, drew up deeds and wills, and sat as judge with several neighbors to hear minor cases.

Law, or, more properly, local custom, varied from county to county, and indeed sometimes from one township to another. It was well into the eighteenth century before a class of lawyers and a system of law began to emerge in the commercial cities on the seacoast.

The very simplicity of the law, the absence of complicated forms, of law books and statutes, made members of frontier communities very ready to have recourse to the law. It was convenient, inexpensive, and accessible to all. More important, the decisions of the sheriff or judges of the county courts were not clouded by legal terminology or drawn from awesome and forbidding volumes. A plaintiff might not agree with the verdict of the court but he generally understood the basis of the decision and respected the integrity of his neighbors who handed it down.

The result of such easy familiarity was a feeling of confidence and trust in the law as it appeared in the village and town. City law of course was something else. It was viewed in large part as the creation of a class of lawyers who served as the pliant tools of the merchants and royal officials, enacted for the purpose of subjecting the country to the rule of the city, of collecting debts owed by poor farmers to wealthy businessmen. As such it was distrusted and frequently opposed.

In the town the law, besides preserving a certain degree of good order under the demoralizing conditions of the frontier, served as entertainment, and more deeply as a means of social redemption and reformation. The role of the law was less punitive than admonitory. Rehabilitation not punishment was its first concern. The town punished its offenders as a father punishes his children, in sorrow and in love. The very informality of its operation made small-town law extremely responsive to what might be called the human factor. The judge was called upon to adjudicate matters within, as it were, the family. The defendant might indeed be a close relative. Thus Mathew Patten noted in his journal that he was "at James Walkers on John Pattens being apprehended by Margret Holms for his Getting her with child for which he agreed with her for 300 £ old Tenor and he pd Charges."[2] John Patten was undoubtedly a relative of Mathew but the case was disposed of with dispatch and apparently to the satisfaction of both parties.

The redemptive function of the law was of greater importance in the non-covenanted communities, which lacked the machinery of public confession and avowal of repentance. In the covenanted communities the law was, in a real sense, auxiliary to the discipline of the congregation, and functioned essentially as a system of arbitration.

Since all towns had the problem of reconditioning the individuals who lacked the stamina to obey the rules of good social order, the law must take the place of the covenant if the town was not to degenerate into a condition little better than savagery, or if, on the other hand, it was to emerge from such a condition. Moreover as the original covenanted community began to disintegrate, the function of the law became of increasing importance and the lawyer rose to take his place beside the minister as a figure of weight and authority in the community.

In many towns a man was measured by his behavior in relation to the law. In such instances the law took on a character at once penitential, expiatory, and ritualistic. When a man had a good case his failure to take it to court suggested moral weakness or bad conscience; litigiousness was valued as a sign of strength and determination if it was not carried to an extreme. It was, in James Williams's words, "regarded by the community as an ordinary and very praiseworthy economic method. The man who won a

[2] Mathew Patten: *Diary* . . . (Concord, N.H.: Rumford Printing Company; 1903), p. 35.

civil suit was regarded as a sort of hero. . . . It was custom-
ary to litigate all, even the most trivial disputes, and a man
was called a coward if he yielded short of a justice's decision." [3] Perhaps above all the town valued the due processes
of law as entertainment. One citizen of Waterbury, recall-
ing the old days with nostaliga, said of the 1820's "so many
went to court in the fall that there wa'nt enough left to do
the chores. . . . We had a lawsuit about every other day,
and, before it was over, the contending parties, the witnesses
and the judge were often pretty drunk." [4] The court docket
for Waterbury showed, in a two-year period, no criminal
cases but 389 civil suits.

"The reason," Williams adds,

> for this respect for law as such and for social cus-
> tom equally with law was the fact that law regis-
> tered custom. Likewise, there was little discrimination
> between more and less important customs. . . . The
> citizen must square his conduct with all customs alike
> —must perfectly exemplify in his character the traits
> of persistence, generosity, honesty, frugality, coura-
> geous resistance to encroachments on property rights,
> peaceableness, sexual morality, law and Sabbath ob-
> servance. [5]

In the small town law was what the community had
ordained, growing directly out of the needs and aspirations
of the people. It was not something remote, alien, imposed
from without.

Here and there a town, feeling that litigiousness threatened the fabric of its common life, made efforts to control
it. Zimmerman cites the case of a town which as early as
1790 passed an act to discourage unnecessary lawsuits. The
act provided for a

[3] James M. Williams: *An American Town* (New York: J.
Kempster Printing Company; 1906), p. 28.
[4] Ibid., p. 57.   [5] Ibid., p. 187.

committee of three discreet freeholders to whom should be submitted for settlement all demands whatsoever held by one citizen against another. . . . Any person refusing to present his claim to the committee for settlement should be deemed unfriendly to the peace of the town, and was to be treated by the inhabitants with contempt and neglect in dealings and intercourse, save in the bare offices of humanity; furthermore, he should not vote for any town office for three years.[6]

The incident is a revealing one; it shows the town's conviction of its right to enact Draconian laws to protect the community. High-handed and indeed illegal as such a scheme might be, it was quite in harmony with the basic concepts of the covenanted community.

As more formal court proceedings developed the courtroom became a theater in which morality plays of a kind were acted out. The lives of people in the community were lifted to the level of high drama. Tragedy and slapstick comedy were intermixed. The town's failings and passions and resentments were acted out before an enthralled audience of its citizens.

The records of the county court of Charles County, Maryland, in the middle years of the seventeenth century contain many such cases. In the July session of 1662 John Neuill brought suit against Thomas Baker for defaming Neuill's wife. The witnesses were numerous, the testimony lengthy. There was obvious prejudice against Baker as "A Common defamor of most of all his neighbours," but in this case he had exceeded his usual level of slander. One of the witnesses was William Robisson, a carpenter who had been building a house for John Neuill and his wife. After he had finished his day's work, Robisson went

to the Loged hows whear thay then lived whear he met with M' Baker and William Empson drincking

[6] Carle C. Zimmerman: *The Changing Community* (New York and London: Harper & Brothers; 1938), p. 289.

of wine, and after this deponant had bin in thear Companie a . . . while Mr Baker sayed to this deponant did you ever heare of such an impudent Que[an] Such an Notorious whore as this Neuills wife is and this deponant asking him why, hee replyed that shee was no sooner got to her bede after her delivery but she Called to Empson to Come get her a boy to her Girle, and Empson turning himselfe about Called of his dogge saying hee was more fitting to doe it and this deponant further sayeth that at an other time Mr Baker tould him that hee and Empson had so Jeared John Blackwood Concerning John Neuills wife that hee swore hee would never hunt a bar[ren doe] againe and further Mr Baker Sayd hang him Ro[gue] I know hee can as well bee hanged as forbaer her Companie for I know hee fukes her oftener then John Neuill himselfe. . . .

After much testimony to the same effect the judges declared that Baker had indeed

maliciously defamed the plaintive and his wife by reason that it was against natur that such a thing coold bee spoken with a desier and thearfor aught not to have bin reiterated as an infamie unto her Whearfor it is ordered beeing a verball iniurie that the sayd Baker shal give them satisfaction by asking them in open Court forgivenes for his offence upon his bended knees and pay the Cost and Charge of suite.
Whearupon John Neuill and his wife desiered the sayd baker to aske god forgivenes . . . not them.

If the community was satisfied, Thomas Baker was not. He turned around at once and sued one of the witnesses in the case against him for defamation. It proved an unfortunate decision, for much of the evidence dealt with Baker's alleged hog-stealing and bawdy talk.
Richard Row swore that while he was working at Baker's house, his friend, William Empson,

taking up a peece of meat out of the Pot sayd it was goode meate the wind had not blowne it and sayd what wind blows at your hows when your meat stincks to which Thomas Baker Replyed and sayd Row['s] Magget Creeps into [P]opes wifes flesh and that makes her meat stinck for I was over the other day and saw her Cunt which is licke a shot bage . . . [and] hee heard Mr Baker say that Mrs Hatch had a Cunt, enough to make souse for all the dogges in the Countrie.

And many similar details that unquestionably entertained the court.

In the May session of the court the following year Dr. Jacob Lumbroso "Surgan" brought suit for defamation against a neighbor who had spread the story that the doctor had tried to seduce the wife of his indentured servant, John Goold. The husband testified that the doctor had indeed offered "one halfe of his boath land and hogs and all that hee had . . . if I woold give Consent to let him ly with my wife." Refusing to be rebuffed, Lumbroso had, Margerie declared, taken her in his arms "and threw mee upon the bed and thear woold have the use of my bodie and I Crying out and then hee let mee goe. . . ." Because there was question of the legality of the oaths of indentured servants the case was referred to the Provincial Court.

The same session John Neuill and his wife were sued by Richard and Mary Dodd for defamation. Joan Neuill, it seems, had accused Mary Dodd of being Captain Batten's whore, or more specifically of lying "with Capt Batten at Patuxon in the sight of six men with her Coats up to her mouth. . . ."

It appeared that the root of the quarrel lay in the fact that Goodie Dodd had trespassed on Goodie Neuill's land. Mary Roe, who seemed to have total recall, had witnessed the episode and gave a blow-by-blow and word-by-word account. Goodie Dodd had led off by striking her enemy in the face and goodie neuill did say tho[u] [j]ade dust tho[u] stricke mee in my owne ground," and with that "goodie neuill strooke her a good blow in the Chops . . . and mary dod sayd goodie neuill doe not you threaten mee for threatened foulkes live long and goodie neuill sayd bauld Eagell get the[e] home and Eate sum of gammer [Be]laines fat Porke and mary dod sayd if shee did eat fat Porke shee did not Eate Rammish boare and goodie neuill sayd who did and goodie dod sayd shee did not . . . and goodie dod say, she was no Scoatchmans whore and goodie neuill sayd that nether scotch Irish or English came amis to her . . . and goodie neuill spit at her and sayd shee scorned to go with such Companie as she was and with that mary dod went away and goodie neuill held up her hands and hollowed at her and further sayeth not.

Doctor Lumbroso was indicted at the same session for seducing his maid, Elizabeth Wild, and when he had gotten her with child, given her a "Phisick" to "kill the Child within." Lumbroso married the girl and the case was apparently dropped. Although Lumbroso, a Portuguese Jew, was charged at one time or another with blasphemy, abortion, attempted rape, and receiving stolen goods, he was "purged" by his successive court appearances and continued to be a prominent and successful member of the community.[7]

The county courts of New England were quite as informal as those of Maryland. Most of the judges were appointed to their offices by the Great and General Court upon the recommendation of the town meetings. As Zechariah Chafee observes, "The magistrates, except for the training derived from their experience in official duties, were as innocent of legal education as the attorney."

[7] *Records of Charles County, Maryland*, Archives of Maryland, pp. 232–3, 234, 235, 357, 377, 379, 387–9.

Moreover because there were no written opinions, and thus no precedents, the courts enjoyed remarkable latitude.

Although the jurisdictions of church and state were kept distinct, many crimes considered serious were more of an offense against the congregation than against the civil community. Reviling a minister was such a crime, which, although committed in church, was punishable in a court of law. In one instance, John Veering was presented "for beeing drunck & abuseing his wife in bad language calling her whore & . . . reproaching Mr Allen & Church members in saying m^r Allen was a black hyprocritical Rogue . . ."

For his crime Veering was sentenced to be whipped with thirty stripes "severly laide on & to stand in the open market place . . . exalted upon a Stoole for an houres time on a thursday after Lecture; with a paper fastened to his breast, with this inscription in a lardge character A PROPHANE & WICKED SLANDERER & IMPIOUS REVILER OF A MINISTER OF THE GOSPEL & church-members; & to pay charges of witnesses & fees of Court."

The law was also invoked against any violators of the Sabbath. Here, as in infractions of the sexual code, discipline in the church was supplemented by discipline before the bar. Some prisoners were sentenced to be admonished in open court, or to make public confession of guilt and ask for forgiveness (as in the case of Thomas Baker), and at other times the convicted lawbreaker could satisfy judgment by public confession.

The cases heard in New England courts were as lurid as those in the Maryland courts of the same period. Mary Druery, taken to court by her husband for refusing to live with him, declared that he was incapable of intercourse and, therefore, since he was a husband in name only, she was not bound to live with him. In her deposition Mary attested that her husband had never had "fellow ship" with her although she slept in his bed for six weeks.

In the Suffolk Court Sammuell Judkin was given

"twenty Stripes" for committing fornication with an Indian squaw, and Christopher Mason, "convict of getting
Mr Rock's Negroe maide Bess with Childe," was sentenced likewise to twenty stripes, to pay court and prison
fees and give a bond of twenty pounds for good behavior.
Mary Plumb, "convict of lascivious carriage by being seene
in bed wth a man," received fifteen stripes and was ordered
to be placed in "the house of correction" until the selectmen of Dorchester found a proper position for her.

Whipping posts, stocks, and pillories seem cruel and
degrading forms of punishment to modern sensibilities, but
it could certainly be argued that they were more humane
than the lengthy prison terms favored by present-day law,
and doubtless more effective in rehabilitating the offender.

Long-term imprisonment was hardly known in the
colonies. The courts preferred to punish briefly and
sharply. "To imprison thieves and other rascals for years
. . . would have cost the taxpayers dear, left the prisoners'
relatives without support, and kept men idle when the
community wanted manpower." [8] Most suits were simply
settled by having the offenders pay fines and damages to
the victims. Bonds posted to ensure good behavior were a
further incentive to reform.

Much litigation arose from efforts of the colonists to
regulate trade and industry. Baking, tanning, making pipe
staves, raising cattle, practicing medicine, and exporting
gunpowder out of the colony were all regulated by law in
Massachusetts Bay. Licenses were required to sell wine and
liquor, to operate coffee and chocolate houses, to maintain a
cook shop, to distill liquor, and to keep an inn. In fact the
network of statutes that controlled the day-to-day activities
of many of the English colonists in the seventeenth and the
eighteenth century had no parallel in America until the
emergence of the modern "welfare" state. Nor is this

[8] Zechariah Chafee, Jr., ed.: *Records of the Suffolk County Court,
1671–1680*, Part I (Colonial Society of Massachusetts Collections),
XXVII, pp. 231, 257; XXX, pp. 837–41; and XXIX, pp. 183–5.

surprising because the assumptions have been the same in both instances—namely, that the well-being of the community, or the "common good," was more important than that of the individual. The colonial assemblies were not distracted by a concept of enlightened self-interest. It seemed evident to them that the private citizen must be restrained wherever his interests conflicted with those of the community.

From the middle of the eighteenth century on, American lawyers and judges worked to impose some system on the disorder of native law. *Blackstone's Commentaries on the Laws of England, Chitty on Pleadings,* and Coke's four *Institutes* (especially *Coke upon Littleton*) came to have wide use in the Republic. But the formalization of law was largely an urban phenomenon. The town was much slower to feel the effects of what were, at least to the city-bred lawyer, the reform of primitive and anarchic practices.

The end of the Revolution, an upheaval in which lawyers had played such a conspicuous part, brought an enormous increase in the number of bar members. Noah Webster wrote in 1787: "Never was such a rage for the study of the law. From one end of the continent to the other, the students of this science are multiplying without number." [9] Yet what was said of Vermont—that its courts "were badly organized and usually filled with incompetent men . . poorly educated and some of vulgar manners and indifferent morals"—could have been said of most frontier communities.

In city and town the lawyers most admired were those who were "copious, fluent, abounding in skilful criticisms and beautiful reflections," who were "familiar with the best classical productions in ancient and modern literature," and were able to give "popular and animated addresses to the jury." The special gifts of rival attorneys were compared and debated. One was acclaimed for his "calm, chaste,

[9] Cited in Warren: *The American Bar,* p. 322.

methodical and logical arguments," another cherished for his apt quotations from the minor Greek poets, or for "his steady flow of sound principles." Cicero and Coke were as often cited in the small-town courthouse as Blackstone or Kent, and with as much authority.[1]

Although de Tocqueville's description of the American bar in the 1830's applies perhaps more directly to city than to small town lawyers, it suggests the status that the profession had won for itself in the span of some fifty years. De Tocqueville called the lawyers "the American aristocracy."

> The special information which lawyers derive from their studies [he wrote] ensures them a separate station in society; and they constitute a sort of privileged body in the scale of intelligence. . . . Lawyers are attached to public order beyond every other consideration and the best security of public order is authority. . . . In America there are no nobles or literary men, and the people is [sic] apt to mistrust the wealthy; lawyers consequently form the highest political class. . . . They have therefore nothing to gain by innovation, which adds a conservative interest to their natural taste for public order.[2]

The legal lag was much in evidence on the frontier where the emphasis continued to be on law as protection for the community rather than for the individual. "Vagrant laws" were popular in the West. The Kentucky legislature passed such an act providing that "any person . . . found without employment or any visible means of obtaining a livelihood" was to be "taken up, and after having been advertised ten days . . . sold to the highest bidder" for a period of indenture as long as three months. All that he earned above the cost involved in keeping him was paid to

[1] Ibid., pp. 321, 296–7.
[2] Alexis de Tocqueville: *Democracy in America* (London: Saunders & Otley; 1835).

him at the end of his service. James Finley recalled a gambler arrested under such a law and sold to a blacksmith who kept him chained to an anvil block until his time was served.

In the nineteenth century the lawyer became, with the teacher and minister, one of the three leading figures in the town. The local politician was almost invariably a lawyer. His legal qualifications were often vague. A brief apprenticeship with an established attorney, an easy familiarity with Blackstone, and an agile tongue were usually sufficient. The law remained crude in the extreme. Often the judges were elected. In Ohio the circuit courts were headed by a "president judge"—a lawyer with some training and experience—and three associate judges, country squires with no pretension to legal knowledge. A wit named the group "the Demarara team," citing the story of the sailor who when fined by such a bench said he hoped the Demarara team was now satisfied. When the clerk asked him to explain the meaning of the phrase, the sailor replied: "In the Island of Demarara a team is composed of three mules and a jackass." Often members of the bar found themselves in court for such offenses as card-playing and drinking. The grand jurors of Seneca County, Ohio, fined absent members a bottle of brandy and there was always a bottle on the table from which the jurors partook freely.

Herbert Quick tells of an Indiana lawyer who convinced the judge before whom he was arguing a case that evidence should be admitted or excluded according to the vote of the crowd present at the trial. Since the lawyer was a popular figure he had the crowd with him and managed to have the evidence damaging to his client tossed out of court. One Iowa lawyer persuaded a judge to forbid a rival to read from *Cooley on Torts* on the ground that Cooley was a Michigan lawyer and a member of the Interstate Commerce Commission in Washington.[3] In this

[3] Herbert Quick: *One Man's Life* (Indianapolis, Ind.: The Bobbs-Merrill Company, 1925), pp. 336–7.

spirit many cases were simply games of wits between rival attorneys. Abraham Lincoln is of course again a classic example of the shrewd small-town advocate who succeeded less by his knowledge of the law than by his use of homespun humor and anecdote.

The lawyer of the country town stuck to the commentaries written by the great jurists of the past long after his city colleagues had started to cite precedents in the form of higher court decisions. The town lawyer was happier with principles than precedents, and the older reliance on principles was perfectly adapted to the needs of the town. The lawyers' clients and the spectators in the courtroom wanted to hear great and immutable principles evoked in the simplest of cases. They took heart at being involved in a drama that comprehended centuries of Anglo-American law. Principles might be used by the Supreme Court to produce an impossible rigidity in the law, or corporation counsels might find them hopelessly inexact, but they allowed the small-town lawyer full scope for his forensic talents, for the marshaling of history, of natural law, of the Almighty himself. Such tactics lifted the most mundane case to the level of a universal drama, placed little demand on precise legal knowledge in lawyer or judge, and could be followed by the layman without difficulty.

The case system on the other hand was designed to meet the needs of city lawyers, the servants of business and industry, and it was resented and resisted by small-town attorneys.

William Maxwell has described this breed in his novel *Time Will Darken It:*

> During the period between 1850 and 1900, when Draperville was still a pioneering community, the ownership of land was continually and expensively disputed. . . . Laws were passed but they were full of loopholes, and consequently for the next two generations, able lawyers were held in the highest respect. In the eyes of simple and uneducated men, the

Law assumed the status, dignity, and mystical content of a religion. The local lawyers . . . sometimes charged very high fees. . . . But the older lawyers also took on a great many cases where there was no possibility of remuneration merely so they could argue in court. They were dramatic figures and people attended their trials as they would a play, for the emotional excitement, the spectacle, the glimpses of truth behind the barn-burning, the murderous assault, the boundary dispute, or the question of right of way.

When the case system penetrated Draperville along with urban ideas and social attitudes,

the great legal actors with their over-blown rhetoric, their long white hair and leonine heads, their tricks on cross-examination [were replaced by university-trained men who] preferred more and more to argue before a judge, to let the court decide on the basis of legal precedent, to keep the case away from a jury, and to close the doors of the theater on the audience who hoped to hear about the murder of Agamemnon and see Medea's chariot drawn by dragons.[4]

The moral and philosophical stature of the law declined. It lost its power to exalt and to instruct. It entered in labyrinthine windings through the tedious minutiae of casebooks and reports where the layman could not and did not wish to follow. Not only was it lost to the town as entertainment, except for the occasional sensational crime, it was lost as a process which the community could understand and in which its members participated. Litigation became expensive, confusing, and uncertain in its outcome. If justice was done, it was not a justice whose sources were recognizable and familiar. Lawyers were no longer the impelling figures that related the town and its

[4] William Maxwell: *Time Will Darken It* (New York: Harper & Brothers; 1948), pp. 46–7.

inner life to immutable principles and great men; they were rather quiet, knowledgeable individuals who could manipulate a law that was complex beyond the layman's understanding. The town's attitude toward the law thus underwent a profound change.

In his study of Plainville James West found, typically, that Plainvillers "dreaded and even hated" the law—feeling "that lawsuits should be avoided and are in no wise considered a safe and sure way to justice." The townspeople said cynically: "The people with the most money win the cases. . . . Only the lawyers make anything out of the law. . . . I don't think much of a man that hollers 'law.' " [5]

Law in the town of course lost its corrective character. As punishment was made more humane and the science of penology arose the town surrendered its offenders to state prisons. Offenses that once brought thirty lashes now brought thirty months in jail, but it might be questioned whether the improvement was as great as champions of reform considered it. Certainly whatever the gains in systematization, in orderly procedure and good court practice, they could hardly balance the loss of confidence in the workings of the law itself, a confidence which the city had perhaps never had and which the town surrendered reluctantly, leaving, as a residue, a respect for the law in its larger implications that has been characteristically American.

The history of law in the town can be traced from an initial hostility and suspicion of English legal procedure and of lawyers brought over from England to a growing confidence in the law or those simplified forms of it that appeared in the town. Simple and accessible, it provided an ideal medium for the development of nineteenth-century American lawyers—an extraordinary breed of aggressive,

[5] James West: "Plainville, U.S.A.," in A. Kardiner, ed.: *Psychological Frontiers of Society* (New York: Columbia University Press; 1945), p. 287.

upwardly mobile individuals who played a vital role in the nation's development. While the lawyer's position in the town remains an important and respected one, it is much diminished from what it once was. The lawyer has shrunk and the law with him in the life of the community.

VIII

Temperance

A S A CITADEL OF CONSERVATISM the town had little taste for general reform, but during its history two causes enlisted its support—temperance, which the town embraced with often fanatical zeal, and the antislavery crusade. Temperance was an almost universal preoccupation of American towns; antislavery concerned only certain communities, primarily those with New England origins.

From the earliest days of settlement colonial Americans had consumed remarkable quantities of rum, hard cider, brandy, and imported wines. The records of church discipline in the New England communities make frequent mention of trials for drunkenness. Every community had its habitual drunkards and problem drinkers, but as long as the covenant held fast it was possible to keep drinking more or less under control.

In 1686 we find Increase Mather writing:

It is an unhappy thing that later years a kind of strong Drink called Rum has been common amongst us, which the poorer sort of people, both in Town and Country, can make themselves drunk with. They that are poor and wicked too, can for a penny or twopence make themselves drunk: I wish to the Lord some Remedy may be thought of for the prevention of this evil.[1]

Cotton Mather, some years later, noted in a similar spirit that "the consequences of the affected Bottel, in . . . [Connecticut communities], as well as ours, are beyond all imagination." Ministers themselves, Mather wrote, often drank freely and sometimes to excess, and "the amount of liquor consumed at meetings of ministers, such as ordinations, became a scandal."[2]

A hundred years later conditions had not improved; an outstanding Massachusetts preacher gave as his reason for joining a temperance movement the fact that among his fellow ministers he knew "forty-four who drank so much as to affect their brains, and he had assisted in putting four to bed on occasions like ordinations."[3]

John Adams was especially offended by the drinking that went on in his native state. The numerous taverns were the root of the evil. In them, he wrote, "the time, the money, the health and the modesty of most that were young and many old were wasted; here disease, vicious habits, bastards and legislators were frequently begotten." Such inns offered "miserable accommodations. . . . Yet, if you sit the evening, you will find the house full of people drinking drams, flip, toddy, carousing, swearing; but especially plotting with the landlord to get him at the next

[1] C. F. Adams: *Three Episodes of Massachusetts History* (Boston and New York: Houghton Mifflin Company; 1903), p. 786.
[2] Ibid., p. 792.
[3] Ibid., p. 783.

town meeting an election either for selectman or representative."

Not only was there continual and excessive drinking in
the town; many of those who left it to seek their fortune in
the city or, later, in the California gold fields became
victims of the habit. "Failure was the rule," Charles Francis
Adams wrote of the emigre youth of Braintree, and the
words " 'He drank himself to death' were so often repeated
by old-timers accounting for those dead and gone, that
they sound[ed] at last not like the exception, but the
rule." [4]

Haying, barn-raising, corn-husking, fence-building
were all occasions for liberal and often excessive drinking
by the entire community. Rum and hard cider were not
only kept at home but were available at every ordinary
tavern and at the general store as well. On training and
muster days the town furnished the rum ration while at
ordinations, installations, and district councils the church
provided the "libation."

Jeremy Belknap reported that in the New Hampshire
backcountry "the thirst for spirits . . . is so ardent, that in
the fall and winter they will sell their wheat for this sort of
pay, and then in the spring and summer go forty or fifty
miles after bread." [5]

Besides the extreme cases many small-town citizens
drank enough rum and hard cider to make them "high" a
considerable part of the time. Mathew Patten, one of the
leaders of the frontier community of Bedford, New Hampshire, may be taken as typical. In 1754–5 Patten purchased
ten quarts of rum in August, six quarts in October (plus
three and a half barrels of cider), seven in February, five
more on the second of March, on the seventh of the same
month four gallons and three quarts, and on the eighteenth
two more quarts. Patten may have traded some rum, and
some may have been sold, although his journal contains only

[4] Ibid., pp. 785, 793.
[5] *Belknap Papers*, Massachusetts Historical Society, III, p. 440.

one reference in this period to such a transaction, but obviously he consumed what would by present standards be enormous quantities of hard liquor.

In addition to rum, twenty to thirty barrels of cider were considered necessary to carry the average family through the winter, and if the cider was harmless when sweet, it became more potent as the winter passed. When some men grew disagreeable and even "ugly" toward springtime, it was commonly remarked that their cider was getting hard. The whisky produced in Vermont in 1810 was of greater value than the maple-sugar crop. In addition there was cider, brandy, maple rum, New England rum, and potato whisky. Potato whisky retailed at fifty to seventy-five cents a gallon and probably it has never been possible to get drunk more cheaply than in the New England towns of the early nineteenth century.

A bad situation seemed to get worse with each passing decade. The historian of Northfield, Massachusetts, writes:

> Hard drink was the countryside's besetting evil. Everywhere the country tavern had its group of drunken loafers. It was tolerated as an inescapable feature. It had its respectable patrons and its political defenders. Village stores, some of them, carried on a more covert but profitable trade out of whiskey barrels. . . . Homes were made wretchedly unhappy, farms were desolated or half-tilled only to have their yield turned into drink.[6]

As the covenanted community disintegrated and the traditional pressures that had ameliorated the vice of drunkenness slackened, the towns were further demoralized by the exodus, year after year, of many of their most able and energetic citizens. The Reverend Sherlock Bristol recalled that in his hometown of Cheshire, Connecticut, there had been

[6] Herbert C. Parsons: *A Puritan Outpost* (New York: The Macmillan Company; 1937), pp. 261, 369.

eight distilleries of cider brandy in full blast, from twenty to thirty cider mills, half a dozen taverns all selling brandy and whiskey at three cents a glass. . . . Was it strange then, that drunkenness was in every other family nearly? Was it strange then that my mother and I counted over fifty drunkards within the circle of our acquaintance? I mean people who occasionally staggered and talked boosily through strong drink? Was it strange, that in one winter we buried ten men who had died with delerium tremens, out of a population of 2,000 people?

It was against such a background that the temperance movement got its start in New England. The movement itself dated back to the last decades of the eighteenth century and there had, of course, been earlier efforts on local scale. In the 1770's the Reverend Ebenezer Sparhawk vigorously attacked drinking. Liquor, he told his congregation, "puts the blood and juices into a most terrible ferment and disturbs the whole animal economy. It vitiates the humor, relaxes the solids, spoils the constitution, fills the body with diseases, brings on meager looks, a ghastly countenance, and very bad tremblings: yea, when the abuse of it is persisted in, it quite ruins the health, destroys the strength, introduces decay of nature, and hastens death faster than hard labour." [7] Moreover, Sparhawk warned, it distracts the victim from his religious duties and thus imperils his salvation. Such vivid denunciations of drinking had little effect. The Reverend Sparhawk's congregation was not notably abstemious.

Not until the 1820's when the movement became associated with the religious awakenings and revivals did it really get off the ground. In John Krout's words: "As the leadership and membership of the temperance societies came largely from the churches, so the appeal of the movement was apt to be religious. The reform took on the

[7] Sherlock Bristol: *The Pioneer Preacher* (Chicago and New York: Fleming Revell Company; 1887), pp. 34-5.

attributes of a huge revival. Temperance workers were evangelists preaching a new gospel. . . ." [8]

The various temperance organizations placed a heavy emphasis on the "testimony" of the reformed drunkard, and the confession and vow of repentance had a striking similarity to the public confession and redemption of the Congregational discipline. The temperance meetings were thus, in part, an effort by the town to recapture the unity of the covenanted community. The meetings were interdenominational; rival congregations forgot feuds and jealousies in an affirmation of common aspirations.

It is moreover of significance that those denominations which held fast to a covenanted relationship offered the greatest resistance to the temperance movement. Some Primitive Baptist churches went so far as to excommunicate members who joined temperance societies,[9] and the Dutch Reformed church, one of the most successful in retaining the covenant unimpaired, roundly denounced the temperance movement. Only when the churches saw the movement as a potential stimulus to religious awakening and had established a measure of control over it did they give it their wholehearted support. They were then quite ready to insist that "the Holy Spirit will not visit, much less will He dwell with him who is under the polluting, debasing effects of intoxicating drink." Drunkenness "counteracts the merciful designs of Jehovah . . . ; binds the soul in hopeless bondage to its destroyer; awakens the 'worm that dieth not, and the fire which is not quenched,' and drives the soul away in despair, weeping and wailing . . . from the presence of the Lord and the glory of His power." [1]

Of enormous assistance to the temperance movement were the utopian expectations of the community. Even where disappointments and defeats had flawed the dream, it was possible to stir some fire from the ashes. Inhabitants of

[8] John Allen Krout: *The Origins of Prohibition* (New York: Alfred A. Knopf; 1925), pp. 67–8.
[9] Ibid., pp. 113, 119.   [1] Ibid., pp. 114–15.

the town might reason that the only impediment to "boundless prosperity . . . coming in upon us like a flood," the only enemy that could "defeat the hopes of the world, which hang upon our experiment in civil liberty . . . , is that river of fire, which is rolling through the land, destroying the vital air, and extending around an atmosphere of death." A universal and rational principle which was to bring America to the golden age was being defied by the uncontrolled sale and use of "ardent spirits." Such words summoned up once again the millennial dream, and inspired the champions of temperance to insist that "this very cause is at once the harbinger of the millennium and destined to be one of the most efficient means of its introduction." [2]

From the ardor of the 1820's the temperance movement achieved a momentum that carried it forward for almost a hundred years. It rapidly became one of the most deep-rooted and persistent themes in American life and it affected the town as no other issue in our history. Moving full cycle from temperance in the specific meaning of the word to voluntary total abstinence and finally to national prohibition, it was given fresh life time after time by the renewed hope that the defeat of alcohol would mean an end to the heartrending problems which beset the town, problems which the town could not comprehend and which it struggled to reduce to a single, tangible issue.

Temperance was strongest in the towns of New England and the Middle States in the years when those towns first felt the full impact of the shattering of the covenant and the defeat of their dreams. Only a sixth of the people of the country lived in New England in the early decades of the nineteenth century, but it contained one third of the temperance societies with one third of the total membership. There was, furthermore, a significant relation between the expansion of New England and the spread of

[2] Ibid., pp. 107, 118.

temperance sentiment. The sections of New York and Ohio most active in the temperance movement had been colonized from New England. There were seven hundred temperance societies in New York State alone, the great majority of whose members were from the "Eastern states." In Pennsylvania a "majority of the societies were supported by the descendants of Welsh and English Quakers and Scotch-Irish Presbyterians. The latter were chiefly responsible for the fact that within the two westernmost tiers of counties lived more than thirty per cent of all Pennsylvanians who had signed the pledge." On the other hand, only ten percent of the country's temperance members lived south of the Mason-Dixon Line and most of these were the Scotch-Irish of western Virginia and Georgia.[3]

By 1834 there were over five thousand local temperance groups in the United States, with a total membership of over a million, but the high tide of pre-Civil War temperance agitation came in the 1850's following the Maine prohibition law promoted by Neal Dow. By 1855 thirteen states had passed prohibitory laws, but states, like individuals, showed a tendency to backslide, and by the mid-1860's only five were left in the ranks of prohibition.

Manchester, Massachusetts, a town of some two thousand people, formed a temperance society in 1829 based on "total abstinence," and seven years later it had nearly four hundred members. In Clinton, New Hampshire, the Clintonville Mechanics Total Abstinence Society was founded in 1844 and six years later the Clinton Division, Number 67, of the Sons of Temperance was instituted and flourished briefly. Such efforts were typical.

It is also perhaps worth noting in passing that the pre-Civil War prohibition movement was most successful in enlisting those very New Englanders who were reputed to be champions of rugged individualism.

[3] Ibid., p. 130.

Temperance

Perhaps the most significant change in the temperance movement came after the Civil War, when the center of power shifted from New England to the Middle West. Important as the crusade had been in the new towns, many of which were indeed started as temperance communities, it was not until after the war that temperance became, in innumerable instances, the towns' central obsession. The sober fact was that drunkenness threatened many towns with dissolution. In the long-established New England communities, widespread drunkenness might be a general calamity, but on the frontier, where the margin of survival for the town was narrow, it could and often did prove fatal.

Much of the excessive drinking on the frontier has been accounted for by the terrible rigors of such an existence—the chilling cold and oppressive heat, the desperately hard work and the bleakness of life. One early settler of such a town recalled:

> The use of intoxicating drinks was our greatest evil. Some would get on sprees, and after taking much whisky, would form a ring, and with bells, horns, tin pans, log chains, or any noisy instrument, engage in a hideous dance, sing, and give Indian war-whoops. Such a state of society was not the rule, entirely however, and was wholly displaced in a short time by the ingress of more refined people, who controlled the moral standard of the neighborhood. That enemy of civilization—whisky—was hard to subdue, however.[4]

On the other hand the most serious drinking problems often came after the pioneer period when the town had become relatively prosperous, stable and orderly. Certainly the drinking that was such a problem in New England communities in the early decades of the nineteenth century could not be attributed to the rigors of a frontier existence.

[4] William Lang: *The History of Seneca County* (Springfield, Ohio: Transcript Printing Company; 1880), p. 95.

After the Civil War undoubtedly the temperance movement proved an ideal channel through which to express the inchoate animosities and resentments that grew up so luxuriously in the town in the last decades of the century. Although such groups as the Independent Order of Good Templars, founded in 1851, grew rapidly, much of the temperance agitation passed to the women of the towns. The women's crusade began in Hillsboro, Ohio, in 1874, when a group of women led by the daughter of a former governor gathered to pray and to read the 146th Psalm, which begins with the words: "O put not your trust in princes, nor in any child of man; for there is not help in them," and ends with a plea for divine assistance "for them that are fallen. . . . The Lord careth for the strangers; he defendeth the fatherless and widow; as for the way of the ungodly, he turneth it upside down."

The embattled ladies of the town resolved to go daily to pray and sing in local saloons in an effort to rout the tavernkeepers. When word of the crusade reached nearby Washington Court House, the wives and mothers of that community formed a "Committee of Visitation" and appealed to the liquor dealers "in the name of our desolate homes, blasted hopes, ruined lives, widowed hearts, for the honor of our community, for our happiness, for the good name of our town, in the name of God who will judge you and us, for the sake of our own souls which are to be saved or lost." The dealers were called upon to "cleanse yourselves from this heinous sin, and place yourselves in the ranks of those who are striving to elevate and ennoble themselves and their fellow men."

While some women remained at the church in prayer, others went with a few hardy males to sing temperance songs before the doors of the town's saloons. The church bells tolled and the women knelt in the snow chanting and praying. Perhaps none of the men who watched this remarkable performance were aware of its implications, but one can imagine their emotions as they saw the saloon-keeper give way and turn his stock over to his besiegers to be emptied into the streets with songs of thanksgiving.

The next day the scene was repeated and another barkeeper struck his colors. After eight days the indomitable ladies had forced the capitulation of eleven saloonkeepers. The crusade seemed at last to have found a means of defeating the "demon rum." Word of the Washington Court House campaign gave heart to militant women in thousands of small towns, and under the leadership of Frances Willard the Woman's Christian Temperance Union had recruited 44,000 members by 1879.

The chapter at Thornton, Indiana, gained fame by the words which a poesy member wrote to be sung to the tune of the "Battle Hymn of the Republic":

> On the plains for bloodless battle, they are gathered
> true and strong—
> All the hero-hearted women who have wept in silence
> long
> At the terrible oncoming of the raven-winged wrong.
> Now God is leading on.
>
> Oh, the beauty and the blessing when the curse is
> swept away. . . .
>
> Then the desert and the wilderness shall blossom with
> the flowers
> Of industry and plenty, in this blessed land of ours.
> And the grace of God unstinted shall come down in
> gentle showers,
> For God is leading on.

The companionship and entertainment afforded by the W.C.T.U. is suggested by a typical program of the Thornton chapter, meeting in July, 1890. The assembled company began by singing "All Hail the Power of Jesus' Name." Then came an "impressive and energizing prayer," and a reading from Scripture. An elocution and singing contest followed, featuring such topics as "Prohibition, the

Hope of Our Country," "The Rumseller's Legal Rights," and "Save the Boy," interspersed with renditions by a mixed quartet of "Sleeping on Guard," "Lift the Temperance Banner High," and "A Child's Pleading." [5]

But the participation of small-town women in temperance activity reached below the surface fact of almost endemic drunkenness. Most obvious was the woman's new consciousness of "rights" and status. In the community where she had gone to war against the man, temperance was the perfect weapon. It was the men, sodden and bestial, who sinned against the community and against its women, who, in defiance of Christian morality, staggered home to despairing families. In the temperance crusade the mother allied herself with the children against the father, and the children appear as a constant symbol searching from saloon to saloon for their father, or dredging his limp form out of the gutter. As the movement spread, it made the rout of the man complete. The pioneer, clear-eyed, devout, powerful in body and spirit, had been defeated by the town, and the woman was left in possession of the dubious spoils.

The preoccupation of the town with temperance reform went beyond the fact of drunkenness. Temperance agitation was strongest in the communities of the covenant and among the children of those communities who wished to reaffirm the integrity of the common life and who, accustomed to group sanctions, sought to invoke them against the common enemy—the producer and retailer of hard liquor.

[5] Lewis Atherton: *Main Street on the Middle Border* (Bloomington, Ind.: Indiana University Press; 1954), pp. 90, 93–5.

I X

Social Life and Social Structure in the Town

T HE SOCIAL LIFE OF THE TOWN centered in the church—indeed, it was the church; the "horse-shedding" that filled the interval between Sunday services was the social event of each week. Weddings, baptisms, funerals, and town meetings brought the people of the community together in ritual acts which affirmed and renewed the covenant. The church did not appear to be in opposition to secular concerns, or a mere supplement to them. The life of the congregation and the community were coterminous. During the early history of the town no anxiety was produced by a struggle between the received religious tradition and changing secular values.

It would be a mistake to assume that because the church

dominated the social life of the community life was grim and joyless. There is abundant evidence to prove that the pleasures of small-town life were as intense, as vivid, and as refreshing to the body and spirit as any modern diversions. Our image of the small town as being harsh, "Puritanical," and pleasure-denying is drawn from a later age when the church, no longer the unchallenged preceptor of the individual's life, still attempted to assert its ancient rights as guardian of the faith and morals of the community.

Even in those communities that remained intensely religious and church-centered down to the end of the nineteenth century, the enormous proliferation of "social activities" borrowed from the city created bitter tensions between "liberals" and "conservatives." In the earlier ages of the town this dichotomy did not exist. The people of the community were hungry for whatever social life the church might provide; the church had no serious rivals except the tavern and the training field.

To John Adams "the meeting house and school-house and training field [were] the scenes where New England men [were] formed. . . ." The trainings were the occasion where the town's militia unit drilled on the common. There were usually two "little trainings" a year plus a regimental muster in which neighboring towns joined.[1] For communities which lived in danger of Indian attacks these were serious occasions, but even so they were invariably enlivened by a carnival spirit, and in those towns safe from Indian forays, the trainings often became Rabelaisian affairs in which the military side was slighted for the social. The lack of a proper martial air was suggested by the jocular names often given to the units by their communities—"Old Salt Hay" and "Slam-Bang" were the names bestowed on the company from Hampton and Hampton Falls, New Hampshire.

On muster day the units from adjacent towns would

[1] Charles F. Adams: *Three Episodes of Massachusetts History* (Boston and New York: Houghton Mifflin Company; 1903), p. 47.

assemble, accompanied by fife and drum. Every musketeer was required to present for inspection a flintlock musket, two spare flints, a priming wire and brush. While the inspectors were progressing with their work, the officers and privates were presented with money by the selectmen of the towns to which they belonged to purchase a dinner. "The old-time musters were sure to attract a large number of pedlers of all sorts of goods, such as hats, jewelry, cutlery, patent medicines, books, pictures, etc., but none of the enterprising traders were better patronized than the venders of candy, gingerbread, and other sweet-meats. . . ."

As time went on sideshows of various kinds became an adjunct of muster days. "Sometimes a bear, a couple of wildcats, or a live rattlesnake could be seen for a few cents." Boxers and wrestlers and runners were generally ready to try their skill and stamina with champions from other towns, and, increasingly, gambling and the sale of liquor became features of the muster day. In 1844 when an effort was made to prevent the sale of liquor at a muster day at Hampton Falls, there was a riot and the rioters were only dispersed when the Seabrook militia fired on them with powder charges at close range.

A witness has left a colorful account of a typical muster day:

> The field was fringed with numerous tents, deal-ing out all sorts and quantities of refreshments, while the "tents of the wicked"—as the temporary gambling hells, were in an adjoining field and we regret to say appeared to be very largely patronized. We saw no drinking but sundry casks and decanters which we observed in different tents had a very suspicious look and two or three men whom we saw extended under the fence in different quarters of the field had evi-dently been *struck by a grape vine*. Peddlers of all description hawked their wares, some valuable, but mostly worthless, with keen wit mingled with stale

jokes. Toward the close of the day the mob made a rush on the gambling quarters and in the twinkling of an eye the tables of the money changers and the poles of their tents were scattered to the four winds.[2]

A fierce fight followed between the gamblers and their supporters and the champions of right, many of whom had suffered at the gaming table.

As in New England, the training field and muster day were a feature of small-town life in the Middle West. There, too, the musters were regarded as time for a frolic. In an account of the day, it was noted that

the hotel keepers and the gingerbread shops made the most of them. . . . [The soldiers appeared in] citizens' clothes and just in such dress as was convenient to each. Some dressed in their best and others came just as they left their work. . . . Some had fur caps on, others straw hats or slouch hats; no two were dressed alike. Standing in line or marching, the men swung their arms, laughed, talked, looked about and generally did as they pleased. If a captain scolded or undertook to be strict in his discipline, they would elect another man next time. Those who had no guns would borrow a piece for the occasion, or use any stick or cornstalk as a substitute for a gun, for there was no time for going through the manual of arms or firing exercises. The captain himself, having no knowledge of military tactics, could give no instructions, and the whole day was spent in marching around, forming line, calling roll, electing officers, drinking, carousing and fighting.[3]

In the years after the American Revolution the celebration of the Fourth of July became one of the central rituals

[2] Warren Brown: *History of the Town of Hampton Falls, New Hampshire* (Concord, N.H.: Rumford Press; 1900–18), pp. 261–4, 266–7.
[3] Ibid., p. 280.

of town life. The unity of the town itself could also be strongly emphasized during these festivities in honor of the national covenant. At first the Fourth of July ceremonies were held in the churches; the Declaration of Independence was read and orations were given—almost invariably these dwelt on the idea of equality and its relation to Christian doctrine.

In the 1830's and 1840's the agricultural fair made its appearance, ostensibly as a means of encouraging improved methods of farming. Like the Fourth of July, it was really a folk festival. A description of the first fair held in Hampton Falls, New Hampshire, gives an idea of the scale of such undertakings:

> The grand entry of the Hampton Falls delegation of members, with their ladies, was a beautiful opening of the display. The band, led by the marshal, went out to meet them a mile from the village and escorted them into the town. Twenty yoke of handsome oxen with their horns tastefully dressed in blue and yellow streamers of ribbon were attached to a car mounted upon four wheels, and containing twenty-seven young ladies of Hampton Falls. The car was roofed over with green corn leaves for a screen from the sun, and carpeted and cushioned like a church. The outside was beautifully decorated with evergreens and bouquets of flowers. Indeed, no part of the wood, not even the wheels, could be seen. . . . Upon the sides, curiously formed in large letters with vegetables of all kinds, was an inscription of the name of the town. Snugly seated among the fair occupants were seen the president of the society and the orator of the day. . . .

The next year, in an effort to outdo its neighboring towns, Hampton Falls produced a carriage thirty feet long carrying seventy-six young ladies and twenty-two young gentlemen, and drawn by forty oxen. Next came two floats in the shape of agricultural implements, one representing "Young America" and the other "Old Fogyism." [4]

Such common ceremonies and festivals as the training days, the fairs, and the Fourth of July observances reasserted the unity of the town. They were, essentially, extensions of the covenanted life of the church congregation, and when that life shrank and diminished, these other ceremonials to a large extent replaced it.

The first social activities to challenge the church and training field were almost without exception "improving." They were moreover conceived as community ventures, designed to draw the community together and to elevate it. Debating, lecture, and library societies were formed in many New England towns by the last decades of the eighteenth century. Although the older and more conservative members of the community often viewed such undertakings as frivolous and distracting, they usually evoked an enthusiastic response in towns hungry for some diversion.

A typical debating society was that organized in Peacham, a Vermont frontier town, in 1810. The society's original membership of fourteen grew in two years to forty, in a town of three or four hundred people. Students of the Peacham Academy were the most active participants, while the townspeople made up the audiences. At weekly meetings members in turn declaimed, debated, or read an original composition. Among the topics debated were: "Are the fine arts beneficial to the morale of a nation?" "Are newspapers beneficial to the United States?" "Are there not too many young men endeavoring after a liberal education?" "Is the spendthrift more injurious than the miser?" "Has government a greater effect upon the character of a nation than climate?" "Are riches preferable to liberty?" "Should every man be obliged by law to pay something for the support of ministers of the gospel?" [Decided in the affirmative.] "Would it be [good] policy

4 Ibid., pp. 282–3.

for the government of the United States to encourage immigrants?" "Ought the poor to be supported by law?" And separate discussions of whether dancing, card playing, and smoking were "proper" and "justifiable." [5]

In many towns the debating society carried on its activities for a few years, then languished, to be replaced by a program of Lyceum lectures interspersed with local talent shows where townspeople read original papers and poems or joined in group singing. Gradually, lectures gave way to more general entertainment—card playing and games of various kinds.

The Lyceum, inspired in part at least by the English movement for workingmen's education, put down roots first in New England and flourished there in the thirties and forties. The constitution of the Lyceum of Manchester, Massachusetts, stated that "the regular exercises of the Society shall be original dissertations, lectures on scientific and other practical subjects, and a debate to be open to all the members." A local savant launched the series by giving three lectures on "Natural Philosophy," while the question, "Ought property to constitute the right of suffrage?" was warmly debated.[6]

Debates were a feature of small-town life in the Midwest as well as in New England. John H. Holmes recalls that there was always a debating society in Mastersville. "There was never a time they were not carrying on, during the winter season, a series of debates . . . on all manner of subjects." In the 1870's religion was a subject much discussed. Was faith achieved through reason or emotion, through intuition or through scripture? The town's most gifted orators argued the issue on numerous occasions.

There were warm debates on whether there should be governmental regulation of trade. The champions of tem-

[5] Darius F. Lamson: *History of Manchester, Essex County, Massachusetts, 1645–1895* (published by the Town of Manchester; 1895), pp. 154–5.
[6] Ibid., p. 15.

perance argued that the government should take over the production of all kinds of liquor, and subject its sale to rigid control. In Mr. Holmes's words: "Our people got to debating tariff. They held a debate on the question of the bank. National questions were debated by them and very intelligently, too." [7] The boys and girls of the community attended such debates when they were old enough to take notice and their entertainment value for the whole community was high.

In towns where some industrial life had developed "Mechanics Institutes" and "Workingmen's Societies" had a brief vogue. The Bigelow Mechanics Institute of Clinton, Massachusetts, was formed in 1846 "for the purpose of mutual improvement and for the further purpose of extending improvement throughout the village in which they reside, and the neighborhood with which they are more immediately connected . . . by sustaining, if their means shall allow it, a school for scientific instruction and education in those branches more immediately connected with their employment, and the collection of a library, a reading room and a repository of models and drawings of useful machines and mechanical inventions."

The preamble to the Clinton Mechanics Institute's constitution stated that its aims were "to promote our mutual improvement in literature, science . . . and mechanical pursuits in the community in which we reside;— and to develop the social, moral and intellectual natures with which we are endowed by one Creator." The covenant was undergoing a transformation, but the accents of its origin were unmistakable. Improvement in Clinton had become the secular analogy to salvation, or indeed a means to that salvation once promised by the covenant, but the enterprise was aimed, not at distinguishing a particular group within the community but at reasserting the unity of the town by drawing in those whose occupations threat-

[7] J. H. Holmes.

ened to mark them off from their neighbors. In this spirit the town attempted to deal with the effects of industrialism. It was an effort doomed to failure because early industry was too unstable and too transitory to provide the base for such ventures. Industry did not establish itself solidly in the town until it was able to draw upon a supply of depressed and docile immigrant labor.

In Clinton as in many other towns the Institute established a library and presented lectures and debates on alternate weeks. In 1848 it offered the mechanics and citizens of Clinton Ralph Waldo Emerson, Horace Greeley, and Henry Thoreau, who lectured to groups of from 100 to 400 townspeople. As the town's leading industry—a carpet factory—flourished the composition of the population changed. By the 1860's Irishmen, Scots, Germans, Englishmen, and Canadians made up more than a third of the population, and the Mechanics Institute, now called the Bigelow Library Association, had given up any pretense of being a workingman's society.[8]

Western towns repeated the pattern of Eastern communities. In Minnesota in the late 1850's dozens of little towns like Austin, Cannon Falls, Hastings, Mankato, Red Wing, St. Anthony, Stillwater, Taylor's Falls, and Winona had active lyceums or literary associations.[9] The Horticultural and Literary Society of Cedar Valley, Iowa, sponsored a lively program of "community entertainments, patriotic gatherings, active debating groups and lecture courses" in the 1870's, and then undertook the responsibility for running the town library. A few years later the Cedar Valley Agricultural and Mechanical Association was

[8] Andrew E. Ford: *History of the Origin of the Town of Clinton, Massachusetts 1653–1865* (Clinton, Mass.: Press of W. J. Coulter, Courant Office; 1896), pp. 409–10.
[9] Carl Bode: *The American Lyceum, Town Meeting of the Mind* (New York: Oxford University Press; 1956), p. 179.

formed along lines very similar to those of the Clinton Mechanics Institute.

The spirit of rivalry, especially among new towns of the West, was often a spur to the development of cultural activity. Waterloo, Iowa, formed a Library Association "to gratify the demand for some kind of recreation; to extend the knowledge of our city, and to gain the reputation we claim to merit as being the best city in central and northern Iowa."

In 1866, through the auspices of the Horticultural and Literary Society, Cedar Valley townspeople heard P. T. Barnum talk for two hours and ten minutes on "The Art of Money-Getting, or Success in Life." The title is significant; it suggests the penetration of the success ethic into the town. Ralph Waldo Emerson, who had packed the Mechanics Institute of Clinton some twenty years before, was coolly received by an audience that applauded the prince of showmen. To the editor of the *Gazette*, Barnum was "a shrewd, high-toned business man, a moral reformer, a wide-awake observer, and possesses a most profound knowledge of human nature and all its failings." Especially applauded was the "scathing yet happy way" in which the lecturer indicted whisky drinking and smoking.

The success theme was thus heavily encumbered with moralism, and the lectures which were most enthusiastically received dealt with such subjects as reconstruction, economics, race relations, and politics. Theodore Tilton, editor of the New York *Independent*, was a youthful prodigy, "the infant Hercules of American freedom," who spoke so eloquently on Negro suffrage that he was asked back for three successive years, an honor unique for Cedar Valley lecturers.

A third lecture series started with Robert Collyer, a Unitarian minister, famous as a champion of reform. Collyer struck an especially popular note in his attack on "the follies of fashionable society." The *Gazette* noted that some of the audience were doubtless displeased at these courageous remarks which "perhaps struck too close to the truth in individuals." [1]

John H. Holmes recalled that in Mastersville, Ohio, one of the favorite topics dealt with the problems of the newly freed Negro. He remembered particularly "a man who came to our town and delivered an evening lecture on Robert Burns [a poet especially popular in the small town because of his egalitarian ideals and his glorification of country ways]. I was just a boy them, but I can see and hear him to this day, talking and reciting Burns' poems." Although Mastersville was too small for a lyceum, no year passed without visiting lectures. [2]

One of the remarkable phenomena of the 1830's and 1840's was the appearance of phrenology, a "science" whose practitioners professed to be able to analyze character by the conformation of the individual's head. Starting in England, it enjoyed its most enduring success in the small towns of America. Initially an urban fad, the talk of society and the darling of the intellectuals, it soon passed into the hands of "practical" phrenologists who toured the country making "manipulations," examining heads for a fee and providing customers with charts showing their strengths and weaknesses in terms of the shape of their craniums.

The new creed hit the towns of Massachusetts first, and by 1844 that state and New York counted the highest number of subscribers to the *American Phrenological Journal*, while Connecticut citizens, too, succumbed in large numbers. Four years later Ohio had the greatest per capita circulation of the *Journal*, followed by Wisconsin and Illinois. In Cedarville, Ohio, one lecture resulted in forty-one subscriptions to the magazine. [3]

While many churches viewed phrenology with uneas-

[1] Luella M. Wright: "Culture Through Lectures," *Iowa Journal of History and Politics*, XXXVIII (April, 1940), pp. 118, 123 n.
[2] J. H. Holmes.
[3] John D. Davies: *Phrenology, Fad and Science* (New Haven, Conn.: Yale University Press; 1955), pp. 59–61.

iness, some enterprising ministers hastened to proclaim it a confirmation of Christian doctrine, collecting such statements as that of the convert who declared: "Phrenology saved me from the rock of infidelity on which I had struck. . . . When I saw, that the mind was *constitutionally* adapted to the great and leading principles of Christianity, I was enabled to comprehend the fallacy of the base and servile doctrines of the infidel."

Another doubter who in his distress turned to phrenology "for salvation from universal scepticism's painful . . . derangement" found that all his "doubts and perplexities fled like morning vapors chased away by a rising sun." [4] Phrenology stressed the traditional values of the ethic— sobriety and virtue, chastity and self-improvement, industry and thrift—but the emphasis was on the individual. The ethic received a new sanction—the sanction of "science." In its older versions it was seen as the proper way to serve God and one's fellowman; in the variation offered by phrenology, it was self which was served. The boy was encouraged to develop his bumps of affluence, acquisitiveness, and industry, and was expected to rely on his own endowments and capacities, aided by phrenology, to make his way "up" in the world.

To those who had already noticed that the older ethic was not as efficacious as its advocates claimed, phrenology provided a new hope. If industry, thrift, and piety would not ensure success, the equation must somehow be incomplete; perhaps the answer lay in the development of one's bumps. This expectation may have enabled phrenology to survive in the small towns of the Midwest for almost fifty years; this, plus, of course, its entertainment value.

In Mastersville, Ohio, every boy who could earn or beg the money had his head examined and a chart made of it. Young John Holmes was advised by a phrenologist to

[4] Ibid., p. 157.

become an auctioneer. As he recalls the experience: "The first thing on the chart was a picture of your head and there were bumps on it. And then [the phrenologist] went over your head. . . . That was the source of a great deal of entertainment to a great many people." [5]

Many of the phrenologists were shrewd and well-intentioned men who, in a time when traditional occupations and standards were badly disrupted, functioned as "career counselors" to many people who needed guidance and assurance because they had lost the Calvinist vision of calling. Phrenologists may well have assigned thousands of young men to jobs which they fulfilled contentedly for the rest of their lives, and they doubtless often fired ambitions that carried able boys far beyond the confines of their hometowns.

Although organizations directed to specific reforms or general community improvements, such as the debating, temperance, antislavery, and library societies, dated back to the latter part of the eighteenth century, the great era of associational activity began after the Civil War.

The seventies and eighties saw the appearance of a remarkable number of clubs and societies of all kinds. Dancing groups, brass bands, musical and dramatic societies, literary and reading groups and social clubs grew apace.[6] Much of this "cultural" activity was urban-inspired. When in 1876 the ladies of Cedar Falls organized the Parlor Reading Circle, they acknowledged the inspiration provided by an article in *Scribner's Monthly* entitled "Village Improvement Societies."

The *Scribner's* author, viewing the vast cultural desert which extended westward from Boston, had written:

> There is really nothing more sadly wanted in the village life of America than the organization of its best materials for purposes relating to the common good.

[5] J. H. Holmes.
[6] Louis B. Wright: *Culture on a Moving Frontier* (Bloomington, Ind.: University of Indiana; 1955), chapter VI.

And then with classic urban condescension:

> So many people must always spend their lives in villages; and these lives, in countless instances, are so barren and meaningless, so devoid of interest, so little sympathetic, that any means which promises to improve that life, should secure the most earnest attention. There is no reason why every village should not be alive with interest in its own culture and its own affairs, or why village life should not be crowded with attractions that have power to hold every villager to his home. There are multitudes who never dream that their village . . . can be the center of a culture as sweet and delightful as a city possesses. . . .[7]

Although the Cedar Falls Reading Circle was limited to sixty members, an effort was made, characteristically, to draw them from all levels of the community. The school superintendent, the president, and a member of the faculty of the new normal school, business and professional people and housewives were all included, and efforts were made to recruit workingmen and farmers.

A typical program opened with a piano solo from *Il Trovatore*, followed by a "very happily rendered reading" from Dickens and some passages from Washington Irving. The group then embarked on a discussion of the New Yorker based on questions drawn up at the previous meeting. The Circle also placed heavy emphasis on "the art of conversation." Not all topics were literary. At one of its liveliest meetings the members debated the English Civil War and argued the merits of John Pym, Sir Henry Vane, William Laud, and Edward Hyde, Earl of Clarendon. Meetings during the winter of 1880–1 were devoted to the subject of "world progress." Science was prominently featured, and after a study of the principles of electricity

[7] Luella M. Wright: "The Cedar Falls Parlor Reading Circle," *Iowa Journal of History and Politics*, XXXIV (October, 1936), pp. 343–4.

the members of the club were given an opportunity to use one of the new telephones.

Peasant life in Russia, economic progress in Argentina, financial booms, strikes, nihilism, and the Chautauqua movement were all examined, but history and literature remained the most popular subjects, and Whittier, Longfellow, Carlyle, Browning, and Macaulay the most popular authors. In the winter of 1894–5 the Circle spent three evenings on Carlyle's *Heroes and Hero Worship* and *Sartor Resartus* and a discussion of Macaulay's *History of England* drew one of the Circle's largest audiences.

After thirteen years of operation the Circle received a warm tribute from the president of the normal school. "One only needs to know Cedar Falls and its homes," he wrote, "to see the wonderful effect that has come as a consequence of good books and the actual reading and discussion of the same. We venture the assertion that no city in the state, large or small, can furnish as many actual readers of Carlyle, of Emerson, of Macaulay, of Ruskin, of Prescott, of the English and American poets and prose writers as can she. . . . It is a fact that Cedar Falls sends more representatives away to college than most towns of double her size." [8]

The activities of groups like the Cedar Falls Reading Circle point up a very significant fact about the changing character of the town. The woman became, by the end of the nineteenth century, the dominant figure in the community. From having been strongly patriarchal in its early years, the town became matriarchal. The mother rather than the father became the central image, the strong, compelling individual. In the founding of most towns the "father-authority" figure was of great importance—the leader, the oracle, the wise judge, the model of excellence. But as the town matured, it pressed in upon the man and defeated him or drove him out.

[8] Ibid., pp. 352, 369.

The man, the perpetually optimistic architect of new enterprises, was better suited for establishing communities than for making them thrive. Far more town ventures failed than succeeded, and the man who still believed that failure was personal, that it was due to one's inability to measure up to the ethic, had no defenses against defeat. So we find him in a hundred novels of small-town life, sometimes vaguely and cheerfully defeated because he would never admit defeat, rather like Sherwood Anderson's father, "Windy McPherson"; sometimes bitterly and hopelessly defeated. But the shocks which revealed the patriarch as the extravagant plunger or the futile dreamer drew the wife and mother to the center of the town's stage.

The town, built by the man, and so often the tomb of his ambitions, was the perfect setting for the woman who emerged in time as the indomitable forerunner of today's Mom. The female presence pervaded the town's life; the female as mother—cooking, baking, admonishing, loyally supporting the beaten husband, sponsoring culture, maintaining the church, upholding the old values, pushing her children, plotting, planning, saving, and finally subduing the town, making it into a larger mother, the place where trust and love and understanding could always be found, making the town one of America's most persistent and critical symbols—the town as mother, comforter, source of love.

Roger Galer's parents were cast in such classic molds. His father was a schoolmaster, justice of the peace, postmaster of the town and "passionately devoted to education for his children. . . ." But one faculty "unfortunately he did not possess—that of making money. He could analyse a business proposition and see how others succeeded, but he had no faculty for executing plans." His mother on the other hand "possessed quite opposite characteristics. She was full of energy, of initiative, of executive talent and foresight. . . . An excellent housekeeper she set a remarkable example of thrift and industry to her children and in addition took an active part in the affairs of the community. . . . For forty years she taught the adult Bible class of the Baptist Church, consisting of some of the most intelligent men and women of the community." But her husband did not go to church.[9]

There was another side to the picture; with the breakdown of the covenanted community and the diminution of the role of the male, the sexual relations between man and woman in the town were subjected to severe strains. One has almost the feeling that as the dream began to fade the women turned on the men. The W.C.T.U. was certainly in part an effort of the woman to capture the temperance movement and use it as a weapon against the demoralized male. The ecstasies, the hysteria, the violence expressed something of woman's sense of alienation from urban culture and her resentment of the inadequacies of her spouse. The small-town woman, having helped to create the image of the sodden and defeated male—that familiar figure of the temperance address—in her struggle for middle-class refinement made the sex act a restrained and pallid experience, and imposed on the male the contradictory image of himself as coarse and bestial.

It is of course impossible to speak with authority on a subject so complex and so inaccessible to the historical researcher, but there is no question that prurient attitudes toward sex that had not existed earlier appeared in the town in the late nineteenth century. These were in part a reflection of urban middle-class mores, but if the relationship between male and female in the town had not already deteriorated—it may be assumed that this deterioration was largely a result of the man's loss of status and self-confidence—the whole sex issue could not have assumed such a morbid character.

· · ·

[9] Roger B. Galer: "Recollections of Busy Years," *Iowa Journal of History and Politics*, XLII (January, 1944), pp. 35–6.

In addition to the cultural activities of the town many purely social organizations appeared. Each new club or society in the town had, as an increasingly important part of its *raison d'être*, the function of defining the role of the individual and binding him in a segment of the wider fellowship that had been lost forever when the primitive innocence of the earlier ages had been destroyed by a growing diversity and sophistication.

Also because many of the associations were more than local (with statewide or national affiliations), they reflected the town's increasing dependence on the greater community. But the remarkable proliferation of such groups can best be explained in terms of an effort to recapture that sense of personal involvement which had been so strong in the original covenanted community.

Aton, Indiana, had a Masonic Lodge as early as 1857, but after the Civil War the Odd Fellows caught hold in the town, followed by the Rebeccas, the Eastern Star, Knights of Pythias, Maccabees, Ben Hurs, Woodmen, and Elks. Albert Blumenthal lists among the clubs and societies of a small twentieth-century Western town such organizations as the Rainbow Girls, Woodcraft, Boy Scouts, Red Men, King's Daughters, Royal Arch Masons, Sons of Herman, Deep Thinkers' Club, Alpine Rose, Pythian Sisters, Knights of Pythias, Pocahontas Club, Priscillas, Westway Club, Yeomen, and a dozen other organizations, many of them related to the various churches in the community.[1] Such a plethora of organizations is obviously a disease of the body politic in communities which have lost all sense of an integrated community life.

A study made of Hamilton showed that in a community of fewer than 2,500 people there were "between 85 and 90 formally organized clubs, groups, societies, and the like." In the words of Baker Brownell "as the community

---

[1] Albert Blumenthal: *A Sociological Study of a Small Town* (Chicago: University of Chicago Press; 1932).

declines in significance and holding power the impulse to make formal organizations seems sometimes to go wild." [2]

The nature of class divisions in the town varied quite widely, but allowing for these variations certain generalizations may be attempted. First of all the town in many instances started as a "classless" community. Certain individuals appeared as leaders, but their leadership was related much less to their worldly possessions than to the moral force they were able to exert in the community. The pace at which the simple equality of the town in its early years gave way to social stratification was determined to some degree by the original ideals of the town. Generally speaking, the colonized community, knit together by some form of the covenant, resisted stratification most successfully. Cumulative towns, on the other hand, sometimes gave evidence of stratification from the day of their founding. If the continuity of a democratic, or more properly an egalitarian, tradition was of importance, so was a slow rate of population growth and of economic prosperity.

Sims notes the absence of class lines in Aton and the town's conspicuous pride in the fact that "everybody is common," that is to say, socially equal. He was told repeatedly that the town was unique in its spirit of neighborliness; that "the unpretentious are most esteemed." Servants were treated as members of the families where they worked. The laundry worker might be more of a belle in the town than the banker's daughter. This situation was in sharp contrast to a nearby town where "an aristocratic class of cultured and thrifty people has kept itself distinct.

[2] Baker Brownell: *The Human Community* (New York: Harper & Brothers; 1950), pp. 249–51. Harold Kaufman's study of a rural community in New York State showed that there was a good deal of overlapping in the membership of a portion of the twenty-eight organizations in the town, but even under the best of circumstances the organizations serve to perpetuate the fragmentation of the community and encourage the formation of enclaves and cliques.

. . . The people of the two towns are conscious of a decided difference in their social ideals." It is Sims's opinion, and it might be added that of the people of the town itself, that the town's democracy stemmed from the democratic idealism of its founders.[3]

While industrialization has often brought rapid stratification with it, especially when it has resulted in an influx of "aliens"—workers of foreign birth or extraction—even here the tradition-bound town has frequently shown a remarkable capacity to resist or at least minimize stratification. Carle Zimmerman noted that despite the presence of a number of Irish and French-Canadian families in "Yankeeville," there was wide participation in its political life by all groups in the community and the wealthy families were not permitted to dominate the town.

In "Babbitt," a prosperous industrial community, the local golf club was made up for the most part of upper- and middle-class members of the town, but mill workers were also active members, and in the rod and gun club, while "mill executives, professional men and officers of the town banks are the principal backers . . . a $20-a-week dyer in the textile mill is president." Correspondingly, here where the sense of community was strong there were few organizations, the most prominent being five literary and study clubs all founded around the turn of the century.[4]

The persistence in many towns of a tradition of equality, a tradition frequently recalled on ritual occasions, softened many of the harsher aspects of small-town class distinctions, for the formation of groups based on some principle of exclusion destroyed the common social life of the town. This came, in many communities, to center increasingly on sports events—baseball, horse races, and athletic contests with neighboring towns, and in such things as locally produced plays and pageants. There were

[3] Sims: *A Hoosier Village*, pp. 92–3.
[4] Carle C. Zimmerman: *The Changing Community* (New York and London: Harper and Brothers; 1938), pp. 477, 369–70.

few towns by the end of the nineteenth century without a baseball team and a band. Often they were the beneficiaries of the town's leading businessmen, like the Northfield bandsmen who wore on their caps "the gold enwreathed letters S.B.B. meaning Stratton Brass Band but commonly translated Some Bum Blowers. . . ." [5]

The persistence of religious attitudes also worked against social stratification and with the development of high schools the activities of the young people of the town formed an important bridge between classes.

Mark Twain recalled that in the Hannibal of his youth, social lines were clearly drawn. There were "people of good family, people of unclassified family, people of no family. Everybody knew everybody, and was affable to everybody, and nobody put on any visible airs; yet the class lines were quite clearly drawn and the familiar social life of each class was restricted to that class. It was a little democracy which was full of liberty, equality, and Fourth of July, and sincerely so, too. . . ." [6] William Allen White likewise recalled that while class lines were not set by money, they were set, nonetheless, "and the community accepted them."

Such class distinctions as did exist often rankled in the town much more than they did in the city. In the town there were daily and inescapable reminders that a neighbor considered himself superior in often small but galling ways. When the more prosperous citizens began to indulge in pleasures that their poorer neighbors could not afford, a sense of alienation between groups grew. In the city class differences, while sharper than those of the town, were often less keenly felt because the city structured itself into neighborhoods and sub-communities where people of similar social and economic status, or of particular national

[5] Herbert C. Parsons: *A Puritan Outpost* (New York: The Macmillan Company; 1937), p. 371.
[6] Mark Twain: *Autobiography* (2 vols.; New York: Harper & Brothers; 1924), I, 120.

origins established themselves. In the town, however, there was no place to withdraw to; the less prosperous were reminded daily of the disadvantages of their state, and these appeared the more unsupportable, in many instances, against the background of a distinguished family history.

However, before conspicuous leisure and conspicuous consumption could appear in the town, the ethic of thrift and self-denial had to be undermined. John H. Holmes recollects that in Denison, Indiana, there were no rich men and the well-to-do took pains not to flaunt their prosperity. The head of the First National Bank was considered very wealthy by the standards of the town, but he was aggressively democratic in his social attitudes. One of the town's more prosperous citizens did indeed buy a fancy buggy and team, but his neighbors ridiculed the display so outspokenly that the poor man sold the horses to a farmer and retired the buggy to his barn.

Initially the towns displayed a remarkable degree of "vertical mobility." With class lines loosely drawn in practice and denied in theory, the boy or girl who showed energy and ambition received friendly encouragement. John Holmes cites as an example the harness-maker of Mastersville, the town's chronic failure whose family lived in destitution. One of his daughters became a high-school principal in Youngstown, two others married Methodist ministers, and a fourth became the wife of a very successful farmer, "so that," in Mr. Holmes's words, "out of what you could call the lower strata of the town good came, just as much as from the good stock." [7]

Dances and town frolics were the common forms of recreation in those towns where the churches had relaxed their ban on secular social activities, and visiting was the principal informal social activity. Parties and "entertainments" were evidences of the town's increasing acceptance of urban values. The old group functions were replaced by

[7] J. H. Holmes.

formal meetings. In Marshall, Oklahoma, "even the young people met formally in the 'sitting rooms' of the new houses and listened to programs of songs, readings, and instrumental music." [8] The social leaders of one town began to form alliances with the socially ambitious of adjacent communities and by so doing escaped the effects of local disapproval. In Waterbury, New York, Williams observed that the growing number of parties, dances, and plays "varied and intensified by economic prosperity" tended to make the town "more and more intimately connected with neighboring towns and to lay a basis for a still wider and more varied activity." [9]

People began to pick and choose "friends" in the community as the idea of "entertaining" caught on among those with social aspirations. In one such town the newspaper dwelt with delighted awe on the details of such an occasion. "Dinner," it reported, "was served at seven, followed by social conversation until the hour of departure at ten." [1]

With entertaining and the conscious selection of friends the town moved further from its Eden-innocence. The destruction of the true community with its network of relationships that are "natural" and do not have to bear the burden of special "liking" or "common interests" meant that a new caginess entered into personal relations in the town. In the early days of the town, as the old pioneers never tired of saying, there had been spontaneous friendliness and everybody had been "on a level" without social pretensions or ambitions. Now there grew up an inevitable element of calculation, the question of whether an individual was a proper friend or suitable to be asked to one's

[8] Angie Debo: *Prairie City* (New York: Alfred A. Knopf; 1944), p. 81.
[9] James M. Williams: *An American Town* (New York: J. Kempster Printing Company; 1906), p. 97.
[1] Quoted in Lewis Atherton: *Main Street on the Middle Border* (Bloomington, Ind.: Indiana University Press; 1954), p. 26.

home, where certain conventions of "polite society" and "conversation" were observed. The new relationships had to bear a heavy burden because friendships were not formed exclusively on mutual liking or esteem but came to have an often bewildering social dimension.

Today in the city and suburb, and to a lesser but nonetheless discernible extent in the town, the individual has business and professional friends and a sprinkling of other friends carefully chosen for compatability of interests, background, and common aspiration. The result has been a progressive constriction and narrowing of personal relationships and their progressive impoverishment. Like accentuates like; boredom and ennui are bred by the homogeneity of subgroups with the larger community; and often a spurious heartiness masks a coldness of response and the careful maintenance of defenses against unsolicited or unwelcome intrusions.

August Hollingshead's study of Elmtown, a Midwestern community, reveals a general breakdown in common community activity. The upper classes in the town use the country club rather than the public parks and, by their style of living, their friends, and their activities, make a special effort to distinguish themselves from the class that Hollingshead calls "Class III." If Class III and Class IV may be considered middle and lower-middle class, they show far more upward mobility than any other group. These groups consider themselves the backbone of the community, scorn the social pretensions of the upper class, and express contempt for the immorality and lack of ambition in the lower classes. Class V, or the lowest class in Elmtown, gave the impression "of being resigned to life in a community that despises them for their disregard of morals, lack of 'success' goals, and dire poverty."

Hollingshead found the lowest class often hostile to religion, and its families showed a higher degree of instability than those of any other level of the community. "Death, desertion, separation, or divorce has broken more than half the families (56%). . . . There are few compulsive factors, such as neighborhood solidarity, religious teachings, or ethical considerations operating to maintain a stable marital relationship." Moreover the odds against a boy in Class V finishing high school were 230 to 1, and for the girls 57 to 1.[2]

The middle-class families of Elmtown are distinguished by their faith in education as a means of social betterment and by their support of the churches. In this respect Elmtown reveals characteristics typical of the small-town community in an earlier age. At the same time the town has suffered, obviously, from the appearance of an upper class which has poisoned the springs of common social life, and a lower class which constitutes a lumpen group without much hope or expectation of improving its status socially or economically. This group, in a town which has become stratified, is if anything more limited in its opportunities for upward mobility than a similar class in the city.

It is hard to make any satisfactory generalizations about the social structure of the town in the twentieth century, but certain things are apparent. Granted that every town has social stratification in varying degrees, it is nonetheless true that the rigidity and visibility of the class structure varies in relation to the size of the town, its economic condition (including whether the town is the trading center of an agricultural area), and the aims and ideals of its original founders. It seems safe to say that, as a rule, the town which has grown slowly, which is still essentially rural, and which was founded on the basis of Christian egalitarianism shows the least evidence of social stratifica-

[2] August Hollingshead: "Selected Characteristics of Classes in a Middle Western Community," in William Miller, ed.: *Class, Status and Power*, pp. 222, 217, 223. In the earlier ages of the town there were usually only two major groups or classes—the middle and the lower. The middle included all who observed the values of the community, and the lower, the improvident or shiftless who by their way of life rejected the standards of the town.

tion, while the cumulative community which has developed without an initial "character" and has grown rapidly and prospered economically is apt to show the most marked stratification and apt most nearly to reproduce the class divisions of the city.

Moreover, whatever the present social structure of the town may be today, taken as a whole, American towns in the nineteenth century were overwhelmingly egalitarian. Most communities in their earliest years approached the democratic ideal in the sense that whatever social and economic divisions might have been discernible to the eye of a trained sociologist or anthropologist were far less important than the fact of the town's unity in common ideals and aspirations and a common Christian faith.

X

The Ideology of the Town

T HE ENVIRONMENT OF MEN is not only artifactual;
it is mental. In towns and cities men build their
environments into their very houses and streets . . .
in every community, primitive or civilized, what most
importantly surrounds and influences the people are the
traditions, sentiments, norms, and aspirations that make
up the common mental life. . . . The world of men is
made up in the first place of ideas and ideals." [1]

What, then, have been the ideas and ideals of the
American small town?

Since at the time of their founding the great majority of

[1] Robert Redfield: *The Little Community* (Chicago: University of
Chicago Press; 1955), pp. 29–30.

American towns were agricultural communities, their first age was that of the rural village whose economic functions were undifferentiated. The minister, storekeeper, and blacksmith were also farmers. Or, it might more properly be said, virtually everyone in the community was a farmer; some added other functions.

In the later ages of the town sharper differentiation of function appeared. The lawyer, storekeeper, or shoemaker became specialists serving the town and the surrounding country. The development of small industries meant further distinction of town from country. The town became, in what was perhaps its most typical form, the "trading center" for an agricultural area. Thus from the beginning the town shared the farmer's values and accepted his cosmos, and, tempted as it came to be by urban yearnings and aspirations, it never wholly abandoned the rural ideals of its youth.

The glorification of rural life is as old as the story of Cain and Abel. The Americans who established the new nation were, in many instances, fervent admirers of Virgil's rural idylls. The French physiocrats gave an eighteenth-century gloss to the classical image of the independent yeoman farmer, and Thomas Jefferson, Michel de Crèvecœur (J. Hector St. John), and John Taylor of Caroline, along with many others, popularized the agrarian dogma in the United States. The ideal figure in their cosmos was "the simple American agriculturist," symbolized, for the French at least, by Benjamin Franklin in a coonskin cap. At its inception this apotheosis of the farmer was directed at the freeholder of Jefferson's Virginia and Jefferson himself was the most articulate champion of this figure of simplicity, innocence, and wisdom. It was indeed the Virginian who gave the dogma its classic expression. "Those who labor in the earth," he wrote, "are the chosen people of God, if ever he had a chosen people, whose breasts he has made his peculiar deposit for substantial and genuine virtue. It is the focus in which he keeps alive that sacred fire, which otherwise might escape from the face of the earth." [2]

The Jeffersonian image, highly flattering as it was, was readily accepted by its subjects. It adorned all rural rhetoric and gave the farmer a conviction of superior virtue that he has never quite relinquished. Throughout the nineteenth century the theme was played with a hundred variations by small-town newspaper editors. One such wrote:

> Corruption of morals in the mass of cultivators is a phenomenon of which no age . . . has furnished an example. It is the mark set on those, who, not looking up to heaven, to their own soil and industry, as does the husbandman, for their subsistence, depend for it on casualties and caprice of customers. Dependence begets subservience and venality, suffocates the germ of virtue, and prepares fit tools for the designs of ambition. . . . Generally speaking, the proportion which the aggregate of the other classes of citizens bears in any State to that of its husbandmen, is the proportion of its unsound to its healthy parts, and is a good enough barometer whereby to measure its degree of corruption.

The town associated itself with this rural nobility, extolling the "real, unsophisticated American; a virtuous, intelligent, brave, hardy, and generous yeoman, who despises alike the trappings of *royalty* or *aristocracy*."

The city, with its glittering riches and dark vice, was a Sodom which "*crushes, enslaves,* and *ruins so many thousands of our young men,* who are insensibly made the victims of *dissipation,* of *reckless speculation,* and of *ultimate crime.*" [3]

[2] Thomas Jefferson: *Notes on the State of Virginia* (Chapel Hill, N.C.: University of North Carolina Press; 1954), p. 165.
[3] Paul H. Johnston: "Old Ideals Versus New Ideas in Farm Life," *U. S. Department of Agriculture Yearbook* (Washington, D.C., 1940), pp. 116–19 quotes *Plough Boy* (June, 1819); and *Prairie Farmer* (1849): "Poetry and Profit of City Life By a Lover of the Country," pp. 18–19.

The romantic image of the "generous yeoman" has demonstrated a remarkable tenacity. Frederick Jackson Turner's frontier thesis was, in essence, a sophisticated restatement of the Jeffersonian ideal. It served to give new life and scholarly respectability to the Enlightenment dogma of the natural man. Turner wrote:

> To the frontier, the American intellect owes its striking characteristics. That coarseness and strength combined with acuteness and inquisitiveness; that practical inventive turn of mind, quick to find expedients; that masterful grasp of material things, lacking in the artistic but powerful to effect great ends; that restless, nervous energy; that dominant individualism, working for good and for evil, and withal that buoyancy and exuberance which comes with freedom— these are traits of the frontier. . . .[4]

The free lands of the West promoted "individualism, economic equality, freedom to rise, democracy." [5] But the frontier that Turner talked about was the "farmers' frontier," and if you looked for the frontiersman who had created the dominant American traits you would be referred to the farmer who was, after all, only an up-to-date version of Jefferson's Virginia yeoman.[6] The terms have changed, the conception is more sophisticated, but the implications are the same—the frontier farmer is God's chosen instrument in the making of America.

The urban business world likewise found enchantment in the image. Business, which was traditionless and revolutionary, displayed a wistful eagerness to establish itself within the ancient framework of values. The tycoon was

[4] Frederick Jackson Turner: *The Frontier in American History* (New York: Henry Holt & Company; 1958), p. 37.
[5] Ibid.
[6] For a perceptive analysis of the essentially rural basis of Turner's thesis, see David M. Potter: "Abundance and the Frontier Hypothesis," in *People of Plenty* (Chicago: University of Chicago Press; 1954), pp. 142–65.

simply, the business spokesmen insisted, the more ambitious farmboy and they enthusiastically subscribed to the doctrine that "when Wall Street wants good business men she usually goes back to the soil to get them. . . . The active officials of most of the large business organizations of America it is said were, with a few exceptions, raised on the farm, and could swim the creek, pitch hay, chop wood, milk the cows, or slop the hogs as easily as they can run worldwide business institutions." [7]

The rural sociologists have perhaps given the classic dogma its most recent restatement. Pitrim Sorokin and Carle Zimmerman (both small-town boys) in their pioneering book *Principles of Rural-Urban Sociology* go to some pains to disclaim any sentimental preference for rural life, yet their words belie their protestations. To them the

> cultivator is exposed more to the weather and climatic conditions, breathes cleaner and fresher air . . . is in a much greater proximity to, and in a more direct relation with 'nature,' soil, flora, fauna, water, river, the sun, the moon, the sky, the wind, the rain, and so on—than an urbanite. The urban dweller is separated from all this by thick walls of vast and huge city buildings and the artificial city environment predominately of stone and iron. . . . Not a free wind refreshes him but a draft of the electric fan; not the sunlight but the artificial gas or electric light greets his eyes; not a soil but a pavement is found under his feet. . . . The miracles and mysteries of nature are seen primarily in movies, theatres, from pictures in his papers and only once in a while on a picnic.

From all this follows, inevitably, the superiority of country to city life and the superior virtue (though such an archaic phrase is not of course used) of the countryman over the urbanite. The rural dweller is healthier and happier than his

[7] Lewis Atherton: *Main Street on the Middle Border* (Bloomington: Indiana University Press; 1954), p. 252.

city counterpart, has "greater forcefulness, vitality, and love for, or satisfaction with life." The city dweller is a "free-thinker," an "open-minded anti-traditionalist," who scoffs at religion, and at values in general, and recognizes no duties or obligations to his fellows, who are "strangers." The farmer, on the other hand, shows "greater stability, simplicity, idealism, religiosity, dogmatism, and generally . . . what may be styled as 'a greater peace of mind.'" He is stronger than his city cousin in "virility, sternness, austereness, patience, endurance, and ability for continued effort. . . ."

Sorokin and Zimmerman reject indignantly the idea that the cities attract the more alert and ambitious country boys, and paint a grim picture of the city dweller who, without friends or purpose in life, commits suicide "either quietly or with curses at the injustices of the world." They have the grace to add in a rather disarming footnote "We are, of course, magnifying the situation somewhat. . . . But this elaboration is the essence of the 'typological' method of analysis. In its essence it is scientifically justifiable." [8]

The appearance of the "new Conservatism" has in recent years served to reanimate once more the apparently indestructible figure of the noble yeoman. The genuine conservative, we are told, is more often found among those "who live on the land." "The Conservative of the field is the prince of Conservatives . . . the hard core of the Conservative temper, is especially marked in the man who 'holdeth the plow . . . and whose talk is of bullocks.'" [9] Since conservatism is true virtue, and the farmer is the most conservative figure, the farmer is still, it seems, the special vessel of virtue.

[8] Pitrim Sorokin and Carle C. Zimmerman: *Principles of Rural-Urban Sociology* (New York: Henry Holt and Company; 1929), pp. 17, 179, 202, 293, 179 and 179 n.
[9] Clinton Rossiter: *Conservatism in America* (2nd ed.; New York: Alfred A. Knopf; 1962), pp. 48–9.

The Ideology of the Town

It is worth tracing in some detail the myth of the wise and virtuous farmer in its various forms because the town has drawn on the myth and associated itself with it throughout much of the town's history. The exaltation of the farming community as opposed to the city has been especially congenial to the town dweller. But the town has given its allegiance to values that go quite beyond, and have often been in unperceived opposition to, the stylized image of the noble farmer. The basic ideology of the American farmer was, to a large degree, comprehended by the phrase "the Protestant ethic." In its most familiar form the ethic exalted the necessary hardships of frontier life into great principles by relating salvation to hard work, thrift, social equality, and simple living. While in this ethic farming was not, as in the Jeffersonian dogma, elevated above other forms of honest labor, it came nonetheless, as the colonial cities grew in wealth and conspicuous display, to embody the ethic at its purest.

Since Max Weber first put forth his thesis concerning the relation of Protestantism to capitalism, historians have argued about the degree to which Calvinism created the psychological atmosphere in which capitalism flourished. In the classic version of Weber's thesis, the Puritan ethic as revealed in such works as Cotton Mather's *Essays to Do Good* is seen as a positive encouragement to the acquisitive spirit. Mather felt, it is true, that the godly man must have a calling—a business—and that he must serve God through his business as he worshipped him at the meeting. He was ready to assert that "contemplation of the good means nothing without accomplishment of the good. A man must not only be pious; he must be useful." Man may "glorify God, by doing of *Good* for *others*, and getting of *Good* for *himself*"; Mather does not promise the industrious young man riches, but what may be merely a modest competence for his old age.

Moreover, he warns, "the way to succeed in our Enterprizes, *O Lord, I know the way of man is not in himself!* Be sensible of this; In our *Occupation* we spread our *Nets;* but it is God who brings into our *Nets* all that comes into them." [1] If Mather was indeed, as Griswold suggests, "one of the first to teach American business men to serve God by making money," [2] he represented, to the extent that he espoused such an idea, a break with the older Puritan tradition. Richard Baxter, one of the great Puritan theorists, had warned a century before Mather that prosperity and godliness were not necessarily related. "Take heed," he wrote, "that you judge not of God's love, or of your happiness or misery, by your riches or poverty, prosperity or adversity. . . ." [3]

And in 1621 Robert Cushman, preaching in New Plymouth, chose his text from the First Epistle to the Corinthians. "Let no man seek his own: But every man another's wealth." Although Cushman conceded that it was "sometimes" lawful for men to "gather wealth, and grow rich . . . a godly and sincere Christian will see when this time is, and will not hoard up when he seeth others of his brethren and associates to want." [4]

It remained in fact for Benjamin Franklin to equate wealth with "*industry and frugality.*" It is Franklin who assured the young man that "he that gets all he can honestly and saves all he gets . . . will certainly become *rich*," but Franklin squares himself with orthodoxy by adding, "if that Being who governs the world, to whom all should look for a blessing on their honest endeavors, doth not, in his wise providence, otherwise determine." [5] The shift from Mather to Franklin is small in degree, but large in impor-

---

[1] Quoted in A. Whitney Griswold: "Three Puritans on Prosperity," *New England Quarterly*, VII (September, 1934), pp. 478–9.
[2] Ibid., p. 483.
[3] Quoted in Winthrop S. Hudson: "Puritanism and the Spirit of Capitalism," *Church History*, XVIII (March, 1949), p. 9.
[4] Ibid., p. 10.
[5] Benjamin Franklin: *Works* (8 vols.; London: printed for G. G. J. and J. Robinson; 1793), I, 59.

tance. It is carried perhaps a step further by Timothy Dwight's suggestion that prosperity is itself an avenue to piety. The man who is determined to be rich is apt "to become in the end a religious man." [6] In Dwight's view "the same sobriety of mind, which is useful to the advancement of your heavenly interests, is the direct means of your earthly prosperity." [7]

Yet even Dwight had deep, and rather typically Puritan reservations about the acquisitive spirit, and on his tour through New England he looked askance at the activities of those early exemplars of the entrepreneurial spirit, the Yankee peddlers, who went about the country hawking the manufactures of Connecticut.

> Many of the young men, employed in this business [he wrote], part, at an early period with both modesty, and principle. Their sobriety is exchanged for cunning; their honesty for imposition; and their decent behavior for coarse imprudence. Mere wanderers, accustomed to no order, control, or worship; and directed solely to the acquisition of petty gains; they soon fasten upon this object; and forget every other of superior nature. The only source of their pleasure, or their reputation is gain. . . . No course of life tends more rapidly or more effectually to eradicate every moral feeling.[8]

Portland, Maine, Dwight viewed with disfavor:

> Such a collection of inhabitants, gathered by business, and by accident, from many quarters, must be supposed to bring with them a corresponding mixture of principles; and, in many instances, may easily be believed scarcely to have formed any principles at all.

[6] Timothy Dwight: *Travels in New England* (2 vols.; New Haven: H. Howe; 1821–2), II, 462–3.
[7] Timothy Dwight: *Sermons* (New Haven: H. Howe; 1828), pp. 24–5.
[8] Dwight: *Travels*, II, 54–5.

Persons of the latter description seat themselves on commercial ground, to amass property; not to find the way to heaven; and of such persons will no small part of such an aggregation ordinarily consist.[9]

"Superiour talents" and "superiour piety" can indeed be united for the glory of God, but such a happy conjunction is not apt to take place in a town established for commercial motives. Prosperity within the true community may be taken as a sign of heavenly favor, but in the cumulative community it is a cause for suspicion, a distraction, and, often, a thing of the devil.

To Dwight it was only men "influenced by some great and commanding motive, connected with a settlement of the soil, such as the hope of civil or religious freedom, or the necessity of providing for an increasing family" who are fitted "to subdue forests, encounter frost and hunger, and resolutely survey the prospect of Savage incursions." Wealth itself is a hazard, and the man who spends his life accumulating money to leave his children is guilty of the greatest folly. "The children are ruined for time and eternity by the labours of the parent; for they are taught, that all good lies in wealth, splendour and luxury; and not in intelligence, and virtue."[1]

Puritanism did not make an easy alliance with the acquisitive spirit or give its explicit sanction to the pursuit of riches. It is, of course, possible to find, especially among the Boston divines, statements that are favorable to the commercial and business interests which were so prominent in that city. It was in such urban centers, dominated by enterprising and successful merchants, that social stratification and worldly accomplishments had most conspicuously weakened the mortar of the covenant. But in the outlying provinces of Puritanism, the Protestant ethic was uncongenial to anything that might be called, in Weber's phrase, "the spirit of Capitalism."

[9] Ibid., p. 209.   [1] Ibid., pp. 233, 397.

The Ideology of the Town

The Puritan ideals of thrift, frugality, and industry had their roots in the rural community. The New England farmer thought of himself as a member of the fraternity of those who lived by the sweat of their brows. His situation in a town prevented him from making that sharp division between the farmer and other occupational groups (or callings) which we have noted in the Jeffersonian dogmas. He was thus less inclined to claim special virtues than he was to emphasize the ethic of work. A suggestive insight into the New Englander's mind can be found in *The Key of Libberty* by William Manning, a farmer of Billerica, Massachusetts. Writing in the 1790's, Manning suggested the founding of a "labouring society" made up of "Farmers, Mecanicks, & Labourers," men who worked with their hands and who obeyed the "erevarsable sentance" of the "Supreem Governour of the Universe" that "in the swet of thy face shall thou eate thy bred."

Everyone has been enjoined by God "to apply himselfe industerously to some honest cauling for the benefit of himselfe & Society." And although there are, Manning admits, "many caulings by which men may live honistly without Labour, yet . . . Labour is the soul parrant of all property by which all are seported. . . ."

Manning did not believe that farmers any more than lawyers or merchants were "naturally" good. "Men are born & grow up in this world," he wrote, "with a vast veriarty of capacityes, strength & abilityes both of Body & Mind, & have strongly implanted within them numerous pashons & lusts continually urging them to fraud violence & acts of injustis toards one another." Man also knows by his conscience the difference between "Right & Rong." "Yet as he is sentenced by the just decrees of heaven to hard Labour for a Living in this world, & has so strongly implanted in him a desire of Selfe Seporte, Selfe Defence, Selfe Love, Selfe Conceit, Selfe Importance, & Selfe Agrandisement, that it Ingroses all his care and attention so that he can see nothing beyond Selfe—for Selfe (as once described by a Divine) is like an object plased before the eye that hinders the sight of every thing beyond."

It is thus the "depravity of the human heart" that made civil government necessary. Moreover "the marchent, phisition, lawyer & divine, the philosipher and school master, the Juditial & Executive Officers," and many others can live without "bodily labours," and the leisure that these groups enjoy was a source of corruption. They looked down on those who labor with their hands; they were possessed by that "superiority & . . . pride & ostentation" so "natural to the humain harte," and they were constantly combining to advance their own interests as opposed to those of the more numerous but less well organized laboring classes.[2]

It was to balance the influence of the non-laboring few by inducing the laboring many to join together in a political association that Manning wrote his pamphlet. His work is most absorbing as a political tract, but it is also an excellent exposition of rural attitudes that were undoubtedly shared by most of Manning's less articulate neighbors.

The theories of the New England farmer present an instructive contrast to the ideology of the Enlightenment. To Manning, man on the farm or in the city was naturally sinful and vainglorious. The best hope of redemption lay in the unremitting labor that God had ordained as man's lot. Those who worked with their hands had common interests opposed to those of the professional and leisure classes. They were purified, not as a result of their condition, but of their labor. The rural town was only in a state of grace as long as industry and self-denial were its highest values. Prosperity, luxury, and ease were its enemies. This is the version of the Protestant ethic that the town adhered to and that yielded most reluctantly to softer doctrines.

Along with the ideals of industry and self-denial went, as essential parts of the ethic, the ideals of neighborliness and social equality. No values were more honored. The

[2] William Manning: *The Key of Libberty* (Billerica, Mass.: The Manning Association; 1922), pp. 67, 8, 14–15.

community had, and acknowledged, a responsibility toward all its members that was a corollary to the ideal of neighborliness. James M. Williams has written of Waterbury, New York, in its early years that "from first to last [it] has been, with reference to the struggle for existence, one group, in which the survival of each and every individual has been, from the mere fact of his or her living within the territory of the group, a practically assured fact." [3] The same could have been said for most small towns. Those who were members of the community must be provided for in illness, disaster, or incapacity. Those who refused to work must be made to work. Drifters and idlers must be warned off. The town, understandably, viewed newcomers with suspicion. Its own poor were burden enough and it had no intention of taking on individuals who would become a further charge on the community.

Northfield, Massachusetts, in the eighteenth century, paid year after year for the support of an unmarried mother and her child, met the doctor's bills, from the one in which he charged fourteen shillings for delivery down through the years for "doctrin and nursin" as long as aid was needed. The town also provided for Thomas Elgar, Revolutionary veteran, buying him a cow, paying for "grain and pasturage," and in time replacing her with another. It bought leather to make shoes for Elgar's wife and paid a cobbler to turn them out, a tailor for making a suit of clothes, and voted funds for help to hoe his corn, for shirts, for doctor's care, for "rhum" and brandy, all given, apparently, without stint. [4]

John H. Holmes recalls that

if there were any persons [in Mastersville] that were not able to take care of themselves they were

[3] James M. Williams: *An American Town* (New York: J. Kempster Printing Company; 1906), p. 241.
[4] Herbert C. Parsons: *A Puritan Outpost* (New York: The Macmillan Company; 1937), p. 207.

cared for by people who were . . . and invariably
if anything happened to one, the whole community
turned in and helped them. And that spirit prevails to
this very day. The only little industry in our community was a woodworking factory. It employed a few
men. Six months ago it burned down and the whole
community turned in and helped the man rebuild it and
it is in full operation now.

For years the town and various neighbors contributed to
the support of an indigent old colored woman who had
been a slave. Usually relatives provided for the ailing or
impoverished, and often the town boarded these unfortu-
nates out to the lowest bidder, a practice sometimes cruel in
its operation.[5]

But neighborliness and equality went beyond provision
for the marginal members of the community. Timothy
Dwight in his travels through Vermont at the turn of the
eighteenth century noted that

a prime enjoyment of these settlers is found in the
kindness, which reigns among them universally. A
general spirit of good neighbourhood is prevalent
throughout New-England, but here it prevails in a
peculiar degree. Among these people, a man rarely
tells the story of his distresses to deaf ears; or asks any
reasonable assistance in vain. . . . To do kind offices
is the custom; a part of the established manners.[6]

And, Dwight might have added, an injunction of the
covenant.

The biographer of Hartford, Vermont, noted sadly the
changes in that town by the end of the nineteenth century.

The reverence paid, and authority yielded to the
clergy, is gone—and with them are gone much of the
peace, order, sobriety and prosperity of our communities, especially in the agricultural regions. The old-
fashioned charity, hospitality, and brotherly kindness,

[5] J. H. Holmes.   [6] Dwight: *Travels*, II, 468.

have vanished away, and their place has not been supplied by any gifts or graces, that should cause their loss not to be lamented.[7]

The theme is a familiar one in all reminiscences of the early days of American towns. In early Waterbury, "common hardships and the common need of help united the entire community with the bond of compassionate sympathy." J. M. Norton, a Michigan pioneer, recalled in a similar spirit:

> It is quite common to speak of pioneer days as times of extreme hardships and privations. In my experience . . . I recall my pioneer days as the happiest of my life. Coarse food and rough diet were the regime of those days, but every cabin was a tent of refuge and relief from want. There were no instances of heaped up wealth or pauper tramps. There existed social reciprocity, a general spirit of charity and free giving, which prevented the extreme poverty of more affluent times.[8]

The town's first value was perhaps equality; it prided itself on being a place where

> the insolence of wealth, and the servility of pauperism . . . are alike unknown. . . . [There were] neither castes nor classes in society then. Some, it is very true, were in better circumstances than others, even then; but their work, their deprivations, their hardships, their sufferings and mutual dependence upon each other in the hours of distress and need, together with their social gatherings, brought all down to a common level, or elevated all to a higher plane of neighborly love . . . thus forming a society that the outside world, away from the frontier, never knew.

[7] William H. Tucker: *History of Hartford, Vermont* (Burlington, Vt.: Free Press Association; 1889), p. 207.
[8] J. M. Norton: "Early Schools and Pioneer Life," *Michigan Pioneer and Historical Collections*, XXVIII (1900), p. 108.

. . . To feed the hungry, to furnish relief in cases of distress and need, and to help each other was the mission of the society.[9]

A spirit of neighborliness, of helpful cooperation, was then one of the principal standards by which the individual was judged. Of equal importance was lack of pretense and the ideal of social equality.

The precarious situation of the covenanted community made it, from the first, excessively sensitive to criticism. The first crises of the Bible Commonwealth were occasioned by those who questioned the covenant. As the earlier core of religious orthodoxy softened, the community enforced other standards of conformity which were, if anything, harsher than the biblical canons. Because they were often without a mechanism of redemption, they bore cruelly on the dissenters and nonconformists. Individualism, such as it was, was only accepted within the pattern of the community's special symbols of unity. The stronger and more specific the central orthodoxy, the greater the variations that could be permitted outside of it. The town without a dominant orthodoxy was often more tyrannical in its insistence on a total pattern of conformity than the community bound to a specific "covenant." As political scientist John Roche has pointed out, in a Southern slavery community Catholics and Jews might have a degree of equality denied them in a Northern "liberal" Protestant community. Similarly, the militant antislavery community of Ohio or Kansas was often as intolerant of gradualism or African emigration as a neighboring town might be of abolitionism.

In Roche's words, "of libertarianism, the respect for views considered fundamentally 'wrong,' there was little: the Populists, for example, were as ready to suppress

[9] Morris Birkbeck: *Notes on a Journey in America* (London: printed by Severn & Redington, for Ridgway & Sons; 1818), p. 10.

economic orthodoxy as the economically orthodox were to expunge Populism." [1]

We have today with the breakdown of the power of the local community a few national orthodoxies rather than many parochial ones. While the hold of any particular orthodoxy upon a specific community has been notably loosened, while the range of orthodoxies insisted upon by a local group has diminished greatly, the key orthodoxies perhaps have to be honored even more wholeheartedly and certainly more unanimously than before. The very variety of orthodoxies, as Roche himself admits, permitted the dissenter to form, with his fellows, his own community of conformity. Almost any heresy could find a home, or if it could not find a home, it could establish one where heresy became orthodoxy and the old orthodoxy, if it appeared, was stoned through the streets.

One measure of loyalty that the town has insisted on is the conviction by its citizens that Cross Roads, Indiana, is the greatest little town in the whole U.S.A. Sims's Aton believed, typically, that it displayed "superior intelligence, morality, and religious devotion." It prided itself on being the cheapest place to live in the United States and the most democratic, the most temperate, the most law-abiding. "In general," Sims notes, "Aton believes that it excels in many things or that it is able to do so, that it is greatly superior to other communities." [2]

Similarly in Hampton, Iowa, the community clung to the illusion that "no one was ever prosperous or content if he permitted himself to be lured beyond the Hampton horizon. . . . Those who returned from ventures in Kansas or Montana . . . were quoted as being penitent." The town prided itself on having the best baseball team in the area, the best band in the state, "the winner of the

[1] John Roche: "We've Never Had More Freedom," *The New Republic* (January 23, 1956), p. 12.
[2] Newell L. Sims: *A Hoosier Village* (New York: Columbia University Press; 1912), p. 81.

district declamatory contest, and the fastest trotting horse to be found at any of the nearby county fairs." [3]

The town's image of itself was of enormous importance to its citizens. It was the last fragment of the utopian dream, and it kept alive a pulse of hope and self-esteem.

Industry, frugality, equality, neighborliness, and loyalty were conspicuous components of the town's ideology. The farmer, nature's nobleman, was also a persistent image who, if he had little correspondence to reality, survived, perhaps for that very reason, after most of the earlier values had been replaced by urban middle-class concepts of "culture."

Anchored in the ancient ethic, the town nonetheless began to feel the terrible pull of city ways and was torn in its deepest soul. Slowest to die was its prejudice against wealth, against the accumulation and manipulation of capital. The historian of Vermontville, Michigan, writing in 1900, dwelt nostalgically on the town's early years, the years of the pioneer.

> The money age had scarcely dawned. . . . The words oftenest used then were home, family, schools, education, churches, religion, virtue and morality; not, as now, gold, silver, riches, wealth, capital, interest, bonds, mortgages, stocks and dividends. . . . Making money out of the labor of others had not become the overtopping ambition, except in the states where slavery existed.

From his vantage point at the turn of the century, it seemed to the recorder of Vermontville's past that life was now

> pervaded by money considerations. . . . Society is diseased by a feverish craving for money; it is more

[3] Baker Brownell: *The Human Community* (New York: Harper & Brothers; 1950), p. 240.

than Heaven, and with it none fear Hell. Big figures with the dollar mark before them are the open sesame to social recognition and political preferment. Such names as Carnegie and Rockefeller are oftener printed than God and Christ. Gold-plating sanctifies moral rottenness. . . . Cash is monarch; character secondary. . . . The pioneer age had no wealthy ruling class. The money age brings new, if not more dangerous, social and political conditions, as unlike those of sixty years ago as special privilege, monopoly and inequality are unlike freedom of opportunity for all, equal rights for all and special privileges for none.[4]

The elite of the large towns and cities was, at the beginning of the nineteenth century, an intellectual or moral elite. As Richard Wohl has pointed out, property was relatively unimportant. "The continuing test for membership was intellectual or moral, not business, achievement. . . . Money-making was not prized, and this especially for boys who had been sent to college." It was in this spirit that the "moral peril" of business was pointed out by an uncle to his nephew who balked at a professional career. "The acquisition of property," he warned, "will not compensate for the neglect of the great interests of eternity." Business meant cities and cities meant relaxed moral standards.

Jeremiah Day expressed an attitude common to the adherents of the older values when he wrote in 1836:

> I have no patience with the rage for speculation that is spread like a pestilence on the community. I believe that some signal calamity will ere long come upon us in a judgment for this insatiable greediness for rapid accumulation. I wish to see honest industry liberally rewarded, but the mere transfer of property

[4] Edward W. Barber: "The Vermontville Colony: Its Genesis and History," *Michigan Pioneer and Historical Collections*, XXVIII (1900), pp. 197–8.

from one man to another adds nothing to the wealth of the community.[5]

Day was alarmed over "what we have called our unexampled prosperity, our rapid strides in opulence and lavish expenditures. . . ."

The town's suspicion of commerce and of urban wealth was fed by lurid newspaper accounts of city sin. One small-town editor, writing in the 1830's, was

> not prepared to say that the cities of our land are yet as corrupt as was Sodom; but it is indisputable that they are filling up with the very sins which destroyed Sodom and Gomorrah. Let thousands of voices be lifted up from our valleys, and the sound be swelled abroad by other thousands from our mountains, until the Sodoms and the Babylons be shaken and purified, lest God destroy them. . . . [In this work of] human reformation [the cities themselves are worse than helpless]. . . . They are governed by the aristocracy who hold not only the rabble at their control, but the city clergy in general, and much of the city press, religious, so-called, as well as political. Reform has got to be pushed forward by the hard-handed, honest-hearted, pure-minded, intelligent inhabitants of the country . . . [who] must be marshalled and drilled into one vast, solid, mighty moral phalanx, that shall come down upon the seats of the Satan with overwhelming power.[6]

In the same spirit the Working Men's Society of Woodstock, Vermont, noted that in

> almost every part of our country . . . power and influence, is passing from the many to a few; that

[5] Quoted by Richard R. Wohl: "Henry Day," in William Miller, ed., *Men in Business* (Cambridge: Harvard University Press; 1952), pp. 158–9.

[6] Orson S. Murray, *Vermont Telegraph* (June 2, 1836), quoted by David M. Ludlum: *Social Ferment in Vermont, 1791–1850* (New York: Columbia University Press; 1939), p. 59.

faction and party spirit, having their origin in the basest passions of the human heart, threaten to extinguish in a great degree the love of country, of justice and our happy institutions, that an aristocracy based and reared in exclusive selfishness, is silently and insidiously undermining the temples of Freedom and equal rights.[7]

For the town dweller the city remained a desert "of depraved humanity, where every one is wrapped up in selfishness, and guards himself against his neighbors while his heart rankles with envy at his prosperity, or his wild, unbridled ambition urges him on the reckless course of outstripping all his competitors." [8] Urban capitalism has brought with it a new kind of slavery, the spokesmen of the town insist—that of "taking and appropriating by one man or class of men for their own use, the services or fruits of the labor of another man or class of men without just compensation therefor." Capitalism is "an octopus which extends its tentacles . . . throughout all christendom." The enemy is to be found in those "vast accumulations of wealth, begotten by unrestrained avarice, absorbing the earnings of other people's labor and toil, and means of subsistence, either by individuals or corporations or syndicates, which oppress their fellow men, robbing them not only of their well earned comforts, but even of the very necessaries of life and often subjecting them to starvation and misery, especially in the great cities of the country." [9]

One of the most vigorous critics of urban capitalism was Leonard Brown, whose *Iowa, the Promised of the Prophets* was a long and inept attack on the new men of

[7] *Working-Man's Gazette* (September 23, 1830), quoted by Ludlum: *Social Ferment*, p. 203.
[8] James B. Finley: *Autobiography* . . . W. P. Strickland, ed. (Cincinnati; 1858), p. 159.
[9] D. C. Walker: "Evolution of Religion, Morals and Legislation in this Country During the Past Century," *Michigan Pioneer and Historical Collections*, XXVIII (1900), pp. 460–1.

power. Brown called for a great rising of the people to drive the moneylenders from the Temple.

> The few grow rich the many poor
> And tramps are dogged from every door
> The millionaire would have his word
> And e'en his very whisper heard
> And Congress bow before his nod
> And Presidents cry "Gould is God!"

The kings of capitalism should be hurled into the Des Moines River. Then, when "grasping Greed and Avarice drown/ And War and Poverty go down";

> Love, Equality and Peace
> Shall bless for aye the human race.
> True Christianity restored,
> Mammon no longer is adored—
> All in one common brotherhood,
> The good for all the greatest good—[1]

One of Brown's refrains, as he recounts the defeat by the toilers of King Gold and his minions, runs "Beware, beware/The millionaire!/A deadly foe, a deadly foe/To thee, O working man, to thee. . . ." To Brown the life of the rural community was a life of Christian cooperation. The welfare state was, for him, simply an extension of the pioneer community. Cooperative farms and cooperative factories were the expression of "a willingness to be equal with our neighbor, and not above him." The unions and the Grange organizations were engaged in educating the people

> up to a higher and truer love and brotherhood. . . .
> Societies and lodges will be merged into the great
> society—the State—of which all are members, and

[1] Leonard Brown: *Iowa, The Promised of the Prophets* (Des Moines, Iowa: Central Printing and Publishing Company; 1884), pp. 64-5.

brethren: a society of mutual helpfulness, of mutual benefits, of mutual love and good will, wherein my neighbor's child will be as dear to me as my own . . . and every helpless creature shall have a lodgement in my heart of hearts . . . then will each man be indeed a very Christ of love, radiant with the spirit of the Divine Teacher.[2]

If the language is that of nineteenth-century evangelical Protestantism, much of the thought is akin to that of John Winthrop's "Modell of Christian Charity."

Many of Brown's contemporaries were still willing to accept the picture of the self-made man who mounted to power and riches through the ethic but Brown knew better. To make his point he gave the example of two boys of equal industry and adaptability.

> They go into business. The one uses as much industry as the other, and is as diligent in business, exercising as much thought and intelligence and physical power. The one makes perhaps five hundred dollars per day; the other not more than five dollars per day. Why the difference? The question is answered in one word— CAPITAL. The one is rich and has capital to invest. The other is poor and depends upon industry alone. . . . What equality is here? . . . The laws are framed to help the rich. . . . Money increases by its own growth, so to speak. . . . "Ten per cent interest will eat the world up." This is a great wrong.[3]

Brown is worth quoting at some length because he represents a number of important currents in the small community: distrust of the city, of the rich and acquisitive, the persistent utopian and millennial expectation, the conviction that drunkenness, avarice, and human exploitation must yield to the unselfish reformer, the belief in the efficacy of Christian love and neighborliness applied to the

[2] Ibid., pp. 65, 82.   [3] Ibid., Appendix pp. 63, 57.

wider economic life of the country in cooperative factories and farms, the latent impulse toward authoritarianism, and perhaps, above all, the Fundamentalist passion that suffused all thought—social and political as well as religious. The town and country, allied against the city, attributed to it the failure of the town's dream of peace and prosperity. It was the city that called into question the old verities, that attracted town youth with its evil glitter, that controlled the flow of money and goods, that held the town and farm in a thralldom more onerous with each passing year.

Bitterness at the destruction of the dream of innocence runs like a sad litany through accounts of pioneer days. The "purse-proud aristocrats" are followed by the "ghouls of greed" and the tones become strident with self-justification, but the theme is the same—the superiority of the town to the city. Yet within the town the older ethic of self-denial, of "character," of unremitting labor gave way slowly to the cities' values of aggressiveness, of enterprise, of deference to riches. Suspicion of those who prospered too much was replaced with admiration for the tycoon. If to the surviving pioneers the millionaire was "no better than the sneak thief who robs your granary or hen roost," their sons admired and envied the few entrepreneurs who brought capital into the community. "They catered to our combined ego," Olney Sweet recalled. "We wanted strangers to see the brick mansion . . . at the edge of town—a house with a turret surrounded by wrought iron work, set well back among tall evergreens. For most of us the medium of exchange flowed meagerly. . . . But there was homage rather than envy towards those capable of lifting the community out of the commonplace and permitting us to gloat together." [4]

The standards of personal integrity often declined in the town and, as the covenanted life disintegrated, the

[4] Olney Sweet: "An Iowa County Seat," *Iowa Journal of History*, XXXVIII (October, 1940), p. 341.

philosophy of "looking out for yourself," a calculating shrewdness, the ability to drive a hard bargain took the place of the earlier emphasis on cooperation and mutual helpfulness. Credit buying won acceptance in the town and consumption was honored over frugality. The increase in land speculation, the hope of quick fortunes, carried in on the winds that blew from the cities, loosened personal morality and depersonalized individual relationships. Indeed American "individualism" appeared only after the older community values, which had balanced the impulse toward individualism with the insistence of the primacy of the common life, had been eroded by urban values. It was not a product of the towns and farms but rather of the depersonalized life of the cities.

The town's acceptance of industry, piety, and thrift as the touchstones of success has been discussed in another chapter. William Allen White was the spokesman of the small-town businessman when, as a young editor, he wrote his famous editorial "What's the Matter with Kansas," in which he lambasted the state for driving out capital by the slothfulness and radicalism of its citizens. Kansas, White wrote scornfully, seemed to think it needed above all else men

who hated prosperity, and who think because a man believes in national honor, he is a tool of Wall Street. . . . We need several thousand gibbering idiots to scream about the 'Great Red Dragon' of Lombard Street. We don't need population, we don't need wealth, we don't need well-dressed men on the streets, we don't need cities on the fertile prairies; you bet we don't! What we are after is the money power. Because we have become poorer and ornerier and meaner than a spavined distempered mule, we, the people of Kansas, propose to kick; we don't care to build up, we wish to tear down. . . . That's the stuff! Give the prosperous man the dickens! Legislate the thriftless

man into ease, whack the stuffing out of the creditors. . . .[5]

Here was the antidote to the Leonard Browns, to the
nostalgic pioneers. What Kansas really needed, White
implied, was a strong dose of urban middle-class respectability and business acumen; proper deference, not scorn,
for the financier and industry builder; appreciation of the
fact that the impoverished farmer was simply a shiftless
worker.

A Chicago paper first republished the editorial and it
was subsequently seized upon by a number of big-city
editors who offered it as a rebuke to the rural radicalism of
the Populists. The Republican party strategists were delighted by the editorial because it could be presented to the
nation as an example of "small-town common sense," and
when McKinley won the election of 1896 over William
Jennings Bryan, the champion of the West, White and
many of his fellow small-town editors hailed the victory as
a triumph over socialism. "The party of emotions, the
party of 'feeling,' the part of classes, the party of revolution
has been rebuked," he wrote.[6]

And all this in the name of the values of the small town.
The truth was these values were not the town's. They did
not come out of the tradition of the noble farmer, nor out
of the town's version of the Protestant ethic with its
emphasis on "calling," on frugality, and self-denial. They
came from the city, which discovered and promoted
"rugged individualism," which developed the Gospel of
Wealth according to which godliness and riches were in
league and the Almighty had delivered into the hands of

[5] William Allen White: "What's the Matter with Kansas," *Empo-
ria Gazette*, August 15, 1896, reprinted in William Allen White:
Forty Years on Main Street (New York and Toronto: Farrar and
Rinehart, Inc.; 1937), pp. 298–9.
[6] William Allen White, "It Is All Over," editorial in the *Emporia
Gazette*, November 3, 1896, in ibid., p. 301.

the financiers the destiny of the country. The town at last had come to accept the city's values, and the city, having triumphed, now claimed that the values which it had imposed on the town were, in fact, the values of the town. And the city lauded the town, and sentimentalized it, and driveled over it, and called it the heart of American democracy, the moulder of men, the ancient defender of American ideals.

If William Allen White lived to repent, his almost equally famous colleague, Ed Howe, the Atchison newspaper editor, stood by the city's version of the small town to the end and was rewarded by the warm if somewhat condescending acclaim of the big-city editors and the admiration of H. L. Mencken, who heard in Howe's Midwestern accents the purest tones of rugged individualism. The principles of Howe that most charmed the Sage of Hollins Street were these:

> The first object of self-interest is to survive. The possession of money makes it easier to survive, Ergo, it is virtuous to get money. . . . Any American of average talents and decent industry can get enough money, barring acts of God, to make himself comfortable. . . . Any man who fails to do so shows an unfitness to survive, and deserves to be exploited by his betters.[7]

Howe's formula for improving the world was for everyone to behave better.

> The young fellow who practices the simple virtues, and is polite and industrious, becomes a high caste man; the young fellow given to bad habits becomes a low caste man, whatever his birth may have been. . . . The story of every successful man is the same in essential details; he began work young, stuck to it, was reliable, dependable, and efficient. He was polite, fair,

[7] Edgar Watson Howe: *Plain People* (New York: Dodd, Mead and Company; 1929), pp. 250, 298, 300–301.

and had respect for the lessons of experience. . . . The man who gets in the bread line, because of too much mental activity and not enough physical, is a mild sort of criminal for whom there should be punishment.[8]

Perhaps Howe's greatest fame came as a fashioner of aphorisms. Many big city newspapers printed them regularly and for a time he published a magazine made up of such axioms for success as,

Take care of yourself . . . is the greatest human philosophy. . . . The men in pursuit of money make less trouble than the big idealists with their experiments. . . . Man hustling to do better than the competitors they hate have done more for the world than the great souls who dream of universal love. . . . Of all the games worth a candle, success is first. . . . Success in life is actually easier than failure.[9]

But if success was the ideal, even poverty was a blessing because the children of the poor "are usually taught industry, acquire good habits, and as a result often become rich."

Howe accepted without question the success ethic of his age. The "noted and successful" of the great world are simply the "especially good workmen" who have stuck patiently to their tasks. Many of these "fine people" began in the country and were "promoted to the big cities on merit."[1] Howe may indeed be taken as the prototype of the small-town man who came at last to accept the city at its own evaluation. When the Howe mentality predominated in the towns of America the fight was over. Howe was singing the battle songs of the enemy. The town had given up the ghost. It was glad now to have a spurious version of itself held up for all to admire and acclaim. The

[8] Ibid., pp. 317, 309, 307.
[9] Ibid., pp. 303, 304.
[1] Ibid., pp. 252–3.

towns congratulated themselves for having nurtured the "rugged individualism" that orators never tired of lauding as the secret of America's greatness; the Ed Howes drowned out the Leonard Browns. The chorus of praise for the great and wise business leaders was seldom disturbed by sour notes which, if they were heard at all, came from crazy agrarian socialists and small-town malcontents, individuals poisoned by "Red" doctrines of the Third International.

Those who counted themselves the heirs of the Puritans concentrated their efforts on a negative morality that was was "anti-liquor, anti-tobacco . . . anti-Mason . . . anti-theatre, anti-dancing, anti-billiards (and card playing) . . . anti-Unitarian, anti-Catholic (the antagonist of civil and soul liberty), and mildly anti-Jew." [2]

The town in its early ages had associated itself with the "agrarian myth." The Jeffersonian vision of the uncorrupted yeoman farmer was grafted on the New England ethic of work and in the resulting montage town and country found comforting assurance of their moral superiority. America was to be made in that image, the image of the country town surrounded by prosperous farms and pious and frugal farmers.

But from the first the farmers bore little resemblance to the myth, and in the second half of the nineteenth century as farming changed from self-sufficient family crop-raising to commercial agriculture the gap between myth and reality grew ever wider. The farmer was no more immune to the speculative fever than the townsman or city dweller. He became a rural businessman, and with this change the town, under the influence of the city, replaced the ideal of the independent, self-sufficient farmer with that of the self-made man—an ideal actually more congenial to the town since it asserted a value that the town could use in making itself in a sense superior to the farm.

In the years following the Civil War, the town, the

[2] Ernest W. Clement: "Jesse Clement: A Yankee Westernized," *Iowa Journal of History*, XXXVIII (July, 1940), p. 280.

traditional ally of the farm against the city, began to transfer its alliance to the city. The old attitudes remained strong, so that this movement was often concealed under familiar diatribes against the corruptions of Sodom, but the town came increasingly to accept the city's version of the rural hayseed, the awkward bumpkin from the farm. This image reinforced the *amour-propre* of the town, and the town took pride in the fact that its most enterprising youth went to the city.

When an Ed Howe could express the city ethic in small-town terms, the town, having emancipated itself from the farm, had lost its soul to the city.

X I

Small-Town Boy

T HE BOY IN THE SMALL TOWN.
Other images of the town may darken. The
novelist may see it hagridden by petty jealousies
and fears; the sociologist may find it obsessed by corroding
class distinctions, but nothing mars the idyllic picture of
town and boy. It remains one constant thread through
many changing visions. From Thomas Bailey Aldrich and
Mark Twain to Sherwood Anderson and Edgar Lee
Masters the myth is untarnished. Even such a skeptic as
Clyde Brion Davis directs his skepticism, not against the
town as the small boy's Garden of Eden but against the
argument that the old days of the town were better than
the present ones, and Davis's picture of his own youth in
Chillicothe, Ohio, is in the classic tradition.

Since the great majority of native-born Americans have

started their lives in small towns and since it may be assumed that environmental factors are of importance in shaping personality, the effect of the small town on the small boy is, presumably, of some significance in the development of "the American character."

In his later years William Dean Howells recorded his recollections of his childhood in Hamilton, Ohio. To Howells the child was a savage whose world has no meaning "but as it relates to him; it is for his pleasure, his use; it is for his pain and his abuse. It is full of sights, sounds, sensations, for his delight alone, for his suffering alone. He lives under a law of favor or of fear, but never of justice. . . ." He feels himself under the power of a "supernal Being who abode in the skies for his advantage and disadvantage, and made winter and summer, wet weather and dry, with an eye single to him; of a family of which he was necessarily the centre and of that far, vast, unknown Town, lurking all around him, and existing on account of him if not because of him." [1]

The world which stretched out around the boy was a world into which he could grow with confidence. It could be encompassed physically as he grew older, and if its psychological limits were wide ones they were not so complex or obscure as to discourage the effort of comprehension. Because there was in the town in its best years a certainty and a confidence in the future, the child grew up feeling that "life wasn't so bad and everything would come out all right." John Holmes feels that one of the town's greatest benefits "was that satisfaction that you were safe. There was no feeling that you would be left behind. . . . There wasn't a feeling of being lost or going to suffer for want of food or lodging."

Equally important was the fact that the boy in the town felt that he belonged to his whole community. In Holmes's

[1] William Dean Howells: "A Boy's Town," *Selected Writings of William Dean Howells*, Henry Steele Commager, ed. (New York: Random House; 1950).

words: "It left you with a feeling when you got out . . . of a kinship . . . I don't know whether it's boasting but I could [always] feel that I was just a part of [any] community and I attribute it to the way that I lived as a boy." A deep sense of security came from belonging to a familiar world. Feeling at home in the town as few city boys could, the town boy often carried this feeling with him wherever he went. Mr. Holmes "never found anybody that was too far above me that I couldn't go right up and meet him nor too far down that I didn't associate with him." He recalls one of the most frequently asserted values of the town was that it gave "the young man . . . a feeling that he is the equal of other men. . . . You get that when you live in a small town. You're on the basis of equality. You're just as good as the other fellow." [2]

Until the defeat of the town the town boy was less conscious of the limitations of his environment than his middle- and lower middle-class counterpart in the city. Where there were social divisions, the boy was at first only dimly aware of them. The boys of the town valued a companion "for his character and prowess, and it did not matter in the least that he was ragged and dirty. Their mothers might not allow him the run of their kitchens quite so freely as some other boys, but the boys went with him just the same, and they never noticed how little he was washed and dressed." [3]

The word "hometown" has deep meaning in America. The town was home. It was an extended family. Arthur Miller has declared that the center of drama, "the more or less hidden impulse antedating social alienation, the unsaid premise of the very idea of 'satisfaction,' is the memory of both playwright and audience of an enfolding family and of childhood." Playwright and audience, Miller claims, believe in a common identity, "a *being,* somewhere in the past which in the present has lost its completeness, its

[2] J. H. Holmes.
[3] Howells: *Selected Writings,* p. 765.

definitives. . . . We cannot go home again, and the world we live in is an alien place."

The town was made up, like the family, of a number of individuals who lived, for the most part, in a face-to-face relationship, a community in which were acted out the great human dramas of birth, marriage, death, sin, and redemption. The remarkable power of Thornton Wilder's *Our Town* comes from its representation of "the indestructibility, the everlastingness, of the family and the community, its rhythm of life, its rootedness in the essentially safe cosmos despite troubles, wracks, and seemingly disastrous, but essentially temporary, dislocations." [4]

The testimony of Eric Sevareid, visiting the town of his boyhood in North Dakota, supports Miller's point. Sevareid confessed that he could find no pattern, "no unfolding of personal life that could be attributed to the town itself, [or] to any of the influences for which we credit or blame the small towns of our country." But he understood why. "I . . . loved . . . its memory always: it was, simply, *home*—and *all* of it home, not just the house but all the town. That is why childhood in the small towns is different from childhood in the city. Everything is home." [5]

The town like the home became the symbol of a world of intimacy, warmth, acceptance, and security. Entangled as it was with the family, the town was searched and yearned for through the restless insecurity of urban, industrial America. In the center of the family group and of the town as the extended family was the mother. She, in Howells's words, "represented the family sovereignty; the father was seldom seen, and he counted for little or nothing among the outside boys." [6] The town was the natural habitat for the woman; in another chapter I have spoken of

[4] Arthur Miller: "The Family in Modern Drama," *Atlantic Monthly* (April, 1956), pp. 35–41.
[5] Eric Sevareid: "You Can Go Home Again," *Collier's* (May 11, 1956), pp. 61–4.
[6] Howells: *Selected Writings*, p. 762.

her triumph over the male in the town. Not only was the world of the small-town boy the proper empire of a mother, she, in her home, had an invulnerability that her husband could not share. The theme of the inspiring mother is not simply small town of course. It is one of the deepest and most persistent themes in history, entwined in every great religion, an article of faith in the American creed. "The testimony of great men," Orison Marden wrote, "in acknowledgment of the boundless debt they owe their mothers would make a record stretching from the dawn of history to today. . . . Few men indeed become great who do not owe their greatness to a mother's love and inspiration."[7] If the mother was the central, loving, inspiring, life-giving figure in the home, and the town was an extension of the home, mother and town merged in the depths of the psyche. The yearning for the security and the love of the mother was part of and fused with the search for the meaning of the town.[8]

It was true that in many towns a boy's life, like an adult's, was desperately bleak and hard. To Eric Sevareid the memories of a "Dakota child" were "laced with these black threads and for some the binding is too tight, too painful, ever to be unstitched." But for Sevareid "the golden threads outlasted the black." The golden threads are "pleasant faces that never die, the creak of saddles and the smell of horses . . . the leafy path to the swimming hole, the mad joy of the circus parade down Main Street, the

[7] Orison S. Marden: *Pushing to the Front* (New York: Thomas Y. Crowell Company; 1894), p. 725.

[8] Against this must be placed the conclusions of the social psychologists that "the successful, upward-mobile man tends to have a positive relation with his father; he does not feel a strong emotional tie with his mother," William Lloyd Warner: *American Life, Dream and Reality* (Chicago: University of Chicago Press; 1953), p. 189. Is this conclusion perhaps based primarily on successful businessmen of the city and suburb where men dominate and the mother's role is very different from her role in the small town?

heady drug of printer's ink in the Journal shop . . . the
stately gravity of the Chautauqua lecturer who made me
feel so wise and grave on the walk home with Father. . . .
We are all alike, we graying American men, who were
boys in the small towns of our country." [9]

The memory of the promptness with which they were
accepted into an adult world was a source of great satisfaction to many of those who tried to account for the special
quality of a small-town childhood. As a boy in Mastersville,
John Holmes always found someone who would listen to
his ideas, however immature, with interest and apparent
respect. Boys and girls participated in such adult entertainment as there was from their early youth. Lectures,
debates, political rallies, murder trials, marriages, and funerals—all adult functions—were available to the child, and
often his attendance was compulsory. The town was the
center of informal debate, of theological disputation, of
political argument, and of endless talk that was a kind of
town ritual, a means by which people asserted themselves,
touched reality or evaded it, made contact, expressed love,
received assurance of love. The boy listened to much of the
talk and was educated by it, and found that he could join
in. The town was in its own view the center of the wide
world, just as the boy thought himself the center of the
town. Boy and town had in common this impulse to relate
themselves to the cosmos. The questions that each asked
were generally simple ones, but they were also the important ones, asked for the most part without the embarrassment or self-consciousness that would have made the more
sophisticated urbanite tongue-tied; and the answers, given
without embarrassment, were essentially simple ones that a
boy could understand.

Even the "bad boys" of the town were seldom delin-
quents. They were pranksters who found an outlet for the
mischievous impulses and latent cruelty of youth by practi-

[9] Sevareid: "You Can Go Home Again," p. 58.

cal jokes and daring adventures. "The boy that might be called a bad boy," John Holmes recalled, "was often the smart boy of the town." He enjoyed a certain status as the "bad boy." We know him as Huck Finn, as Aldrich's Bad Boy, as Penrod or Sam, and in a hundred other guises.

This suggests another attribute of the town as a small boy's haven. The town offered the boy an extraordinary degree of freedom within the security. A suburban neighborhood might rival the town in the secure world that enwombed the growing boy, but it was generally a world of barriers, of barred exits, of nurses and solicitous aunts.

In every recollection of the town we find the symbol of water. In its classic form it is the old swimming hole or the broad Mississippi of Tom Sawyer or Huck Finn. It is the symbol for freedom and also for mystery and perhaps for something deeper. In the swimming hole, clothes and the conventions of the town are discarded. The adult world is rejected in this unique arena which custom has allowed as the American boy's special preserve. The pond, the lake, the river, the swamp, the stream; it is as though here the small-town boy is dimly aware that he touches the source of life—dangerous, strangely loving and enfolding.

But most important is the freedom. The virtue of the town is that despite its hard and settled forms (forms that the boy has for the most part yet to feel pressing cruelly upon him) it offers the boy such freedom as no child of the urban middle class can know. It is most obviously a freedom to run and race, to adventure into fields and woods, to hurtle through a generally hospitable space. The boy roved through the town like Adam through the Garden before the Fall, though not in Adamic innocence.

The small-town boy saw life around him at firsthand; he was spared none of its more intimate details, sordid though they might be. Part of the town myth has held that the town-bred boy was somehow purer in body and spirit, more protected from dark knowledge than his city counterpart. The opposite was true. The city probably knows no vice that was not invented by the country. Gross sexuality has been a conspicuous feature of town life from the days of the Puritans to the present. It is probably fair to say that the middle-class boy who grew up in a small town knew far more about the problems of Eve and the apple than the middle-class city or suburban child. Herbert Quick has written:

> I have often wondered what city boy ever had more evil associates than did I out there on the prairie. . . . The simple innocence of the Deserted Village was absent. . . . The boy with whom I played most, and whom I liked for his sense of humor, developed into a village drunkard, and, after a dreadful debauch, committed suicide in a town far from the old home. How a boy of that age could have had more vices I can not imagine.

Quick mentions five of his close friends who turned into drunkards and thieves, adding:

> Now if I had lived in the worst slum in any city I could not have had associates more evil than were these boys. Their language was unspeakably profane.[1]

And O. J. Laylander recalls that his village "was a center for the circulation of vile pictures and vicious literature."[2]

William Allen White wrote in a similar vein that there was little to teach a boy who had grown up in a pioneer town

> around the slaughterhouse and in the livery stable, who had roamed through the romantic woods where the peripatetic strumpets made their camps, who had

[1] Herbert Quick: *One Man's Life* (Indianapolis: The Bobbs-Merrill Company; 1925), pp. 147–8.
[2] O. J. Laylander: *The Chronicles of a Contented Man* (Chicago: A. Kroch; 1928), p. 23.

picked up his sex education from the Saxon words chalked on sidewalks and barns, who had taken his Rabelaisian poetry from the walls of backhouses, and who had seen saloons spew out their back door their indigestible drunkards, swarming with flies . . . as it was in the beginning of civilization.[3]

The Victorian attitude toward sex infected the town in the post-Civil War period. In the early history of the town the harshness of Puritan sanctions had been softened by the practical wisdom of a rural community which, if it expected its members to excel in virtue, was not surprised when they failed. The fact that there were, in the period of the town's decline, an increasing number of frustrated and unfulfilled people contributed directly to the atmosphere of sexual severity and repression. As urban attitudes toward sexual matters pervaded the community the town's voice grew strident and hysterical. Much was said and written about the danger of "impure thoughts." Newspapers exhorted parents to warn their children that they must keep their minds on noble things; remedies were advertised which were guaranteed to cure the victim of impure thoughts without "use of the knife."

For ten cents a boy could obtain a widely advertised pamphlet written by Dr. E. C. Abbey of Buffalo on *The Sexual System and Its Derangements*, which told of the terrible consequences of thinking about girls. Such thoughts could produce, in an unhappy youth, nervousness, sexual debility, languor, "tiresome feelings," despondency, unfitness for business, unsociability, cowardice, bashfulness, irritable temper, lack of confidence, unfixedness of purpose, broken sleep, trembling dizziness, staggering, soft muscles, weak back, pasty skin, hollow eyes, blunted senses, eruptions, scanty beard, and a number of other symptoms which in turn brought on more serious failings,

[3] William Allen White: *The Autobiography of William Allen White* (New York: The Macmillan Company; 1946), p. 67.

such as epilepsy, palsy, idiocy, insanity, and nervous break-down. Such were the ills that threatened the boy whose mind dwelt on sex.[4]

The sexual education of the small-town boy can hardly have been considered ideal in any age, but it had such virtues as might adhere in explicitness and a kind of coarse naturalism. The small-town boy seldom reached manhood inadequately informed on such matters. The Victorian era, applying to the sex problem its own unhealthy veneer of prurience and repression, did nothing to improve the situation, but it can be said with some confidence that whatever damage was done in the town was less than in the city or suburb. Moreover when the town is judged on its attitude toward sex, it must be remembered that sex was one of its most critical problems. There were many towns which, like the one described by Herbert Quick, simply became pestholes of corruption and vice that sank under the burden of their own iniquities or that were uprooted by neighboring towns conscious of the danger of contamination. Much of the town's harshness on the sex issue was a result of its vulnerability. It was well aware of the brutal force of the libidinous, and having abandoned its most effective control through the operation of the covenant the town found no satisfactory substitute.

If the small-town boy received an informal education from the community of which he was a part, he was also educated more formally in school and academy. One of the most persistent American themes has been devotion to education. The first settlements in New England struggled to provide an education, however crude, for their youth. Given the conditions of frontier life, the determination of the pioneers to establish schools and colleges was by practical standards a strange folly. Beginning ostensibly as a means of ensuring that every Puritan would have direct access to the word of God through the Scriptures, educa-

[4] Lewis Atherton: *Main Street on the Middle Border* (Bloomington: Indiana University Press; 1954), pp. 91-2.

tion became an article of faith in the covenanted community. The school followed the church as an essential institution in the new community. Charles Chauncy expressed the Puritan attitude toward education in a commencement sermon delivered at Harvard College in 1656.

> Be at the cost [he told his audience] *to trayn up thy towardly children in good literature:* parents are commanded to *trayn up their children Ephes. 6.4. in putting understanding & instruction* into them: as if children were like bruit beasts without it. . . . If ye be poor, yet *pray for posterity* and means of education, and *pray for the peace of Jerusalem;* and that *Bethel,* the house of God may not be turned into *Bethaven* the house of iniquity, that schools of learning be not poysoned, or the fountains corrupted. . . . This point may serve for Information, To teach us, that schools of learning are approved and appointed of God, and of great importance for the benefit of Gods people: Seeing that the Lord works with, & blesseth this means, for the laying up of provision, & making of supplys for the work of the ministry; and the Lord here reckons it up as the chiefest of all the blessings mentioned: and this was always one way (even when there were extraordinary Prophets) of raising up of Prophets &c: And there is much need of schools now, when those extraordinary Prophets are wanting. . . .[5]

Over two hundred years later James Finley, a Methodist circuit rider on the frontier, wrote in a similar spirit:

> The subject of education was of great importance in the early settlement of the country; but its importance increases in proportion to its growth and advancement. The mind of man on his entrance into our disordered world is destitute of knowledge of every kind, but is capable of vast acquirements and prodi-

[5] Quoted in Perry E. G. Miller and Thomas H. Johnson: *The Puritans* (New York and Cincinnati: American Book Company; 1938), pp. 705–6. Italics in original.

gious expansion; and on this his happiness and usefulness depend. But it must be acquired by education; and whatever opens the door to facilitate this object, will be productive of the greatest good, both to the individual and the community at large. . . . The whole world, and every man and woman in it, ought to regard the improvement of the mind as the most valuable acquisition within their grasp, both for here and hereafter. It was the purpose of God, in the very constitution of the human mind, that he should be wise; and that in this consists alone his true greatness and unending consummate felicity. On this depends the happiness of social intercourse, the enjoyments of all civil and religious privileges, the advancements in the arts and sciences, and the commerce of the world. Indeed, it raises man from the common level of a beast and brutish enjoyments, to the exalted dignity of a rational being. . . . Every good man, every lover of his country, every bad man ought to use his influence to encourage and sustain, with his property and by the education of his children, every effort to banish the cursed monster ignorance from our happy country.[6]

Although the passage is imbued with a more rationalistic faith in the redeeming power of education than might be entirely consistent with orthodoxy, it nonetheless expressed the view of the majority of Americans in Finley's day. Frontier ministers, missionaries, and circuit riders like Finley stimulated the founding of thousands of schools and colleges in the nineteenth century.

C. W. Cruikshank, writing of Denmark, Iowa, recalled that "the Academy and its needs seemed to fairly obsess the very souls of these people as they planned and labored to promote the welfare of Christian education. . . ."[7] Sus-

[6] James B. Finley: *Autobiography* . . . , W. P. Strickland, ed. (Cincinnati; 1858), pp. 40–1.
[7] C. W. Cruikshank: "Denmark Academy As I Knew It," *Iowa Journal of History*, XXXVIII (April, 1940), p. 183.

tained by the hope for a better life that had brought them
to the frontier, most newly founded towns in their earliest
years showed remarkable enterprise in school and college
building. The elementary school was generally followed—
before the advent of the high school—by a grammar
school. Between the grammar school and the college came
the academy, which charged tuition but which was at least
in part supported by the community; "every ambitious boy
or girl planned to attend . . . one or more terms" at the
academy, but "only rarely did one get as far as college." [8]

These early schools often did little more than inculcate
the community values of persistence and self-denial. The
teacher's maintenance of discipline was generally considered more important than the teaching function, and a
pedagogue's fitness was more apt to be measured by his
ability to keep a roomful of unruly children of all ages in
order rather than by his fluency in Latin or Greek.
Nonetheless, in many instances the school system became
the focus of the town's pride. Where some communities
found satisfaction in their rate of growth, their acquisition
of a railroad line, their temperance record, or the performance of local athletes, others prided themselves on their
schools and on the numbers of preachers, missionaries, or
lawyers they had produced.

John Holmes recalls that the Mastersville school was the
social center of the town. "All the various societies had
meetings there, and closing days were great events with us.
They put on holiday attire and had a general program." [9]
But this passed with the appearance of the consolidated
school and the children of the town now go to a large new
school several miles away.

If the schools were second in importance only to the
churches, this did not mean that they were effective
educational institutions. When present-day sentimentalists

[8] Roger B. Galer: "Recollections of Busy Years," *Iowa Journal of
History and Politics*, XLVII (January, 1944), p. 8.
[9] J. H. Holmes.

contrast modern education with that of the little red schoolhouse in order to disparage progressive education they have in mind the small-town school at its idealized best. It seems safe to say that in eighty to ninety percent of the small towns schools, elementary and secondary (where the latter existed at all), were far below modern levels, poor as these levels may in fact be. Such critics are remembering the best of the private schools or "academies," and the denominational seminaries which were in most instances little more than high schools. Of course it must also be said that the instructional competence of many schools varied widely from decade to decade depending on the resourcefulness and ability of a single teacher or superintendent. The average situation was not far different from that of the town of Northfield, Massachusetts, a community of three thousand: it had thirteen school districts, some with an average attendance of seven to ten pupils, and the classes were often taught by poorly prepared teachers. One such school, named optimistically the Bee Hive, had no specific course of study and hardly the form of a class. "Each pupil advanced as far and as fast as he could be led to travel. He stayed shorter or longer as his parents saw fit to have him, gained no diploma but could pass, if such was the plan, to any college, albeit none did." [1]

In Waterbury, New York, in the 1850's there were eight schoolhouses, each with a single room, but as the town's historian writes, "if each of them had one or more of the many faults that Horace Mann was vigorously assailing, they were centres of neighborhood interest and pride." [2] The pride, if often misplaced, was justified when a particular teacher was skilled and devoted. Then, despite severe limitations, real education took place. In a system of

[1] Herbert C. Parsons: *A Puritan Outpost* (New York: The Macmillan Company; 1937), p. 374.
[2] James M. Williams: *An American Town* (New York: J. Kempster Printing Company).

this type a gifted teacher could give the gifted pupil such stimulus and attention as he seldom receives today in a more pretentious "plant" or from a more elaborate curriculum. And we know from a multitude of reminiscences and memoirs by small-town émigrés that this indeed happened.

Roger Galer recalled that the school in his Iowa hometown, although carried on in an "old-fashioned, inadequate building," was an outstanding institution. "The rooms were small, with plain seats and no teaching apparatus except a blackboard, but a succession of able teachers from 1870 to 1880 made the school notable. Students ambitious for academy and college had unusual facilities for that day. In addition to the common branches there were advanced classes in algebra, physical geography, natural philosophy and higher arithmetic." From here Galer went to Howe's Academy at Mt. Pleasant. Provided with a cookstove and some odds and ends of furniture contributed by his father, he did his own cooking and acted as janitor at the school in return for his tuition and room rent.[3]

The curriculum of the academy at Denmark, Iowa, was typical of the better among those institutions. The junior class studied arithmetic, grammar, and Anderson's *Popular History of the United States*. Those students who had mastered Caesar and Cicero progressed on to algebra, natural philosophy, botany, and Nordhoff's *Politics for Young Americans*. As a senior, C. W. Cruikshank studied astronomy, political economy, rhetoric, chemistry, trigonometry and surveying, commercial law, "moral science," Mark Hopkins's *Evidence of Christianity*, Butler's *Analogy*, Shakespeare, Virgil, more Cicero, and Milton's *Paradise Lost*.[4]

O. J. Laylander, having exhausted the schooling available in his hometown, managed to save enough money by

[3] Galer: "Recollections," pp. 8, 37–8.
[4] Cruikshank: "Denmark Academy," pp. 189–90.

teaching to go to Professor Carver's Academy in Medina, Ohio, and there was introduced to the heresies of Huxley, Tyndall, Darwin, and Spencer. He bought Winchell's *Doctrine of Evolution* and used it to badger the Fundamentalists. Raised in Calvinist orthodoxy, he savored such forbidden fruits as Rousseau, Voltaire, and Renan, and found in Emerson's "Oversoul" the perfect image of transcendental truth.[5]

The great majority of small-town boys and girls advanced no further than the local elementary or grammar school, where their principal nurture was drawn from the famous *Eclectic Readers* of McGuffey. The *Readers* were undoubtedly of enormous importance in "making the American mind," but they were not the means, as some writers have tried to maintain, of preparing the way for industrial capitalism. In actual fact they carried over to the end of the nineteenth century the small-town and rural version of the Protestant ethic. They taught "that village and country life surpassed that in cities," and urban ways were either ignored or used as examples of corruption.[6]

Only religion and education, the *Readers* maintained, could save the Republic from anarchy and disaster. The stories, poems, and articles that made up the *Eclectic Readers* were chosen for the most part from the best literature of the Western world. They were selected to reinforce the doctrine that thrift, industry, and piety were the ingredients of modest worldly success. The selections were improving, highly moral morsels that usually made vivid and exciting reading. The pallid stories of Dick and Jane and Spot and Puff that are the product of today's new morality fall, by any standard that an educated person would recognize, far below the literary and intellectual level of the *Readers*. Laylander recalls that "McGuffey was our all, and constituted the only study of English literature open to us. . . . The result was that we read the

[5] Laylander: *Chronicles of a Contented Man*, p. 58.
[6] Atherton: *Main Street*, p. 66.

books over and over. The reading was all oral. We vied with each other in intonation, in inflection, in interpretation." [7]

The *Readers* have been accused of fostering the American success ethic, but they warned constantly against the dangers of excessive worldliness and materialism, enveighed against the acquisitive instinct, and placed their primary emphasis on character, generosity, and goodness. Riches were indeed a curse unless used for the greater glory of God. As a student of the *Readers* has expressed it, their most persistent theme is that "human ambition and knowledge come to nought" unless supported by God's wisdom. "Wealth, rightly got and rightly used . . . power, fame, these are all worthy objects of ambition," the *Fourth Reader* admits, "but they are not the highest objects, and you may acquire them all without ever achieving true success." A "noble and beautiful character" is "not only the best of possessions in this world, but also is about all you can expect to take with you into the next."

The ideal figure in the *Reader* was not the businessman or industrial tycoon, but the teacher or missionary. In Richard Mosier's words, "With respect to matters of religious and racial tolerance, with respect to simple piety and healthy morals, the McGuffey readers were, and are, supreme." [8]

Perhaps the most significant fact about the *Readers* was that they reaffirmed constantly the American creed that all problems were susceptible to faith and industry. There was in them no hint that the United States was undergoing the travail, torment, and psychological dislocation that marked

[7] Laylander: *Chronicles of a Contented Man*, p. 28; see also Herbert Quick: *One Man's Life*, Chapter XVI, for a tribute to the McGuffey *Readers*.

[8] Richard D. Mosier: *Making the American Mind* (New York: King's Crown Press; 1947), pp. 86, 98, quotes McGuffey's *Fourth Reader*, Eclectic Series (Cincinnati: Van Antwerp, Bragg & Co.; 1879), p. 154.

its transition from a predominantly rural to an urban industrial society. The *Readers* mirrored the placid, optimistic agricultural society of a generation past whose values had survived into a ruder and less congenial age. They can be rightly read as a résumé of much of the American mind, but they did not make or modify that mind—they reflected and preserved its conservative and indeed archaic character —and when new forces had changed that mind the *Readers* fell from favor. They contained a compendium of eighteenth- and early nineteenth-century American moralities; they were a summary of the ethic. Cotton Mather and William Holmes McGuffey spoke much the same language.

The great educational reforms brought by the high school, the normal school, the professionalization of teaching, and finally by school consolidation changed the school system of the town beyond recognition by the end of the nineteenth century. If these changes did not result in an education as superior to the older ways as their protagonists believed, they marked a great advance in orderliness and a vast extension of educational opportunities. The disappearance of the "rock-ribbed" academy was a real loss. Great things were hoped for from the new high schools, however. The dreams of growth and wealth so often defeated turned now to the school. The school, so up-to-date, so new and magnificent would somehow redeem the town and bring at last the better days so long hoped for. When Marshall, Oklahoma's first high school class was graduated, the whole town turned out to fete the students. The seniors "were given a banquet, with the juniors as hosts and the woman's club as humble cooks and waitresses, with hothouse flowers and a formal program and fearful concentration on forks and etiquette . . . and the whole town showered them with presents. . . . To a people less than twenty years removed from a three months' term of school in a sod building, high school graduation represented the ultimate in academic achievement." The seniors went on a picnic and their young teacher told them: " 'You must begin to assert yourselves . . . ten years from now, you will be the leaders of this community.' " But none of them became leaders and only two remained in Marshall. The rest scattered, going for the most part to the cities.[9]

Sims's observations in Aton were similar. Of 299 high school graduates in the years from 1877 to 1910 ninety percent left the community. The high school did not provide the town with leaders; it simply encouraged migration to the cities. It brought in city ideas and city values. It loosened the ties of community; it gave the small-town boy or girl a kind of cosmopolitan contempt for the town with its pokey ways, its narrowness, and country manners. It encouraged restlessness as it discouraged ambition. The system of public education created by devoted men and women, the great majority of whom came themselves from small towns, was captured by theorists who replaced the ancient morality with programs of "life adjustment" and "creative play." At the same time, the consolidated schools brought a variety of social activity that was often highly congenial to the increasingly urban-oriented community. Thus the schools became the agents of the city's values and the community was attacked at its most vulnerable point.

Eric Sevareid, visiting his hometown in North Dakota, found "the 'well-rounded, socially integrated' personality that the progressive schoolteachers are so obsessed with" very apparent in the community.[1] The town high school is thus producing a character type of remarkable uniformity who finds his way in the city as well as in the town, who has an easy assurance that is the same in Algona as in Chicago, in Four Corners as in Kansas City or Philadelphia.

Mastersville, Ohio, which once turned out Methodist ministers and teachers now turns out young men and

[9] Angie Debo: *Prairie City* (New York: Alfred A. Knopf; 1944), p. 148.
[1] Sevareid: "You Can Go Home Again," *Collier's* May 11 1956.

women who, thinking of jobs rather than careers, go to work at the pottery factory in an adjoining town. In Mr. Holmes's words:

> In my day the girls tried to fit themselves to be the wives of ministers or lawyers, but today they simply go to work for themselves. . . . I don't hear of anyone in my community who has taken up a profession lately. We had some excellent physicians . . . the patron saint of the town, my uncle Joseph Masters, his grandson became one of the famous doctors of Ohio. And today I don't hear of anyone talking about professions. They go to work.[2]

It seems safe to say that American towns never got a proper return for their investment in education. The boys who went to an academy and later the great majority of those who went to high school were lost to their home-town, and most of those who went on to college likewise never returned.

Proof of the town's folly in educating its young people beyond the elementary level can be found by comparing the history of the average covenanted community with those communities that consciously restricted the education of their youth and took positive measures to discourage them from continuing their training beyond the community itself. Such communities, together with those towns which we have been primarily concerned with in this study, shared the desire to establish utopian societies standing in a special relation to God and marked by a conviction of salvation. They differed most notably in their cautious and restrictive attitude toward education, an attitude determined in large measure by their suspicion of the national community. The covenanted community, on the other hand, never relinquished its missionary expectations or its assumption that it would in time dominate the national community. It therefore accepted a concept of education

[2] J. H. Holmes.

that in practical terms worked against the best interests of the particular town by encouraging its ablest young people to acquire capabilities that the town could not utilize. The fortress communities, such as the Moravians, Mennonites, Shakers, and dozens of Christian communist communities, showed an extraordinary ability to maintain themselves over the years with a minimum of social and institutional change.

John Holmes has remarked that the young man or woman of today's Mastersville "doesn't think of fitting himself for the future." [3] The phrase is a significant one. The town in its best years led the child to conceive of a "life style" rather than to simply prepare himself for a job. The life style was compounded of many elements, among them of course the ethic which for some time after it had been abandoned by the adult world remained, as a residue of the past, a critical factor in forming the child's mind. The ethic, because it dealt with ultimate ends and purposes that reached beyond practical goals, projected this life style. Children's awareness that "God himself could not save them against themselves . . . helped them to realize the serious responsibility they were under to their own after-selves." [4] The most feckless boy knew that, like his parents, he lived "close to God's will." He might indeed suffer terrible pangs of guilt and fear because he had offended an omniscient and implacable God, but he was never uncertain as to where the proper path lay.

The city child generally suffered from the absence of a coherent society into which he could graduate. [5] The same could not be said of the average small-town boy. He understood the expectations and requirements of his community and soon learned the small deceits and evasions that afforded some relief from the straitjacket of conformity.

[3] Ibid.
[4] Howells: *Selected Writings*, p. 720.
[5] Alexander Comfort: *Sexual Behavior in Society* (London: Duckworth; 1950), p. 59.

Within this framework he could grow, often joyfully, until he was tall enough to look the village in the eye. Then, when it pressed upon him, he might go, or stay to face, or find means to evade, defeated expectations.

Church, school, and town in an amalgam uniquely American shaped the boy. The smaller the town the closer it was to its heroic age, the more binding its original covenant, the deeper its imprint was apt to be upon its boys. Hundreds of thousands of such boys could say with Thomas Wolfe, "You can't go home again," and add, "nor can you escape it."

X I I

... *Makes Good*

THE SMALL TOWN PRODUCED CITIZENS who became the settlers of thousands of other small
towns, but year after year it also produced the
greater part of the urban population of the United States.
The town exported its most able and energetic youth, who
found places in the higher occupational ranks of the cities
and in many instances carved out distinguished careers on
the national scene.

Important as the town was in accomplishing the orderly
settlement of the country and in maintaining a received
tradition and custom virtually intact, its greatest contribu-
tion to the development of the United States may have
been in the creation and preservation of a remarkable
character type. This type, often failing to find suitable
opportunities within the town, migrated in large numbers

to other towns, to smaller cities, and to the great urban centers. They filled up the professions; they became business leaders; they controlled large areas of political life; they constituted a self-conscious, articulate, aggressive company of "inner-directed" men and women prominent in all areas of national life.

While everyone is generally aware of this movement from town to city, historians and sociologists have given surprisingly little attention to this "great migration": the sociologists apparently because of their practice of studying communities as more or less isolated segments of our society; the historians because their attention has been directed elsewhere—primarily to the frontier and the city —and because they have been generally reluctant to embark on "cultural" studies of the kind best suited to reveal the contributions of the town. The Warner-group studies of small communities, for instance, have slighted the critical question of "residential mobility" by concentrating on "small economically stagnant communities, and failing to give a systematic accounting of what has happened to persons moving out of the community. . . ." The emphasis on economic opportunity or "access to facilities" as the critical factor in upward mobility has obscured the problem of motivation. Talcott Parsons, for one, feels that the economic aspects are "less important than is generally supposed," adding that "if this is correct, then an unexpectedly heavy emphasis falls on the factor of *motivation* to mobility, on the part both of a boy himself, and of his parents on his behalf, as distinguished from objective opportunity for mobility."[1] In most studies of the community, as another critic has noted, "examination of emigration and the subsequent careers of emigrees from these

[1] Talcott Parsons: "A Revised Analytical Approach to the Theory of the Social Stratifications," in R. Bendix and S. Lipset, ed.: *Class, Status and Power* (Glencoe, Ill.: The Free Press; 1953), pp. 126–7.

communities were not included in the research designs." [2]

Certain social psychologists have stressed "an unequivocal relationship between parental status and scholastic aptitude," which for our purpose can be restated as "an unequivocal relationship between the ideals and aspirations of the parents (and the community) and the career motivations of the child." [3] Certainly all the evidence that is available in regard to "successful" small-town boys reinforces the theory that motivation is far more important than "accessibility."

The Army General Classification Tests, given to all recruits in World War II, revealed that many individuals of superior intelligence as measured by the test occupied positions far below those which their intelligence scores suggested they were capable of filling. For instance, although the median ratings of truck drivers and mechanics placed them near the bottom of the occupational scale, a number of them tested better than persons in occupational groups at the top of the scale. The significance of these figures for the small town is obvious. They underline the importance of motivation rather than intelligence as a factor in "upward mobility."

Moreover if the family of the small-town boy was lacking in ambition for him, he might quite readily receive his stimulus from individuals in the community, or from

[2] W. Lloyd Warner and James C. Abegglen: *Occupational Mobility in American Business and Industry, 1928–1952* (Minneapolis, Minn.: University of Minnesota Press; 1955), p. 18.

[3] Theodore Caplow: *The Sociology of Work* (Minneapolis, Minn.: University of Minnesota Press; 1954), p. 78; and see also Lewis M. Terman: *Genetic Studies of Genius*, vol. I, *Mental and Physical Traits of a Thousand Gifted Children*, 2nd ed. (Palo Alto, Calif.: Stanford University Press; 1926); Mapheus Smith: "University Student Intelligence and Occupation of Father," *American Sociological Review*, VII (December, 1942); Edward L. Thorndike and others: *Prediction of Vocational Success* (New York: The Commonwealth Fund; 1934).

the explicitly stated values of the community. The town thus offered the optimum situation for the boy or girl of ability. Between family, outside friends (teacher, minister, family doctor), and the community itself, few capable young people failed to receive the stimulus (or motivation) that would spur them to make the most of their potentialities. The Protestant doctrine of calling, which held it a kind of sin not to perform up to the limits of one's ability, remained strong in the towns, and the promising boy or girl was encouraged to associate a worthwhile career with service to God.

Just as many towns produced particular products for which they enjoyed some slight fame, so did they in innumerable instances produce individuals who followed particular callings. Peacham, Vermont, for instance, in a period of thirty years, turned out a remarkable number of missionaries. Three went to work among the Cherokee Indians in Tennessee; another to the Sandwich Islands (Hawaii), where he built a church and translated the Bible and Watts's hymns; another to Ceylon, and still another to India. Two domestic missionaries went to Indiana in 1831 and one helped found Wabash College. A Peacham girl went to Green Bay, Wisconsin, where she labored among the Indians for forty years.[4]

Vermontville, Michigan, in addition to producing several dozen Congregational ministers turned out five college professors, four of them in the Kedzie family, and four surgeons and assistant surgeons for the Union Army.[5]

Granville, Ohio, colonized from Granville, Connecticut, produced teachers at an astonishing rate. In 1820 the township had furnished forty schoolteachers and by 1846 seventy Ohio schoolteachers had come from the town, of whom, it was proudly noted, "62 prayed in school."

[4] E. L. Bogart: *Peacham, The Story of a Vermont Hill Town* (Montpelier, Vt.: Vermont Historical Society; 1948), pp. 184–6.
[5] Edward W. Barber: "The Vermontville Colony," *Michigan Pioneer and Historical Collections*, XXVIII (1900), pp. 248–50.

In the 1920's eight out of fifty-eight officers of flag rank in the United States Navy were from small towns in Texas, and communities within twelve miles of Paris, Texas, were the homes of four of the nation's most prominent contemporary political figures—John Nance Garner, Tom Connally, Sam Rayburn, and Pat Wrightman.

The choices of career that lay ahead of the town boy were limited and clearly defined. They were, specifically, the professions—the ministry, teaching, law, and medicine. A business career, at least until the end of the nineteenth century, was a far less desirable alternative. Roger Galer writes that "as an ambitious boy I had no thought of a business career. Mine was to be a profession." [6] A small business in a small town carried with it little prestige and was moreover apt to be a highly precarious operation. To start a local industry, however modest in scale, required capital, always in short supply in the town, and was if anything more hazardous than storekeeping. Only the exceptional boy with the prosperous and successful relative in the city to act as his sponsor had much hope of becoming another Horatio Alger. In most instances he did not wish such a future. If the small-town boy had a model it was more likely to be Horace Mann or Mark Hopkins than John Jacob Astor or Jay Gould; Peter Cartwright or Henry Ward Beecher rather than Commodore Vanderbilt or Diamond Jim Brady.

Prior to the Civil War the ministry was the goal of most gifted small-town boys and indeed it remained the most respected calling in many towns down to the end of the century. Henry Severance recalls the doctor in his hometown, who was "interested in boys and girls, and encouraged them to make the best of themselves. He was especially interested in the Butcher's fourth son, who joined the Baptist Church when he was ten years of age, and was

[6] Roger B. Galer: "Recollections of Busy Years," *Iowa Journal of History and Politics*, XLII (January, 1944), p. 71.

nicknamed the 'little deacon.' The Doctor said: 'That boy will make something of himself. He will be a minister.' " [7]

The Denmark Academy in Denmark, Iowa, prided itself on its twenty-six prominent alumni, seven of whom became college professors, two university and college presidents (Cornell University and Knox College), three distinguished lawyers, three writers, six teachers, including three who became superintendents of schools, six missionaries, and two businessmen. Out of twenty-six, twenty-four were in the professions, primarily teaching and the ministry, and only two in business. The proportions can be taken as representative.

Theodore Munger, writing a book of advice for young men "on the threshold" of their careers, had more warnings of the dangers of riches than exhortations to acquire them. He urged his readers to aim for a noble calling rather than material gain. The important thing was "not learning, talent, energy, nor money, but training. . . . A call, or calling, is a divine thing, and must be obeyed." The ambitious youth is admonished to place the love of God before all else, to "listen evermore to conscience. Keep the heart responsive to all sorrow. Love with all love's divine capacity and quality." Such advice is supplemented by chapters on thrift, manners, self-reliance and courage, reading, amusements, and faith. It was to such voices as Munger's that the town-bred youth was most responsive. [8]

Like Munger's work, William Mathews's *Getting On in the World*, one of the most popular books of its genre, placed great emphasis on piety and morality, and spoke

[7] Henry O. Severance: "The Folk of Our Town," *Michigan History Magazine*, XII (January, 1928), p. 62.

[8] Theodore Munger: *On the Threshold* (Boston: Houghton Mifflin Company; 1885), pp. 11, 19, 28. See also *Men Who Have Risen, Book for Boys* [author anonymous] (New York: Miller; 1859).

scornfully of "certain classes of writers and lecturers" who teach our youth "to look with scorn upon, and to struggle out of the sphere or place in life to which, if a lowly one, Providence has assigned them, and to become 'great men,' that is, governors, members of Congress, foreign ministers . . . railroad kings, *et id omne*, which they are told they may become, if they only will to do it. . . . The mercantile profession," Mathews warns, is especially to be avoided since statistics show that only "three out of a hundred merchants are successful; all the others becoming bankrupt or retiring in disgust." While Mathews admits that "rank, talents, eloquence, learning, and moral worth, all challenge a certain degree of respect; but, unconnected with property, they have comparatively little influence in commanding the services of other men," he nonetheless insists that "money-getting . . . impoverishes the mind, or dries up the sources of the spiritual life. . . . Any beginner in life . . . may hope to become independent, if not rich, if he will but work persistently, be temperate, and save part of his earnings. Mediocre abilities will suffice for this end, nay, may prove more advantageous than the most dazzling mental gifts." To save a few pennies a day will result in the accumulation of "enormous sums." In forty years, a saving of 14 cents a day will amount to $7,700, "thus securing a snug provision for old age."

Mathews's book is distinguished from many of its kind by its determined realism in certain areas. The author stresses repeatedly the small chance of success in business. The president of the Union Bank has collected figures which show that of a thousand persons doing business with the bank in 1798 only six remained at the end of forty years —"all the rest had failed or lost their property" (or, it might be assumed, died). Mathews warns that of every hundred young men who come from the country to the city to make their fortune ninety-nine fail.

The small-town boy could read and ponder Mathews's disheartening picture of the businessman's "endless struggle for pelf," which left him at last an exhausted "bond-slave of Mammon." "Do not deem yourself," he warns his readers, "authorized to pity those who prefer incorruptible treasures to a balance at their banker's." These are indeed the true successes, those "who have been successful as *men*, though they may have failed as lawyers, doctors, and merchants." [9] To one small-town boy, Mathews's book was an inspiration. "It was surcharged with the old self-help philosophy, filled with quotations, and consciously intended to spur the ambitions of young men. But . . . the success held up to the young men of his clientele was literary or professional success." [1]

In order for the impulse toward mobility to be translated into actual mobility, the town needed channels through which her most talented sons and daughters could advance. The channels of "upward mobility" were to be found in the extraordinary number of denominational colleges founded, primarily, by the covenanted communities. The extent of this college building can hardly be imagined today. Colleges sprang up overnight only to disappear in many instances almost as quickly. All that was needed to establish a college was an aggressive president—who was also responsible for teaching much of the curriculum—a building or two, a handful of students, and the support of churches in the vicinity.

Of course many colleges were from the beginning established on a firmer and broader basis with considerable financial backing from the more prosperous denominations such as the Presbyterians, Congregationalists, and Methodists. Some, like Oberlin, were in a sense missionary enterprises founded by graduates of Eastern seminaries, but all were animated by a large measure of Christian idealism,

[9] William Mathews: *Getting On in the World* (Chicago: S. C. Griggs & Company; 1873), pp. 8, 37-8, 284-5, 293, 295-6, 305, 331, 348.
[1] Herbert Quick: *One Man's Life* (Indianapolis: Bobbs-Merrill Company; 1925), p. 180.

mixed with strong democratic and egalitarian sentiments. Oberlin College stated its purpose was

> to educate the youths of both sexes, so as to secure the development of a strong mind in a sound body, connected with a permanent, vigorous, progressive piety—all to be aided by a judicious system of manual labor. . . . To beget and to confirm in the process of education the habit of self-denial, patient endurance, a chastened moral courage, and a devout consecration of the whole being to God, in seeking the best good of man. . . . To establish universal liberty by the abolition of every form of sin. . . . To avoid the debasing association of the heathen classics, and make the bible a textbook in all the departments of education. . . . To raise up a church and ministers who shall be known and read of all men in deep sympathy with Christ. . . . To furnish a seminary, affording thorough instruction in all branches of an education for both sexes, and in which colored persons, of both sexes, shall be freely admitted, and on the terms of equality and brotherhood.

The program was an odd mixture of New England orthodoxy and liberalism. The founders of New England had never considered the "heathen classics" debasing, nor had they considered "making the Bible a textbook in all the departments of education." Such sentiments were as alien to the older colleges of the East as was the determined egalitarianism of Oberlin's founders.

By 1840 Illinois had twelve colleges. McKendree College had been founded by the Methodists in 1828. The Reverend George Gale had founded Knox Manual Labor College in 1836, and Illinois College had opened its doors in 1830. Beloit was established a few years later. Blackburn, started by two of the Yale band from the Theological Seminary at New Haven, was formally incorporated in 1857 as a Presbyterian institution, and the Whipple, Dover, and Princeton academies had collegiate ambitions, while

Monticello, Jacksonville, Rockford, and Galesburg were the locations of "female seminaries."

The same story was repeated in every Midwestern state. The covenanted communities took the lead in college founding as they did in the establishment of academies and seminaries. By the 1890's Kansas had seminaries, colleges, or universities organized by seventeen church denominations. The Methodists led the parade with Baker University, Blue Mount College, Southwest Kansas College, Kansas Wesleyan University (founded in 1886); they also made an unsuccessful attempt to found an institution at Topeka.

Like so many of its counterparts, Mastersville, Ohio, a town of a few hundred, was obsessed with education. In the 1880's it could count three colleges within a radius of seven or eight miles from the town: one Presbyterian, one Methodist, and another Christian, which later became Hopeville Normal. Athens, the Presbyterian college, held strictly to the classical curriculum requiring four years of Greek and Latin, and in John H. Holmes's words, "they turned out some great men, preachers and school-teachers, and the mathematician who prepared text-books used all over the Middle West." [2] Scio, the Methodist college, requiring but two years of Greek and four years of Latin, graduated scores of Methodist ministers before it closed down and united with another Methodist institution some forty miles away.

In addition to Athens, Scio, and Hopeville Normal, the boys and girls of Mastersville had, for several years, a "university" on the outskirts of town. Its founder and president was an educational reformer who named his institution the One Study University. Each student was required to take up one subject at a time and study nothing else until he had mastered it, whether it be mathematics, language, science, or history, and proceed in this fashion through the curriculum. The university failed as did the

[2] J. H. Holmes.

founder's plan for an extension program in which students might study at home and take examinations at the school. The depression of the middle seventies knocked out the One Study University, but the Methodists took it over and made it into a grammar school that was responsible for the education of most of the boys and girls of Mastersville. Such institutions as those in the vicinity of Mastersville, transitory as they might be, provided channels of mobility that for a few years or a few decades were filled with ambitious young men and women.

Thousands of towns literally went into the "education business," and hundreds found in it a modest livelihood. For a community struggling to maintain itself, unable to attract a railroad or develop a local industry, an academy or college often meant the difference between extinction and survival. Often the competition between towns for colleges was as bitter and ruthless as the competition for railroads, and it was hardly surprising that such communities should produce a high proportion of "upwardly mobile" young men and women who crowded into the professions.

Aton, the "Hoosier Village" of Newell Sims's study, noticed that a nearby town had prospered, apparently as a result of a local college. Through the efforts of some of Aton's most energetic citizens a seminary and an academy were started but both of these failed. Finally, a teacher's college was established. It was a private, nondenominational institution, which at first drew 78 percent of its student body from Aton itself. Sims's description of the college could be applied to thousands of similar institutions scattered throughout the country in the last half of the nineteenth century. The ideal of the college, he writes, has been "a narrow utilitarianism that sacrificed academic thoroughness." He found that "a premium had been put on certain qualities of character, such as religious devotion, moral rectitude, and 'servicefulness.'" As a result many of the graduates went into social service and reform work. Of 394 graduates prior to 1910, 80 had become ministers, missionaries, and "reform workers." At the Aton college "truth is considered static, and the modern view of the world in philosophy and science is combated with religious zeal." The student is, in Sims's words, "trained for political, religious, moral and intellectual conservatism and bias." At the same time fraternities, clubs, and cliques are forbidden and "social equality is inculcated and practiced. The poorest and humblest student is quite as much at home in the atmosphere as any other. The spirit of the institution is a democratizing force, and its operation is manifest in the life of Aton." [3] The college is thus a projection of the values of the covenanted community—intense political, social, and theological conservatism, with high ideals of unselfishness and service, and an insistence on equality.

If training for the ministry was the first concern of the colleges, and continued to be one of their principal concerns for many years, the production of teachers became of increasing importance in the years after the Civil War. The "teacher's institute" and the "normal" school appeared, and by drawing together an "intellectual elite" from dozens of small towns in every state, they made possible the systematic improvement of elementary- and secondary-school education and the development of the high school. Perhaps equally important they helped to break down the isolation of individual communities and, by providing an acceptable alternative to the older professions, enabled each state to utilize many of its ablest youths. Herbert Quick describes his experience at the teachers' institute at Grundy Center. "I was now," he writes, "one of a group of the most intelligent people in the county; for school-teaching was then a calling in which most of the energetic, thinking and developing personalities engaged—for a while at least. The teacher then stood in this respect far higher than now." [4]

Roger Galer went to the State University of Iowa. It

[3] Newell L. Sims: *A Hoosier Village* (New York: Columbia University Press; 1912), pp. 74–7.
[4] Quick: *One Man's Life*, p. 247.

was small, shabby, and poor, but "in all the great essentials of a liberal culture the University gave us excellent facilities," he recalled, "with as good results, as have been attained with all the vast array of buildings, apparatus, books, museums, and specialized instruction of these later years." Galer was able to take mathematics up through analytical geometry, two years of Latin, three years of German, one year of political economy and English literature, two courses in history, and one each in mental and moral philosophy, international law, comparative philology, and the English constitution.[5]

Many individuals went on from school to college teaching, or to medicine, or, more frequently, to law. Others found business opportunities in the course of their teaching. It thus seems safe enough to say that from the end of the Civil War to the turn of the century teaching, increasingly professionalized, not only drew a very large proportion of the town's best talent but also provided an important and much-used avenue to other occupations in smaller cities and in the great urban centers.

R. H. Knapp and H. B. Goodrich in their study of the *Origins of American Scientists* found that the colleges that produced the highest proportions of scientists were virtually all "founded by Protestant denominations for the training of ministers and teachers." In this first stage of development the institution was invariably small, its religious commitment inflexible, its social and moral standards severe, its curriculum classical, and the position of the sciences not yet secure. "Gradually," as the authors describe it, "this phase of development gave way to a second stage, which might be characterized as the period of 'first secularization.' In this second stage, religious preoccupations began to lose their hold, the curriculum was usually modified to provide for specialization, secularization of student interests became clearly manifest, and the sciences

5 Galer: "Recollections," pp. 46–7.

moved into a position of great prestige and popularity. . . . Gradually this second stage gave place to a third, in which the processes of secularization proceeded to a point at which sectarian commitment became virtually indiscernible." In place of the "earlier provincial and lower-middle-class constituency" these institutions attracted the more prosperous students. "Urbanity and cosmopolitanism grew apace, and the sciences suffered a comparative decline as other fields of interest, such as medicine, law, and managerial vocations attracted increasing adherence." [6]

Stephen Visher's study of the origins of 4,340 Indiana scientists suggests further conclusions about the avenues of mobility in American small towns of the nineteenth century. Visher found that certain towns produced a disproportionate number of scientists. Communities such as Aurora, Brookville, Columbia, Crawfordsville, Garrett, Goshen, Greencastle, Hammond, Huntingburg, Lebanon, Madison, and Mt. Vernon contributed far more than their quota.

Visher discovered that, at least in Indiana, there was no truth in Frederick Jackson Turner's statement that the yield of outstanding individuals "seems to be largely a matter of topography; the level lands yield[ing] leaders as well as crops, while rugged land produces few of either." Visher found, apparently to his surprise, that much of the nearly level land of the state was unproductive of leaders while some of the hilly areas were highly productive in terms of scientists. He also noted that there seemed to be no relation between the per capita wealth of a section and the number of scientists it produced. "The parts of Indiana having the greatest tangible wealth," he wrote, "are not the most productive of scientists; large sections of relatively rich and prosperous land have yielded few." Indeed one of the state's "exceptionally poor counties" contributed a

[6] R. H. Knapp and H. B. Goodrich: *Origins of American Scientists* (Chicago: University of Chicago Press; 1952), p. 293.

higher number of "notables" in proportion to population than some of the most prosperous counties.

Visher found that college towns and county seats generally yielded a high proportion of scientists, but "on the other hand, five of the six counties which had the highest yield of [outstanding] scientists in proportion to population lacked colleges." Small towns turned out proportionately many more scientists than did the cities, and the small cities were more productive than the larger ones, except, interestingly enough, in the production of men of "exceptional distinction," where the large cities led. Furthermore, professional men fathered more than twice as many "notables" as did businessmen, twenty times as many as did farmers, and a thousand times as many as did unskilled laborers. It is Visher's conclusion that there is a "far greater" correlation between "type of place of birth and yield of notables" than between yield and topography, soil, climate, material resources, or age of settlement.

Visher does not make a systematic effort to describe the "type of place" which has produced the greater proportion of scientists, other than to distinguish between college towns and county seats. A more thorough investigation would show that towns in which the "covenant" had been most in evidence, and which had as a result been more deeply marked by the town version of the Protestant ethic, had produced the larger proportion of scientists. Other factors would include local tradition, perhaps represented by a particularly gifted teacher, which guided the student into science rather than into the ministry or to law.

Visher's study of some 2,600 outstanding American scientists supports the conclusions based on his Indiana study. Visher claims that the higher productivity of certain areas can be correlated with the predominance in those areas of New England settlers, i.e., areas where the covenanted communities were strongest.[7] In Ohio, for instance,

[7] Stephen S. Visher: *Indiana Scientists* (Indianapolis: Indiana Academy of Science; 1951), pp. 8, 9.

the ten southern counties, sparsely settled by New Englanders, produced no starred scientists, while the central and northern counties produced a large majority of the state's top-ranking figures. Ohio's large cities produced twice as many starred scientists as the state average, while towns of under 8,000 yielded five times the state average and the farms only a fifth of the average for the state as a whole.

In Illinois, the story was much the same. The southern half of the state, settled largely by Southerners, produced only 16 of the state's 72 starred scientists. Chicago yielded scientists at the rate of 1 per 23,000 persons, slightly above the state's average, but such towns as Galesburg, Rockford, Aurora, and Jacksonville contributed at the rate of 1 per 5,500, while for Decatur and Pekin the rate was 1 per 3,500; Centralia and Dixon 1 per 1,800; Henry 1 per 800; Geneva 7 per 600; and Granville 1 per 120.

The most unproductive area of Michigan was the populous southwestern corner of the state, contiguous to an equally sterile section of Illinois. These Michigan counties were settled early by people from southern Illinois who were attracted by the lead deposits, while the northern regions were again the stronghold of the colonized communities of New England.

Statistics for the other Midwestern states are less carefully broken down, but the pattern that emerges is quite clear. Certain areas in every state are far more productive of starred scientists than other areas, and, while towns and cities contribute approximately equal numbers of outstanding scientists, the most productive towns far outdistance the most productive cities; there is indeed a very wide variation in the productivity of individual towns. On the other hand, the number of scientists born or raised on farms is statistically insignificant.[8]

Visher's works and the study by Knapp and Goodrich

[8] Stephen S. Visher: *American Men of Science* (Baltimore: Johns Hopkins Press; 1947), *passim*.

supplement each other. The latter investigators have focused their attention on the education of scientists, attempting to find out what social and cultural factors have drawn young men into the various scientific fields. Their survey of 18,000 scientists revealed a number of facts that have relevance for this study. The small denominational liberal arts colleges of the Northwest, Midwest, and Far West have had a much higher "productivity index"—that is, turned out far more scientists in proportion to their total graduates—than have the larger colleges and the great universities, which latter, even "after the most charitable adjustments had been made, were seen to be less productive" of scientists, although producing a high proportion of "lawyers, physicians, and graduate students in general."

The authors went behind these statistics to consider the type of student drawn to such institutions and the superior opportunities afforded in them "for the development of the most creative of student-teacher relationships." "Formative historical influences" were identified by Knapp and Goodrich as one of the critical factors in producing scientists. Among these the authors list "liberal Protestantism," and the "psychology of the American frontier," which, they suggest, "engendered an empirical orientation of thought, a fluidity of social organization, and an emphasis on individualism highly propitious to the development of scientific interests." Combined with these factors, they feel, was the "lower middle-class" origin of most scientists which impelled them to try to ascend the socio-economic ladder. If adjustments are made for different terminology the conclusions of Knapp and Goodrich tend to support certain hypotheses put forward in this study. The authors of *The Origins of American Scientists* are still under the spell of the "frontier thesis." Since the scientists covered in their survey did not come from anything we could call "the frontier," but rather came in large numbers from small towns, we might venture to correct their generalizations somewhat to this effect: "Protestant orthodoxy and the psychology of the small town engendered an ideal of professional 'calling,' a fluidity of social organization, and an ethic of service to the larger good that, in an increasingly materialistic and secular society, made science a most attractive field for young men from thousands of small-town communities."

The fact that a very large proportion of scientists were the sons or grandsons of Protestant clergymen would seem to give added emphasis to this substitute generalization. Knapp and Goodrich state that great "importance must be attached to the cultural background of the students, specifically the types of communities from which they come, their religious affiliations, and their class membership," and they voice their suspicion that individuals from small-town environments "possess in common certain distinguishing attributes of character, among them strong individualistic incentives to achievement, pragmatism . . . democratic ideology, rationalism and empiricism of outlook, and frequently sobriety, thrift, and other fundamental Protestant virtues." [9] If we exclude the essentially meaningless references to small-town "pragmatism . . . rationalism and empiricism" as an untenable part of the Turner myth, we will recognize at once that the colonized towns produced in large numbers the character type described above.

Unfortunately no adequate statistical studies have been made of the origins of other professional and academic groups. We do know of course that great numbers of ministers, teachers, and professors came out of the same institutions which in the late nineteenth and early twentieth centuries were producing such disproportionately large numbers of scientists; it is hard to believe therefore that the academic disciplines covered by the terms "humanities" and "social sciences" did not recruit a large proportion of their members from the same environment which produced so many scientists.

[9] Knapp and Goodrich: *Origins of American Scientists,* pp. 291–3.

. . . Makes Good

There is some evidence that as the cities began to produce a larger proportion of the outstanding scientists, the towns began to produce the great majority of engineers. In the 1920's, exactly 61 percent of the American engineers came from towns with populations of under 25,000. As a professional group these individuals were overwhelmingly of Protestant northwestern European stock and of the character type that we are already familiar with as a typical product of the small town. The average engineer accepted the town's version of the ethic without question. Again education was the channel which carried the aspiring small-town boy upward. The residential mobility of the engineers is indicated by the fact that 59 percent left their own states after graduation as opposed to 38 percent of all other graduates leaving home for greener pastures. Herbert Hoover, "the great engineer," was the classic success story of the profession. A small-town boy, Hoover combined the ethic of service with the ethic of success, and thus suggested to his fellows how the old might be profitably amalgamated with the new. Moreover as engineers moved in increasing numbers to the management side of industry, the profession provided access to the inner circles of the business elite.

In general however the town provided a relatively small proportion of the business leaders of the country. From the early colonial days the commercial towns produced their own merchants and tradesmen. It was only with the great expansion of commerce and industry in the first decades of the nineteenth century that many ambitious small-town boys made their way in the world of business and industry. As late as the 1870's approximately 64 percent of the leaders of one key industry (textiles) had been born in towns of less than 8,000 and 80 percent of the railroad tycoons and 77 percent of the steel entrepreneurs had come from such communities. Yet the picture shifted rapidly; Francis Gregory and Irene Neu, investigating the origins of the American industrial elite, conclude that "the typical industrial leader of the 1870's" was not a refugee from the slums of Europe or from a paternal farm, but "American by birth, of a New England father, English in national origin, Congregational, Presbyterian, or Episcopalian in religion, urban in early environment . . . born and bred in an atmosphere in which business and a relatively high social standing were intimately associated with his family life." [1]

W. Loyd Warner and James C. Abegglen likewise argue that the small towns and small cities of America "are not important sources of the business elite." However, "when the occupation of father, the region of birth, and the size of the birthplace are considered jointly, the very small part played by the small-town and rural South in business leadership is sharply revealed." [2] In C. Wright Mills's words, "for the whole of United States history: the typical member of the American business elite is of northeastern origin. . . . He did not migrate westward to success. He was definitely of the Upper classes by birth . . . and was educated well above the level of the general population. . . . The father of the business elite has typically been a business man." [3]

The truth has not shattered the myth which is expressed in classic form in the following quotation:

Most of the men who have battled their way up the steeps of life and occupy places of prominence in the

[1] Frances W. Gregory and Irene D. Neu: "Industrial Elite in the 1870's," in William Miller, ed.: *Men in Business* (Cambridge, Mass.: Harvard University Press; 1952); see also Chapter XI, William Miller: "The Business Elite in Business Bureaucracies: Careers of Top Executives in the Twentieth Century," in ibid.

[2] W. Lloyd Warner and James C. Abegglen: *Big Business Leaders in America* (New York: Harper & Brothers; 1955), pp. 17, 26.

[3] C. Wright Mills: "The American Business Elite: A Collective Portrait," in "The Tasks of Economic History," *Journal of Economic History*, Supplement V (December, 1945), p. 44. See also Irwin G. Wyllie: *The Self-Made Man in America, The Myth of Rags to Riches* (New Brunswick, N.J.: Rutgers University Press; 1954).

world, particularly in the business world, have come from the small town or the farm. The list is an imposing one, too lengthy to be quoted here, but almost without exception it is the small town boy who wins his way to fame and fortune. Perhaps this is not true because he possesses any greater ability than his city cousin, but because he has learned to burn the midnight oil, to sacrifice his desires and pleasures to duties. He has learned not to be distracted by the bright lights. So all he knows is to work, and as work makes for success, and success makes for prominence, he acquires both.[4]

This passage, written in 1936, demonstrates the durability of the myth. Here is the ethic in its pure form, unclouded by any doubt.

The town then contributed disproportionately to the professions, but to business it contributed very little. Taking a more general category of "notables," in this instance individuals who attained sufficient prominence in life to be included in one edition or another of *Who's Who,* the record of the town is an impressive one. The suburb is, as one might suspect, the highest producer of "notables" because it is a sub-community segregated according to income, educational opportunity, and social position. Thus it is or has been the residence of a more or less self-perpetuating business elite. But close behind the suburb in the production of outstanding individuals comes the town. Since the town is predominantely middle and lower-middle class in character, its production of "notables" is far more impressive than that of the suburb, which is already the result of a process of natural selection. According to Stephen Visher's figures the large city suburb had a relative productivity index of 10.9 while the town (up to 8,000) had one of 8.9 and the city (over 50,000) one of 5.6. The farm takes a very poor last place as a producer of outstand-

[4] Edwin P. Chase, "Forty Years of Main Street," *Iowa Journal of History,* XXXIV (July, 1936), p. 229.

ing individuals with a productivity index of 1.0, giving the towns a productivity nine times greater than that of the farms. When one takes into account the fact that many towns were entirely unproductive, the role of the productive towns is all the more remarkable.[5]

It is apparently in the fine arts and in business that the city has made its principal contributions. According to a skimpy but suggestive survey of occupational origins made in the late 1920's, almost 90 percent of the individuals in the field of the fine arts were city-bred. On the other hand 68 percent of the scientists had come from small towns, while the Army and Navy had drawn some 70 percent from the towns, the ministry 73 percent, and education 76 percent.[6]

The failure of the town to produce artists can perhaps be attributed in large part to the traditional hostility of American Protestantism to the plastic and visual arts. Puritanism, and most of its offshoots among the radical Protestant sects, rejected adornment while they revered oral and written eloquence and honored education. The bright boy was the boy who read omnivorously and showed a precocious facility with words—the minister, teacher, writer, and later, the scientist who could accomplish practical magic.

The overall picture that emerges is one of extraordinary upward mobility from the towns to the cities and the wider arenas of national life. All towns exported their youth in large numbers, but the fate of such young people varied widely, often in relation to the type of town from which they had come. The cumulative town, the essentially inchoate community, dispatched the great majority of its

[5] Stephen S. Visher: "A Study of the Type of the Place and Birth and of the Occupation of Fathers of Subjects of Sketches in 'Who's Who in America,'" *American Journal of Sociology*, XXX (March 25, 1925), p. 551.
[6] Roy H. Holmes: "A Study in the Origins of Distinguished Living Americans," *American Journal of Sociology*, XXXIV (January, 1929), pp. 670–85.

youth to other towns and to the cities to constitute again a lower-middle- and middle-class element, if they did not indeed often sink to even lower occupational and social status in the city.

Of those who "made good" the vast majority came from communities given coherence by some form of the covenant, towns where the Protestant ethic retained much of its force and where channels were created through which the energetic and ambitious got a leg up for their ascent to higher strata of the society.

The towns moreover served as staging areas and conditioners where upwardly mobile individuals, or, more properly, families, stopped off on the way from the farm to the city. Studies of the origins of business leaders and what data we have on the background of professional men show that, while very few ever made the transition from farm to upper strata of the city, a great many successful individuals were the grandsons of farmers whose sons had moved to town.

As the farming population contracted the importance of the town as an intermediary between the farm and city grew. The town, with its essentially rural tradition and its relatively sophisticated and complex social and cultural life, prevented the development of a rural peasantry in America and bridged what in most cultures has been a wide gap between farm and city.

But more than this, the town produced a highly mobile character type that proved ideally suited to play a succession of virtually important roles in the development of the United States: the small-town boy who generation after generation made good, and making good, helped to make America.

XIII

The Town in American Literature

U NTIL THE LAST FEW DECADES the overwhelming majority of American novels have had a small-town setting. We might thus take the novel and the short story as an index to the importance of the town in the "American experience." Not only did most Americans live in towns down to the end of the nineteenth century, but the literature they read was concerned with town life; whether the town was accurately described in such fiction or whether it was transmuted by the writer's particular vision, at the very least these images of the town tell us a good deal about how many Americans viewed the small community. The town was the setting the vast majority of American writers prior to the present generation used, because these men had been brought up in towns and their basic apprehension of America was a small-town apprehension. In most cases not only was the town the only environment that the novelist knew intimately, it was also the only coherent community, the only arrangement of people living together that was manageable in terms of the existing conventions of the novel. Nineteenth-century English novels dealt with classes and their relation to each other or simply with the relations of members of a particular class to one another. These were classes defined by tradition, quite visible and quite recognizable. In the absence of a plainly demarcated European class system, the human group that the American novelist had to deal with was, if only by default, the small town.

It was not until the mid-1920's that the city emerged as a common locale for the American novel. Henry James of course used Boston as the setting for several of his novels and Henry Adams's *Democracy* is laid in post-Civil War Washington. William Dean Howells's *The Rise of Silas Lapham* recounts the move of a country boy to the city, and a number of other nineteenth-century novels deal with this theme. But generally when the city appears it is seen in contrast to the town and the town predominates until the rise of the so-called proletarian novel of the 1930's. It might be argued that indeed it only gives way to the city with the appearance of the second-generation immigrant novelist and most conspicuously perhaps with the Jewish novelist who takes the big-city ghetto as his subject. And this subject after all might be called the small town *in* the city, since the racial neighborhood is almost invariably the setting. Because the city—not the ghetto or the neighborhood—as a *place*, as a part of the American landscape, presents such staggering problems of assimilation for the writer, the town continues to reassert itself, generally the New England town, now a refuge of the exurbanite. James Gould Cozzens in *The Last Adam* and *By Love Possessed*, John Cheever in *The Wapshot Chronicle* and *The Wapshot Scandals*, John Updike in *Rabbit, Run,* and *The Centaur*, Peter De Vries in *The Tunnel of Love* and *Reu-*

ben, Reuben and *Comfort Me With Apples,* and John P. Marquand in *Point of No Return* all have made use of small-town settings. But these are vastly different towns of course. They have been appropriated by the rootless middle-class intellectual whose origin, orientation, and income are all urban. Such towns, valued for their charm and the vestiges of history that cling to them, are inhabited by refugees from the cities; they have become to all intents and purposes urban dependencies.

Although novelists starting with Charles Brockden Brown used small-town settings, it was New England women who in a sense invented the town as an aspect of our literature. Harriet Beecher Stowe was the first of a long line of female writers that extended from Sarah Orne Jewett and Mary Wilkins Freeman to Alice Brown and Edith Wharton, and moved West at the turn of the century to include Zona Gale and Willa Cather. The town may thus be seen as the most successful genre of the American female novelist. It is of course impossible to say whether the lady novelists and short-story writers made such a mark in nineteenth-century literature because of the happy coincidence that they made the town their own special preserve, discovered and explored it, or whether their relative eminence was incidental to the town rather than the consequence of their exploitation of it.

Certainly it is tempting to speculate about the social currents of the time that drew women's attention to the town. Did the town offer a quintessential opportunity for the particular gifts of observation and sensitivity that may be special feminine attributes? Or were women moved to examine its meaning by a sense of personal loss that came with the growing decadence of the town or from witnessing the more vigorous males leaving the town (especially the New England town from the early years of the nineteenth century on) for greener pastures?

The nineteenth-century woman was of course far less mobile than her present-day counterpart and vastly less mobile than the small-town male. The woman's exploitation of the town may have been in part a consequence of the fact that a number of unusually intelligent and energetic ladies were marooned in towns that had lost their most enterprising and adventurous men.

But if women like Harriet Beecher Stowe and Rose Terry Cooke turned their attention to the New England village because they were marooned there, there was little hint of bitterness in the idyllic scenes of small-town life that they painted. Harriet Beecher Stowe provided the prototype in *Oldtown Folks* (1869). Old Town was a place of pleasant intimacy whose center was the general store

> where the post office was kept, and where there was a general exchange of news, as the different farm-wagons stood hitched around the door, and their owners spent a leisure moment in discussing politics or theology from the top of the codfish or mackerel barrels, while their wives and daughters were shopping among the dress goods and ribbons.[1]

Sarah Orne Jewett, the daughter of a country doctor, developed the genre with more skill and sophistication than did Mrs. Stowe. William Dean Howells sponsored the publication of her *Deephaven* (1877), a collection of stories about the Maine town in which she grew up. Rose Terry Cooke mixed realism with Victorian sentimentality in a series of books that convey with a good deal of humor and sympathy the lives of small-town people: *Somebody's Neighbors* (1881), *Root-bound and Other Sketches* (1885), and *The Sphinx's Children and Other People* (1886). Alice Brown was another writer whose subject was the decadent New England town. Her novels, short stories, and her play *Children of Earth* (1915) show a sympathetic insight into frustrated and impoverished lives;

[1] Harriet Beecher Stowe: *Oldtown Folks* (Boston: Fields, Osgood & Co.; 1869), p. 2.

she is best known for her collections of stories about New England life, among them *Meadow-Grass* (1895) and *Tiverton Tales* (1899). With Alice Brown we come virtually to the end of a genre started fifty years earlier by Harriet Beecher Stowe.

Nathaniel Hawthorne's novels *The House of Seven Gables* (1850) and *The Scarlet Letter* (1851) may be taken as examples of tales in which the small-town locales presented are, at least to a large degree, incidental to the unfolding lives of particular characters. The same thing could be said of St. Petersburg, Missouri, the setting for *The Adventures of Tom Sawyer* (1876) and *The Adventures of Huckleberry Finn* (1884). The town in these novels is largely assumed, a part of the landscape. But Twain came, step by step, to see the town first as opposed to the city and then as a microcosm of the larger world. "Human nature," he wrote, "cannot be studied in cities except at a disadvantage—a village is the place." And gradually, as Twain soured on the world, the idyllic setting of Hannibal came to be peopled with fools and knaves. In *The Man that Corrupted Hadleyburg* (1889) we have a bitter story of human corruptibility set in a small town.

But it is not clear that Twain's disillusion was concurrent with the clouded image of the town. The object of his scorn was human nature as expressed in the greedy, hypocritical people of Hadleyburg. There is no suggestion that it is small-town life which has made them what they are. Human nature, not the town, was Twain's villain.

As early as Hamlin Garland's *A Son of the Middle Border* (1917), with its vivid portrayal of the bleakness of life in a Midwestern community, we begin to get the pictures of the dismal side of the small town. In *Main-Travelled Roads* (1891) Robert Bloom speaks for Garland when he says of the townspeople:

> They talk every rag of gossip into shreds. 'Taters, fish, hops; hops, fish, 'taters. They have saved and pinched and toiled till their souls are pinched and

ground away. . . . Talk about the health of village life! It destroys body and soul. It debilitates me. It will warp us down to the level of these people. . . . Their squat little town is a caricature of themselves. Everything they touch they belittle.[2]

But it is in Sherwood Anderson's *Winesburg, Ohio* (1919) that we can identify most clearly the second stage in the literary career of the town. In a ten-year period that extended from the publication of Willa Cather's *O Pioneers!* (1913), Anderson's *Windy McPherson's Son* (1916), and Edgar Lee Masters's *Spoon River Anthology* (1915) to Sinclair Lewis's *Main Street* (1920) and *Babbitt* (1922), the image of the American town changed dramatically from a place of semi-rural innocence to a symbol of the crassness, the cultural aridity and ugly materialism of American life. The shift can perhaps best be measured in the work of one writer, Zona Gale, who took a small town as the setting for her novels and short stories and whose active writing career spans the two dominant eras of the town as it appears in our literature. In *Friendship Village Love Stories* (1908) Miss Gale spoke of the fellowship that characterized Friendship:

> I think that in this simple basic emotion lies my joy in living in this, my village. Here, this year long, folk have been adventuring together, knowing the details of one another's lives, striving a little but companioning more than striving, kindling to one another's interests instead of practicing the faint morality of mere civility. "I declare [she has one of her characters exclaim], it wasn't so much the stuff they brought in, though that was elegant, but it was the Togetherness of it. I couldn't get to sleep that night for thinkin' about God not havin' anybody to neighbor with." [3]

[2] Hamlin Garland: *Main-Travelled Roads* (New York: The Macmillan Company; 1899), p. 2.
[3] Zona Gale: *Friendship Village Love Stories* (New York: The Macmillan Company; 1909), p. 6.

In the same year that Sinclair Lewis published *Main Street*, Zona Gale's *Miss Lulu Bett* appeared and was hailed by many of the same critics who praised *Main Street* as a cruelly accurate picture of the pinched and constricted life of the Midwestern town. What had happened in the interim? From Hannibal to Hadleyburg, from Oldtown to Main Street, from Friendship Village to the sterile, greedy community that was the home of Miss Lulu Bett, the town seemed to have decayed, or at the very least changed almost beyond recognition. Was the change in the town or in the eyes of the beholders? Certainly the theme of change was already a familiar one in the towns themselves, as we have seen. And the change was almost invariably for the worse. Such at least was the opinion of pioneers reminiscing about the early days. In Miss Cather's *O Pioneers!* and later again in *My Ántonia* we have the lament so common to the older settlers: the spirit of unity, of neighborliness, of community that was so strong in the early stages of the town has been replaced by selfishness and suspicion. Edgar Lee Masters took the town as a symbol of the growing materialism that was poisoning the springs of American life. In his *Domesday Book* (1920) he finds "cleanness, high-mindedness and idealism" lacking in the town. "It seems devoid of normally happy men and women, its citizens dominated by greed, grossness and cynicism." [4]

Sherwood Anderson's *Winesburg, Ohio* was the most famous of his books, but *Poor White* (1920) is his most searching treatment of the theme of change in the town.[5] It

[4] The towns in their darkest hours had their fervent defenders. Vachel Lindsay spoke with the voice of an older generation when he wrote, "O you who lose the art of hope, whose temples seem to shrine a lie,/ Whose sidewalks are but stones of fear,/ Who weep that liberty must die,/ Turn to the little Prairie towns,/ Your higher hope shall yet begin." Athens, Oxford, and Florence were all small towns in which the human spirit had flourished. (*Collected Poems* [New York: The Macmillan Company; 1923], p.72). [5] (New York: Modern Library Edition; 1926), pp. vi–vii. Ander-

is the story of the son of a lower-class Southerner in a little Missouri town. Hugh McVey, the hero, is befriended by Sarah Shepard, daughter of a family of New England origin, a woman who has the proverbial Yankee drives for education and self-improvement. She sends him off to find the idyllic town of Bidwell, Ohio, full of bustling, efficient people of New England stock; this was where she had grown up. Hugh sets out searching for this "earthly paradise in which lived bright, clear-thinking men and beautiful women." In a way Hugh's search is the classic American odyssey. Like the search for the Holy Grail, it belongs more to a legend than to life. It is only the latest chapter of the story that began with Winthrop's little band setting out to build "a city upon a hill."

Of course Hugh's search ends in disappointment. Industrial growth had changed Bidwell almost beyond recognition. "All over the country," Hugh realized, "in the towns, the farm houses, and the growing cities of the new country, people stirred and awakened from their dream of rural innocence." What was happening—the transformation of the towns into noisome industrial cities—was part of a terrible but necessary step in the creation of the great community, "the newer, broader brotherhood into which men are some day to emerge, in extending the invisible roofs of the towns and cities to cover the world." And this new brotherhood must be built on the crushed and broken bodies of those who stood in its way or who could not adapt themselves to the changing times.[6] At the end of the novel Joe Wainsworth, the harness maker who bitterly resents the intrusion of the machine, goes berserk and kills

---

son, writing an introduction to a later edition of the book, argues that Bidwell, Ohio, was really the hero of the book though none of the critics had noted the fact. "What happened to the town," Anderson wrote, "was more important than what happened to the people of the town."

[6] Ibid., p. 129.

the opportunistic Jim Gibson and attacks Hugh. Hugh overcomes Wainsworth, but the assault awakens him to the dehumanizing effect of his beloved machines and to a sharp sense of his unwitting complicity.

Since much of American literature has had in it elements of the morality play, city and town have alternated as hero and villain. Most characteristically the town has been the hero and the city the villain, but about the time that the successful urban businessman began to applaud the town as the embodiment of American virtues, of the Protestant ethic of thrift, industry, piety, hard work, and rugged individualism, the writers began to take this same personified town and use it to expose the crassness, greed, complacency, and self-righteousness of American middle-class culture. If the town was to be made into a symbol of "Americanism," then the Philistines would have their nose rubbed in it, in its pettiness, provincialism, and moral shoddiness. We might pair E. W. Howe with Sherwood Anderson, William Allen White with Sinclair Lewis. The situation was shot through with irony. The town did not truly become the object of the novelist's attack until it had been largely integrated into the dominant urban culture and had accepted as the price for this recognition the imposition of the city's values upon the town. The town then, in its primal innocence, was fair game. The city was still largely unmanageable as the setting for the novel, so the town had to do as a rather incongruous substitute. Babbitt was not *sui generis* a small-town figure. He was the middle-class American businessman; he was pre-eminently the man who admired the pseudo small-town aphorisms of E. W. Howe. He was more in evidence in the city, big or small, than in the town. And this, of course, was at once recognized. Babbitt was taken to be not a typical small-town figure—that was still perhaps Anderson's Windy McPherson—but "the representative average American."

Another ponderable may be found in the not unreasonable assumption that the small town suffered from the

The Town in American Literature

dominance of the liberal critical intelligence in the American literary scene. The liberal imagination in the half century from 1890 to 1940 was primarily urban. The liberal critics dominated the literary scene as surely as their neighbors, the big-city entrepreneurs, dominated the business and financial scene. They were in revolt against that which remained of what they conceived of as Victorian prudery and hypocrisy; they were the relentless critics of "the genteel tradition." Again because the town was the only element of the American experience that was manageable in traditional literary terms, the town to a degree had to stand as a surrogate of the wider and now essentially urban culture which it had been persuaded to profess that it represented. There was more to it than this of course. There was the fact that the town showed its least attractive qualities in the period of its decline. Moreover since the liberal imagination was inherently utopian and perfectionist, those human failings and frailties which were so apparent in the town—in what was doubtless their general proportion throughout the species—were thought of as being the special qualities of the town, where it was assumed they flourished in a soil rich in bigotry and provincialism.[7]

Thorstein Veblen, born in Cato Township, Wisconsin, and the beau ideal of the small-town boy in revolt against his background, wrote in 1923 of these small towns:

[7] It is interesting to note that the rise of the great school of urban sociology in Chicago was coincident with the literary attacks on the town. As Maurice Stein has pointed out, Robert Park was a small-town boy and many of his most gifted disciples likewise came from small towns in the Middle West. Stein suggests that while "the rural backgrounds of the Chicago sociologists did lead them to view their sprawling city with a slightly jaundiced eye, on the whole these men saw the rewards as well as the costs of urban living." Their revolt against their hometowns made them in a sense the first generation of Americans to see the city in some perspective. (*The Eclipse of Community* [New York: Harper & Row; 1964], p. 16.)

One must be circumspect, acquire merit and avoid offense. So one must eschew opinions, or information, which are not acceptable to the common run of those whose good will has or may conceivably come to have any commercial value. The country-town system of knowledge and belief can admit nothing that would annoy the prejudices of any appreciable number of respectable townsfolk. . . . In this sense the country town is conservative, in that it is by force of business expediency intolerant of anything but holdovers. Intellectually, institutionally and religiously the country towns of the great farming country are "standing pat" on the ground taken somewhere about the period of the Civil War.[8]

By the end of the nineteenth century American literati were traveling abroad, and in the charming villages of Europe they saw the antithesis of the towns of their homelands, the endlessly repeated main streets with their raddled storefronts, blatant drugstores, and dreary cafés whose decor bespoke nausea as surely as their menus. These travelers became suddenly aware that one could search history in vain to find human communities as bleak and graceless as the American town.[9] The result was a kind of cultural trauma that expressed itself most commonly in flight and rejection.

A writer like Floyd Dell made this flight from small-

[8] Thorstein Veblen: *The Portable Veblen*, Max Lerner, ed. (New York: Viking Press; 1961), p. 424.

[9] Waldo Frank, another town boy, spoke for those of his generation who had been expatriates when he apostrophized Paris in the opening pages of *The Rediscovery of America:* "Suddenly came Europe to me—my Europe, whose heart is France; and it was the draught I needed of freshening wine. The mellow farms, the peasants sure as their trees. The luminous eye, not of France alone but of all the western world—Paris I saw again that masterwork of modern life—intricate, mouldering, subtle, immense, intimate, generous Paris: fruit of the autumn of all the Mediterranean summer." ([New York: Charles Scribner's Sons; 1929], p. 3.)

town Midwestern America the theme of half a dozen novels and short stories. Sometimes, as in Dell's *The Briary-Bush* (1921), they fled simply to the nearest city but increasingly they fled to Europe and even, in the case of Michael Shenstone, to the Far East to find a brief haven amid that beautiful alien world. For a time it seemed indeed as though the literary landscape was filled with unhappy figures in flight from one harsh and dreary town or another.

Glenway Wescott's hero in one of the stories in *Good-bye Wisconsin* (1928) looks at his town and finds it "like any other not too new or too large or too small. . . . Main Street down the middle—beef-red brick and faded clapboards . . . lamentably unimpressive." All the young people of any ability or energy dream only of getting away and there are indeed "already a fair number of Middle-Westerners about the world; a sort of vagrant chosen race like the Jews," a group of vagabonds who really having rejected the barren ugliness of America "have no native land left. Upon these renegade children—voluntary exiles, adventurers and emigrants, brothers, cousins, or acquaintances—the others, those who have not yet taken flight, even those who never will, speculate a great deal in their own interest." [1]

And Wescott perhaps speaks for most American writers who have struggled to say something intelligible about their country when he writes of the Middle West:

> However earnestly writers proud of being natives of it may endeavor to give it form and character, it remains out of focus, amorphous and a mystery. . . . And yet—there is the sluggish emotional atmosphere, the suavity of its tedium, the morbid grandeur of its meanest predicaments; or are these illusions of those who take flight, who return? There is no Middle West. It is a certain, a certain landscape; and beyond

[1] Glenway Wescott: *Good-bye Wisconsin* (New York and London: Harper & Brothers; 1928), pp. 16, 26.

that, a state of mind of people born where they do not like to live.[2]

But where, after all do Americans "like to live"? They cannot all live in Rome or Paris, nor do they wish to, because being an American is not simply a question of nationality, but an inescapable condition of being in a way quite different from being a Frenchman or an Italian. For one thing, to be a Frenchman or a German or an Italian is to also be a European. The Frenchman (or the Englishman) after all has a place and a history, or a place saturated with history. Americans cannot all live in New York or San Francisco—but it almost comes down to that. If you cannot bear to live in the particular graceless small town in which you were born and if you have in addition a literary bent, you go to New York (once it was Chicago *or* New York). If the disheartening winters of the Midwest have broken your spirit, you go to the great expanded city of Los Angeles, five hundred square miles of sun-thickened ozone.[3]

So Americans are true Ishmaels, the rootless, "going to and fro in the earth," the perpetual migrants, and the small towns, if our literature is to be believed (and it is certainly quite possible to argue that it should not be) are railroad

[2] Ibid., p. 39.

[3] Sinclair Lewis touched on the same theme (search through the world) countless times. "He knew then," wrote Lewis of his hero in *World So Wide*, his last novel, "that he was unalterably an American; he knew what a special and mystical experience it is, for the American never really emigrates but only travels; perhaps travels for two or three generations but at the end is still marked with the gaunt image of Tecumseh." (Quoted in Mark Schorer: *Sinclair Lewis* [New York: McGraw-Hill, 1961], p. 790.) Thomas Wolfe saw himself in Lewis, "this wounded lion, this raging cat of life, forever prowling past a million portals of desire and destiny, [who] had flung himself against the walls of Europe, seeking, hunting, thirsting, starving, and lashing himself into a state of frenzied bafflement." (*You Can't Go Home Again* [New York: Harper & Brothers; 1941], p. 510.)

stations on the way to the metropolis, all comfortingly (or frighteningly) the same. Americans looked on their raw wilderness and saw Paris and Athens rising splendidly from the dark earth. They dreamed of beauty and created ugliness, for beauty was not their destiny.

As I have suggested elsewhere, the theme of the town as purity and innocence, opposed to the city as sophistication and corruption was coeval with the birth of the Republic. Charles Brockden Brown's Arthur Mervyn, in the prototype of all such experiences, went from the town to the city and in the city experienced evil, alienation, coldness of heart and greed, the antithesis of the life of the genuine community.[4]

In his footsteps followed hundreds of literary characters, small town or farm boys going from home to the wilderness of the American city. Paul Piehler argues that a classic theme of literature from the Gilgamesh Epic through medieval times has been that of the hero who ventures from the city into the wilderness for a time of testing in which he typically encounters terror in the form of some frightful beast and seduction in the form of a temptress. In the American epic the form is reversed. The hero leaves the town, which is in a sense in the wilderness, and goes to the city, which is the true wilderness, where he experiences the terror of loneliness and the various seductions of the metropolis which has idolized an abstract

[4] Only one play forces itself upon our attention as part of the literature of the town. Thornton Wilder's *Our Town* appeared in the 1930's, when the town was still generally in disrepute. Its mood is one of frank sentiment and nostalgia for the classic form of American community life. But Wilder chose the town as a symbol of the enduring rhythms and the everlastingness of existence—the cycle of birth, marriage, and death the unchanging nature of the town. Wilder subordinates one of the basic characteristics of the town—change—to the unchanging drama of life and death. The play has about it, in muted tone, much of the poignance that characterizes Wolfe's work and Ross Lockridge's *Raintree County* (Boston: Houghton Mifflin Company; 1948).

sexuality. Of course the notion of the city as evil is not new, as witness Sodom and Gomorrah and Babylon. This notion is perhaps predominantly Judaeo-Christian, but it is undoubtedly the case that a Bible-oriented culture picked up much of its suspicion of the city from scriptural sources.

Whatever its origin, the suspicion of the city is in the literature as surely as it is in the political and social thought of America. Willa Cather's heroine in *O Pioneers!* cries out passionately to Carl Linstrum, who tries city life and returns to the farm, "I'd rather have had your freedom than my land." Carl's answer contains the classic Jeffersonian indictment of the city:

> "Freedom so often means that one isn't needed any-where. Here you are an individual, you have a back-ground of your own, you would be missed. But off there in the cities there are thousands of rolling stones like me. We are all alike; we have no ties, we know nobody, we own nothing. When one of us dies, they scarcely know where to bury him. . . . We have no house, no place, no people of our own. We live in the streets, in the parks, in the theatres. We sit in the res-taurants and concert hall and look about at the hun-dreds of our own kind and shudder." [5]

In Booth Tarkington's novel *The Gentleman from Indiana* (1899) we have much the same theme. John Harkless, the editor of the *Carlow County Herald*, who has gone East to college and then returned to his home town of Plattville, is restless and dissatisfied. But he had left the city because he was "heart-sick" over "the rush and fight and scramble to be first, to beat the other man. . . . I saw classmates and college friends diving into it, and bound to come out ahead," and too busy to ask, "What does it get me?" He had been repelled by "the cruel competition, the

[5] Willa Cather: *O Pioneers!* (Boston and New York: Houghton Mifflin Company; 1913), p. 123.

thousands fighting for places, the multitude scrambling for each ginger-bread baton, the cold faces in the streets. . . ." He came to value the people of Plattville for their kindness. Not rich, nor smart, nor fashionable, but kind. And when he was elected to Congress by his fellow citizens, he told them: "To represent you is to stand for realities—fearlessness, honor, kindness. . . ." [6]

A hundred similar examples could be quoted. Through all of Thomas Wolfe's boyhood in Asheville "the great vision of the city burned forever in his brain." [7] Yet when he went to the city he found it, as had all those small-town boys who had preceded him, a place full of glittering artificiality. The city is Mobway, the home of Standard Concentrated Production Units of America and its symbol is the suicide of the "unidentified" man, C. Green, who leaps to his death from the Admiral Drake Hotel. Wolfe wrote feelingly of "the sweat and noise and violence" of the city; the "grimy brick and stone . . . months of tainted air and tainted life, of treachery, fear, malice, slander, blackmail, envy, hatred, conflict, fury, and deceit . . . frenzy and tension of wire-taut nerves and changeless change." [8]

[6] Booth Tarkington: *The Gentleman from Indiana* (New York: Doubleday and McClure Company; 1899), p. 369.
[7] Thomas Wolfe: *You Can't Go Home Again* (New York: Harper & Brothers; 1941), p. 305.
[8] Ibid., p. 531. There is of course no indication that Americans today are any more at peace with themselves about the city than they have been in the past. The city, like the town, remains an ambivalent image. From the simpler, older notion of the city as the particular residence of the Dark One we now see the city as the most critical "problem" in American life. The urbanites have fled to the suburbs and the central city is more and more the preserve of marginal Americans, predominantly, of course, of the Negroes. It is a curious paradox that at the very moment when we have become an overwhelmingly urban culture the heart of the city is rotting away from abuse and neglect.

In some ways the classic fact about the small town as it appears in American literature is the obvious ambivalence of the authors who write about it. Certainly Sherwood Anderson could be taken as one of the harshest critics of small-town life. He found in the communities of the Midwest a symbol of the "cheapness and materialism" of American life. Yet when in his later years he came to settle in the town of Marion, Virginia, in the classic role of a small-town newspaper editor, he wrote in *Hello Towns!* (1929) a final testament to the saving qualities of small-town life.

Similarly, Grace Lewis argues that her husband's *Main Street* is full of nostalgia for the true community. Carol Kennicott with her touching yearning for culture, for a wider, more generous life, was a real heroine to Lewis, who had in fact a very commonplace, middle-class notion of life and yearned for nothing so much as a rose-covered cottage to share with his socialite bride. The letters that Lewis wrote to his fiancée would have been perfectly appropriate to a young man in Gopher Prairie or Sauk Centre. If we may trust Grace Lewis, her husband was surprised that his painstaking effort to depict small-town life accurately was hailed by the critics as satire.[9] It is certain in any case that Lewis's relation to Gopher Prairie or Sauk Centre was a classic love-hate relationship, and Lewis, uprooted from Sauk Centre and wandering about the world, remained a small-town boy looking for but never finding the consolations of home. There is a curious poignance in the story that Grace Lewis tells of their son, Lance, killed in World War II. Lance, for whom Lewis had never been able to function as a real father, had planned before his death to write a novel about a famous writer, a deracinated intellectual, who roamed through the great cities of the world seeking peace and came at last to find it in the very kind of small town he had once scorned.

[9] Grace Hegger Lewis: *With Love from Gracie; Sinclair Lewis: 1912–1925* (New York: Harcourt, Brace & Company; 1955).

The most biting critics of the town came back, ultimately, chastened and repentant.[1]

Perhaps of all the American writers whose work is suffused with a sense of the town Thomas Wolfe is the most significant. From *Look Homeward, Angel* through *You Can't Go Home Again* Wolfe's childhood in Asheville, North Carolina, is a recurrent theme. In *Look Homeward, Angel,* it is as though all the longing, the anguish, the wild and despairing search for meaning and beauty that tore at the bowels of every young man in every American town had come to a focus. Wolfe's father, "melodramatic, opinionated, fond of spouting poetry and denunciations of fancied perils or enemies, a lover of beauty . . . a spree drinker of terrifying endurance and violence," a casual and inept provider, is the archetypal small-town male whom we have already met in a hundred variations, and his mother, Julia Westall, is equally the archetypal mother, shrewd, vital, indefatigable, terrible in her love and in her ambition for her son.

The archetypal town, the great unfathomable town, was so deeply in Wolfe's blood that after he had gone to the University of North Carolina he would leave Chapel Hill and rush off to towns nearby to register at shabby hotels as John Donne or William Blake or Robert Browning. In his mind's eye he saw on these wild journeys "ten thousand sleeping towns," and speculated on "the infinite rich variety of all the towns and faces: behind any of a

[1] One of Sinclair Lewis's last books, *Work of Art* (1934), reaffirmed the values of small-town life. Ruth Suckow in *Cora* (1929) showed her nostalgia for what is plainly Hawarden, Iowa, the town of her childhood, and in a subsequent volume of short stories she uses several variations of the theme of the small-town boy who becomes a wealthy city man but finds that his success is dust compared to the simple virtues of his hometown. Helen Merrell Lynd recalls that the classic description of a Baptist revival meeting in *Middletown* was hailed by an urban critic as scathing satire and acclaimed by the church itself as an accurate and sympathetic account.

million shabby houses he believed there was strange buried life, subtle and shattered romance, something dark and unknown." [2]

In the college community he longed for the wider world. Beyond Chapel Hill lay

> the ugly rolling land, sparse with cheap farmhouses, beyond all this, America—more land, more wooden houses, more towns, hard and raw and ugly. . . . Only the earth endured—the gigantic American earth, bearing upon its awful breast a world of flimsey rickets. . . . There was no ruined image of Menkaura, there was no alabaster head of Akhnaton. Nothing had been done in stone. Only this earth endured. . . . Within its hills he had been held a stranger. . . . And the old hunger returned—the terrible and obscure hunger that haunts and hurts Americans, and makes us exiles at home and strangers wherever we go. [3]

Returning from Chapel Hill Wolfe found he could not remain in Asheville. He went to Harvard and later to New York, but the ghost of his home dogged his footsteps. When *Look Homeward, Angel* came out he was devastated by the reception that it received in Asheville. "So overwhelming was his sense of loathing and guilt that he coveted the place of murderers on whom the world visited the fierceness of its wrath." [4] He went back at last, to encounter the contempt and anger of his former neighbors. Evil, blind Judge Bland had spoken to him on the train returning to Asheville the fatally prophetic words—"You can't go home again." And he found it to be true. Only in the cemetery, as yet undisturbed by the town's mad lust for real estate speculation, did Wolfe have the sense of things as they had always been. "But the town of his childhood, with its quiet streets and old houses, which had been

[2] Thomas Wolfe: *Look Homeward, Angel* (New York: Modern Library edition), p. 597.
[3] Wolfe: *You Can't Go Home Again*, pp. 423–4.
[4] Ibid., p. 131.

obscured below the leafy spread of trees, was changed beyond recognition, scarred now with hard patches of bright concrete and raw clumps of new construction." Everything had changed as everything inevitably did in America.

Wolfe left Asheville once again to return to New York and to go from there to a Germany already infected by Nazism. But Asheville was never far away: "He remembered how many times he had thought of home with such an intensity of passion that he could close his eyes and see the scheme of every street, and the faces of the people, as well as the countless things that they had said and the densely-woven fabric of all their histories." [5]

When Wolfe traveled to England, a dramatic encounter in London brought together two small-town boys, one (Sinclair Lewis) world famous; the other (Wolfe) younger and much less well known. They were in a sense partners, though strangely ill-assorted ones, in a doom-haunted search whose most persistent themes were loneliness, the seeking of a father, the love and hate of America, and the strange triangle of small town, great city, and ancient impenetrable Europe. From Lewis Wolfe learned that fame was no real balm and that the search, the journey through the world, must bring him back to America to the death he sought and anticipated in the final moving postscript to Foxhall Edwards at the end of *You Can't Go Home Again:* "My tale is finished and so farewell. But before I go, I have just one more thing to tell you: Something has spoken to me in the night, burning the tapers of the waning year; something has spoken in the night, and told me I shall die, I know not where." [6]

Granted that all novels are autobiographical in the sense that the author begins with his own experience and fantasies from it, the degree to which the novel is autobiographical is a matter of considerable importance. The more completely the author invests his work with the form

[5] Ibid., p. 99.   [6] Ibid., p. 369.

and details of his own life, the more rapidly he exhausts the raw material of creation. Wolfe was so lavish in this that his life and his art were in a sense coterminous. One had to end with the other; life and art were fused and Wolfe did not even care to wait until what would have been his last novel was published.

Wolfe's one great book, made up of all his books, is not so much a novel as it is a kind of great American utterance, a long, exaltant, and tormented testament to what it has meant in its most memorable and bitter way to have grown up in and then left the small town, seeking America. It is both not a novel and the great American novel. While Lewis worked in the much more conventional forms of the novel Wolfe had the courage to be at once the first and last great autobiographical novelist in the sense that he pursued himself to the edge of death, and when he had nothing more to say about the "Wolfean Writer in Search of the Meaning of America" he willed his death as Ross Lockridge later committed his. (And this is why critics, especially the more academic ones, have hardly known what to do with Wolfe's book. They have walked around it, prodding at it with their pens, awed by its immense and crude vitality, and dismayed by its vast chaos and disorder.) In its own strange way it is the last nineteenth-century American novel and the first modern American novel of tortured introspection. But Wolfe was saved from the thinness and air of exhaustion that cling to so many novels of this latter genre by the fact that he still looked outward to discover the meaning of himself in the meaning of America, an enterprise that if it staggers us with its presumption nonetheless created for Wolfe an enduring place in literature.

Wolfe was the last major writer before the disappearance of the town to grasp it and shape it into literature in the wild, flamboyant prose that speaks so much of American dreams and yearnings. The small town as an independent, self-reliant, vital, optimistic social entity, as the classic American social entity, has disappeared. An adjunct of the city, a suburb integrated into the dominant culture of the megalopolis, it is no longer available to the writer as a symbol for America. And it seems unlikely that the city, changing, inchoate, diffuse, sprawling, and unmanageable can soon replace it.

Ross Lockridge's *Raintree County* has, with the exception of Wolfe's extended autobiography, as good a claim as any single work to the title of "the great American novel." Lockridge, born and raised in Bloomington, Indiana, had the inspired notion of deriving his novel from the classic town and county histories that form such a rich and unmined literature of the small town of the American past. The endpapers of the original edition of Lockridge's book are marvelously evocative of all such histories—the large, ugly courthouse, the stiff churches, the farms lithographed on commission from their proud owners. These "memoirs" differ from the more orthodox late nineteenth-century town histories, especially those of New England, in that they are simply raw material—the faces, farms, businesses, and vital statistics, primarily of the subscribers. On the foundation of the memoirs Lockridge re-creates the town of Freehaven and a cast of small-town characters—the revival minister, the Reverend Lloyd G. Jarvey; Cash Carney, the town's tycoon; Professor Jerusalem Webster Stiles and his Academy; Senator Garwood B. Jones; and the hero, young John Shawnessy, foot runner extraordinary, Union soldier, teacher, and archetype of the small-town boy.

Lockridge puts all of the historic town in this book— phrenology; the Teachers' Institutes; a small-town Fourth of July; a Temperance drive; a revival meeting; the drama of the Civil War; the graveyard of Danwebster, where lie "the beloved sleepers in the earth of Raintree County," a symbol likewise of the strange and unperceived destiny of the land itself; the train—its thunder "the voice of years and fates, crying at the intersections; it is the bullhead beast, who runs on a Cretan maze of iron roads and chases the naked sacrifices hither and thither." [7]

John Shawnessy is obsessed by the meaning and the fate of Raintree County: "Nothing would remain at last except the name itself, itself a legend, beautiful and talismanic, a sound of magic and of recollection, a phrase of music and strangeness—Raintree County." [8] Like Eugene Gant, young Shawnessy struggles to penetrate the meaning of America: "What ever the days of a man? Where did the small brown roads lead him at last? Who could preserve the ancient verities of Raintree County?" This is the book's refrain. John Shawnessy seeks the hero (himself?) and discovers that his hero is Humanity "and the place in which the Hero strove for beauty and the good was the Republic. Both Hero and Republic were immense fictions. . . . For he had localized the great myth of the Republic in Raintree County." [9]

Again like Wolfe, Shawnessy can't go back to Raintree County, "because it won't be there. . . . *Not one little thing* [italics in original] can escape change and death." The novel ends on a falling note of sadness and of dreaming, the dreams of the great strange land where John Shawnessy, the mythic hero, carrying under his arm the immense *Historical Atlas*, walks home through Waycross in the soft evening, "lost and yet not lost, away and yet at home, forever awake and yet forever dreaming," [1] a note hauntingly like that of George Webber in *You Can't Go Home Again*. Within a year Lockridge, like Wolfe, exhausted by his struggle to articulate America and emptied of all he could ever say, was dead by his own hand, one of the briefest and strangest literary careers in our history. It is almost too pat—the tragedy of the towns, Freehaven and Waycross absorbed into the vast indifference of urban America intermingled with and almost indistinguishable from Lockridge's own tragedy, as though he had written

[7] Lockridge: *Raintree County*, pp. 232–3.

[8] Ibid., p. 45. [9] Ibid., pp. 234, 1020. [1] Ibid., p. 1060.

himself into the material actual person of his hero, Shawnessy, and then had, like him, to pass into "the legend of a
life upon earth and of a river running through the land, a
signature of father and preserver, of some young hero and
endlessly courageous dreamer" [2] who had come to the end
of his dreams. And mixed in of course was the myth of
American success. *Raintree County* was a Book-of-the-
Month Club selection, a best seller purchased for the
movies, acclaimed in *Life* magazine, certain to make its
author rich and successful.

It is hard to read *Raintree County* without feeling the
passion and anguish of the book's creation. To try to put
the essence of America into a novel surely requires considerable courage. What resulted could hardly, like Wolfe's
vast autobiography, be judged as a novel. As an historian I
am, I suppose, peculiarly vulnerable to a novel such as
Lockridge's (the "such as" is inaccurate since there are no
others like it), which shows so profound and sympathetic
an understanding of America's past. *Raintree County* asks
to be judged as something more or less but certainly
different from the conventional novel. It might better be
placed between a sad, wild poem and an imaginative
narrative history. At the very least it seems safe to say that
no novelist has employed the materials of small-town
history to better effect.

In that terrible self-consciousness, that torment and
agony that have been the particular burden of many
American writers, they could not seem to write without
addressing themselves to the meaning of America. One
cannot imagine European writers trying to explicate the
meaning of France, or England, or Germany. Only a
Tolstoi or a Dostoevski was capable of conceiving a novel
that might try to tell "the meaning of Russia." Yet hardly
an American author from Hawthorne to Thomas Wolfe
has failed to make such an attempt. Space and place are
obliterated in American fiction (with the important excep-
[2] Ibid.

tion of the Southern writers) and Time reigns supreme. William Faulkner, perhaps the truest American novelist of the twentieth century, had the incredibly sure instinct to create a world of almost inexhaustible richness which he could explore for a lifetime. By the same token he understood what Wolfe was doing and he realized the dangerous and ultimately tragic investment of himself that Wolfe made in his great extended novel. Thus Faulkner was generous enough to place Wolfe ahead of himself.

I wonder if it is going too far to suggest that at least part of the contemporary novelist's preoccupation with interior states is a consequence of several irredeemable facts. The novelist is no longer a small-town boy, for the small town no longer produces such progeny; moreover the small town, having vanished, is no longer accessible to the novelist. America, if it has classes, has none worth talking about or writing about. The city is at the moment unmanageable, and the American imagination in any event is not ready to accept it as the symbol of our national experience. If one cannot go out to the world, one must turn in, to the self. Thus, as Nelson Algren has put it, the question that the contemporary novelist addresses himself to is, "Who am I?"—and a very dull question it is—rather than the equally unanswerable but infinitely more interesting question, "What does it mean to be an American?" But even the latter question, like the former, is presently irrelevant. Perhaps the only question any longer worth asking is, "What is man?" Perhaps when America is willing to lose its soul, that haunted, wandering, fatherless soul, that soul lost in space, searching for home, it will find it at last, or at least make a beginning of finding it, in a somewhat larger category—that of the human race.

To be sure such an issue lies outside the sphere of this book. We mean only to say what is plain enough: that the American small town has in our literature stood for America, been the one common experience accessible to the vast majority of our novelists who have dealt with it well or ill according to their lights and their times; and that, as the setting or the subject of a short story or novel, it can no longer convince us of its value as a universal symbol or even I suspect as a very interesting or important fragment of American life.

What is perhaps most worth remarking is that the town should have appeared as the archetype and image of America, and in that role should have pre-empted the greater part of our literature. Art, in perhaps all the high cultures of the past, has been principally an artifact of the city, where leisure, sophistication, and learning resided. In nineteenth-century America the cities were, as they always have been, the marketplace and distribution point of the culture we had borrowed or were hesitantly and uncertainly creating. But, if we except Boston, it was from the towns that the creators of American literary culture largely came and it was the town that they wrote of and the town that they called the real America, accepting the city grudgingly or guiltily.

Their themes were ones that we are by now familiar with: the purity and innocence of the town; the change and corruption of the town; the sense of spatial loneliness and isolation; the search for beauty and grace; the search for the father; the town for better or worse, as the symbol of America; the town against the city; the town as the haven of boyhood; the town as the lost home.

If anything were needed to persuade us of the centrality of the town in the experience of Americans our literature at the very least should do so.

X I V

Conclusion

A COMPARISON OF AMERICAN TOWNS with communities of comparable size in other societies may point up some of their unique characteristics. The village of Rampura, India, in the state of Mysore presents an exaggerated picture of class or caste stratification. The town, with a population of five or six hundred, contains nineteen Hindu castes, each with clearly marked and often impenetrable boundaries and each with its own court of law. It is worth noting of these courts that their peasant judges, like the lay judges of an earlier age in American towns, judge cases that come before them less on points of law than on "the judges' knowledge of the individuals involved and their sense of justice." [1]

[1] M. N. Srinivas: "The Social System of a Mysore Village," in McKim Marriott, ed.: *Village India, Studies in the Little Community* (Chicago: University of Chicago Press; 1955), pp. 17.19.

Conclusion

The Indian village on the other hand is more cosmopolitan than most nineteenth-century American towns because its extraordinary kinship system preserves relationships that sometimes extend, as in the case of Rani Khera, over a network of 400 villages. Yet the community, fragmented by the caste system, has little sense of general responsibility and little feeling of solidarity. Oscar Lewis, comparing Rani Khera with Tepoztlan in Mexico, found the Mexican town a far "more clearly organized and centralized community." Tepoztlan moreover had a spirit of rivalry with adjacent communities that is entirely lacking in Rani Khera. But the pressures in the Mexican town to "get ahead," and its increasing orientation toward competitive values showed in the faces of its citizens. "In Tepoztlan, outside the home, faces are generally unsmiling, unrevealing masks. In Rani Khera faces seem more secure. Children are more open-faced and laughing, old men are bland and peaceful, young men restless but unrebellious, women straight and proud. Here too there is individual reserve and formalized behavior, but it does not seem to mask so much of an undercurrent of hostility and fear as in Tepoztlán." And perhaps significantly the women of Rani Khera are bolder, stronger, gayer, and more independent than the peasant women of Tepoztlan. The Indian village pays for its sense of security and inner freedom by its rigid social system.[2]

Undoubtedly many of the anxieties and tensions of the American town are the result of the absence of clear-cut class distinctions, or at least of the fact that it is not only possible but expected that the enterprising individual will be "upwardly mobile." Tepoztlan, having chosen to move beyond the level of peasant life, suffered severely in the early stages of this new venture from feelings of uncertainty and from the anxiety produced by the transition from a primitive traditional society to a more complex and

[2] Oscar Lewis: "Peasant Culture in India and Mexico: A Comparative Analysis," in Marriott, ed.: *Village India*, pp. 161–2, 164.

self-conscious one. In America the covenanted community was always fortified by its conviction of ultimate triumph through being part of God's plan for human redemption. When this conviction weakened it was replaced by secular substitutes which, if they lacked the vitality and power of the older imperatives, nonetheless carried the community and the nation forward with a minimum of uncertainty and self-doubt.

Hsiao-t'ung Fei, in his study of a Chinese rural community, is well aware of the contrast between it and comparable American towns: "The traditional town," Hsiao-t'ung writes,

> is the seat of the gentry. The gentry class symbolizes political and financial power. The town in which I was born, and which I know very well, mainly consists of residences of the gentry, rice stores, pawnshops, tea houses, and private gardens. There are also a number of tailors, carpenters, blacksmiths, and goldsmiths and other craftsmen. . . . Tea houses, big gardens, and magnificent residences are also the paraphernalia of the gentry. From morning until nightfall, the leisured gentlemen gather in the tea houses to amuse themselves in sipping tea, in listening to the storytellers, in talking nonsense, in gambling, and in smoking opium. It would appear to a New Englander that such a town is no better than a concentration camp of voluntary deserters from life. But, to them, leisure means prestige as well as privilege." [3]

Laurence Wylie's study of the French town in the Vaucluse which he calls Peyrane offers some fascinating similarities and contrasts with American towns. Wylie discovered that the apparent changelessness of the town was an illusion, families left Peyrane and new families

[3] Hsiao-t'ung Fei: "Peasantry and Gentry: An Interpretation of Chinse Social Structure and its Changes," in Reinhardt Bendix and Seymour Lipset, eds.: *Class, Status, and Power* (Glencoe, Ill.: The Free Press; 1963).

moved in; the population was surprisingly transient. The town's air of permanence and stability was created by a relatively few vigorous and colorful individuals, who were fixtures in the community, and by the buildings themselves, whose unchanging façades suggested endurance and continuity.

Yet Peyrane had preserved the classic attitudes of a rural commune. Its citizens were deeply conservative. They viewed the government as something remote and threatening, to be propitiated, manipulated when possible, or better avoided entirely, except for the largesse it dispensed, which was gratefully received. It was in the education of the children of Peyrane that one finds perhaps the sharpest contrast with the American town. Conformity was the goal of the educational system and shame the principal means by which it was achieved. The mores of the town reflected the classic pessimism of the peasant, for whom life was full of inscrutable powers with the capacity to harm or humiliate. The best way to ameliorate the effect of such powers (since their malice could not in any event be entirely avoided) was to remain as inconspicuous as possible. Education in Peyrane had little of the openness and orientation toward mobility that characterized the American town. Education for the small-town American was an avenue of advancement; in Peyrane it was a means of protection. Another marked difference between Peyrane and its American counterparts was the low level of organizational activity (or indeed its virtual absence) in the French community. "People," Wylie notes, "say they do not want to belong to an organization because they do not want to put themselves in a position where other people will spy on them, boss them, make them the butt of gossip and ridicule, commit them to action against their will." [4]

To the citizen of Peyrane organization meant power, and power meant the oppression of the individual. The

[4] Laurence Wylie: *Village in the Vaucluse* (New York: Harper Colophon Books; 1964), p. 330.

American attitude has been startlingly different. Americans have been inclined to deny the fact of power while busily organizing in order to assert it. We are already familiar with the fever of organizational activity which characterizes the American town and which is apparently essential to the individual, placing him securely in the community, promoting his self-esteem and advancing his business and professional interests.

When Wylie returned to the town some ten years after his original study, he found that the "telé" had worked certain obvious changes. The common life of the community—the games, the festivals, the gatherings at bars for convivial glasses of wine—had been eroded by the private ritual of television-watching. On the other hand much of the characteristic pessimism of Peyrane seemed to be yielding, doubtless as a consequence at least in part of the country's prosperity, to a belief in the efficacy of common political and social action as expressed in the "tool-sharing" cooperative (the C.U.M.A.). Thus although the cooperative served primarily the needs of the "peasant workers," it showed the ability of the farmers of the commune to draw on a long tradition of "community" as opposed for example to the basic "individualism" represented by the proliferation of organizations in the American town. At the same time it must be said that the organizational activity of the American town drew its support essentially from the business and professional class, a group poorly represented in Peyrane.

Yet in Wylie's opinion the town retained much of the human drama that made it such a fascinating subject for study. The community that is the consequence of history (a community that we sometimes call "organic") is bound to be more interesting and will usually be more human than the community that is "ready made." But the ready-made community seems to be the kind that an increasingly large number of Americans are destined to live in; a community without a past and with an uncertain future. "Developments," one feels, provide an arid soil for such classic human qualities as loyalty, kindliness, and responsibility to grow in.

The "New Towns" of Great Britain suggest some of the problems inherent in the most ingenious planning of community life. Harold Orlans's study of the new town of Stevenage shows the complex problems that beset those who attempt to determine how others should live. Orlans quotes the minister of Town and Country Planning as desiring "not merely to get different classes . . . living together in a community, but to get them actually mixing together. . . . Unless they do mix, and mix freely, in their leisure and recreation, the whole purpose of . . . a mixed community disappears." And the chairman of the Stevenage Development Corporation expressed himself in a similar vein. "We want," he declared, "to revive that social structure which existed in the old English villages, where the rich lived next door to the not so rich and everyone knew everybody. . . ." The "balanced" community was to be created as a balance of classes, but what neither the minister nor the chairman understood was that generally speaking such a "balance" is the product of a historical development and cannot be reproduced at will by a planner, however well-intentioned.

It is true that in the early days of the "new towns" a rough equality existed.

> Everybody without exception went to the same meetings and functions, to the same religious meetings, political discussions, dances, social gatherings, tennis parties. . . . The first wedding, the first christening, the first funeral, the first event organized by some new society . . . were matters of at least curious interest to all. There was no established social hierarchy . . . nobody who by traditional right must be asked to be chairman or secretary of anything.

But such an idyllic state of affairs lasted only a few years and was due, as Orlans suggests, to the "pioneer environment" of the new towns. After the "pioneering" phase was over, the individuals of the town grouped themselves according to class and income.

Such planned communities have been marked by the utopian expectations of their sponsors. Human happiness was to be achieved, in the planners' view, by certain physical arrangements. They were fired by the conviction that universally valid architectural and sociological principles could be developed "for engineering the happiness and success of a neighbourhood or community." To distinguish them again from American towns, the latter were founded by people who themselves held some kind of utopian expectation, while the twentieth-century English communities have been planned by people who wished to create utopias for others. Moreover the American town builders saw utopia as being achieved through the conquest of the human heart, while the British planners have seen it as a triumph of the mind, a victory for "scientific principles." [5]

Of all the towns of the world, those of Australia have perhaps come closest to reproducing the American experience in terms of frontier settlement. A survey of country towns of Victoria by A. J. and J. J. McIntyre presents some interesting parallels and contrasts to American towns. In Australia those towns with a dramatic and historic past (especially the gold-rush towns) seem to have had the greatest capacity to survive. In addition, the towns which have "a sense of community" due to a common religion or nationality have fared better than more heterogeneous towns. Minyip, a Lutheran center in the Wimmera, has held its own better than neighboring towns because of its character as a "covenanted" community. The McIntyres's description of Saturday on Main Street in an Australain

[5] Harold Orlans: *Stevenage* (London: Routledge & Paul; 1952), pp. 82, 89, 101.

community with its common gathering places for farmers and townspeople "in the street—outside the pub, on the corner under the pepper tree, round the fountain" is reminiscent of an American small town.

One of the most marked differences between Australian and American towns lies in the area of education. Out of 180 towns investigated by the McIntyres, only 66 had state secondary schools, of which 22 were high schools and 44 "higher elementary schools." According to the authors only a small percentage of primary-school children go on for further education; out of 24,228 children attending school in Victoria at the age of thirteen only 4,157 remained in school until their sixteenth year. The McIntyres moreover found no deep-rooted tradition of education in the towns they studied. The children themselves were anxious to leave school and the researchers frequently heard from parents such comments as: "There doesn't seem much sense in them staying at school any longer. They don't learn anything that helps them get a job." As for more advanced work at the Melbourne University, it is seldom even considered and only 14 percent of the University's students come from outside the city.[6]

There are almost as many rival religious denominations in the towns of Victoria as there are in the average American community but except for such towns as Minyip, they seem to exercise little influence on the life of the community and their strength is declining. Although the same thing could be said of many American small towns in the present day, there is no evidence that religion has had a role in Australian towns comparable to that in the small communities of the United States.

In "associational activity" the Australian townspeople rival their American counterparts, and as in America much of the social life of the community is dominated by women

[6] A. J. and J. J. McIntyre: *Country Towns of Victoria* (Melbourne: Melbourne University Press in association with Oxford University Press; 1944), pp. 28, 147.

who belong to many "helping organizations" and auxiliaries as well as to the popular Radio Clubs. The men's organizations are mostly Friendly Societies, Masonic Lodges, Returned Soldiers Associations, Mechanics Institutes, and, in some instances, "gentlemen's clubs." In one town, members of the gentlemen's club also belong to the workingman's club. Such service clubs as Rotary, Carry-On, Apex, Legacy, and Toc-H are active and, as in America, their membership is confined largely to the middle-class business and professional groups in the community.[7]

The attitudes of residents of the small towns of Victoria are again similar to those of Americans toward their communities. The McIntyres often heard such comments as:

> "I'd hate to live in the city." "I know everybody here. When I walk down the street I can have a word with everyone I pass. In the city nobody knows who you are and nobody cares." "In the city you're a little fish in a big pond. Here everyone knows who you are and you know who they are."

Those dissatisfied with town life also expressed themselves in classic terms:

> "Country towns are too narrow; everybody just talks about everyone else, you don't feel your life's your own; you can't do anything but it's picked to pieces by the gossips." "All the interests here are personal. Of course the wireless is a help, but there's no one here to discuss anything with. I feel like a fish out of water." "You can't pick your friends here. You've just got to know everybody, whether you've got interests in common with them or not."[8]

The authors discovered that

> sexual promiscuity is . . . very general throughout country towns, but those who expressed indignation

about it were in a minority. These are typical comments: "There's a good deal of sexual immorality in this town, but where's the town where there isn't?" "There seems to be more here because everybody knows about everything." "Most of the marriages here are pretty hasty, but there's no social stigma attached to that." "There's a good deal of immorality here, but it's not held against people." [9]

Such attitudes have obvious parallels to the realistic sexual mores of American towns of the Puritan age before middle-class urban mores had invaded the town and brought with them prudery and hypocrisy. At the same time it should be emphasized that the "Puritan" community conditioned and controlled the sex drives of the town and through public confession and repentance used them to increase the solidarity of the community.

The country towns that the McIntyres observed were obsessed by a feeling of insecurity due in part to their dwindling population. These communities, again like many of their American counterparts, were convinced that industry was the answer to their economic plight. If only industry could be attracted to the town, it might yet be saved. But, in the authors' words, "in some towns—often those which have some industry and know its insecurity—government institutions and services are desired and worked for." [1]

The conclusions of the McIntyres are worth quoting at length:

The over-all impression which we ourselves got from this medley of kindliness, bitterness, generosity, meanness, community effort and struggling for individual gain, was of anxious and to some extent thwarted people. They are under the necessity of earning a livelihood, but they are never sure that circumstances will allow them to do so; their education and experi-

[9] Ibid., pp. 258–9.   [1] Ibid., p. 267.

ence have not shown them any alternative way a livelihood may be earned except by individual struggle, one against the other, and have indeed sanctified this to a certain extent. . . . As communities, country towns have an atmosphere of their own, quite different from that of a big city, and eminently satisfying to many people; it is essentially neighbourly; but the anxiety and frustration springing from economic insecurity and from the lack of a wide social consciousness, tend to make it also small minded and intellectually stultifying.[2]

The similarities between the towns of Australia (as far as those of Victoria may be taken to be representative) and those of the United States are striking, but they are perhaps, ultimately less significant than the differences. Moreover they demonstrate present rather than historic similarities. The Australian towns have apparently lacked the extraordinary dynamism of comparable American communities. Most Australian towns have had cumulative rather than colonized origins. The covenanted community has been a rarity; and the town has never been dominant in Australian society. Although evangelical Protestantism has been an important element in the life of the Australian community, it has not played a role equal to that of religion in the American towns, nor has education been an absolute value as it has been for most American communities. Australian towns have not bred other towns nor have they produced the aggressive, upwardly mobile individuals so conspicuous in the American story.

The superficial similarities may thus be taken to underline the unique characteristics of the American town. The Australian communities have as much and indeed perhaps more racial and religious homogeneity than the average American town. They were established under "frontier" conditions by individuals with virtually the same cultural

[2] Ibid., pp. 269, 271.

heritage as those who founded the majority of American towns. The decisive difference was perhaps in the American ethic, in the ideals of the covenant, in the dream of a city set upon a hill.

Despite the defeats that the American town has suffered, it has not lacked champions who have insisted upon its superior virtues and called for it to assume national leadership. William Allen White described the superiority of the Western community as based on the "practical acceptance of the Christian philosophy and its corollary tenets of . . . credit and . . . democracy." Moreover the West is a purer America since "populations from the ghettos of southern and central Europe are negligible in the West." Western Protestantism is "a descendant of New England Puritanism" but a purer creed, purified by Western life. "As pure Protestantism, it is founded upon a tolerant liberalism. . . ." [3]

The county-seat town of the West is, White insists, the new purified community. Typically it contains

> from 1,500 population, on the high plains east of the Rocky Mountains to 150,000 population on the rich alluvial areas of the Mississippi Valley. These western county-seat towns house their citizens more satisfactorily, give them more breathing space, provide more of the physical and spiritual blessings of life today for the average citizen than any other kind of human habitation. . . . These new thriving county trade centers of the West are the social safety valves which carry forward into the twentieth century all the energy which realized the vision of the nineteenth century pioneers. [4]

[3] William Allen White: *The Changing West: An Economic Theory About Our Golden Age* (New York: The Macmillan Company; 1939), pp. 26–7.
[4] Ibid., pp. 82–3.

This middle-class society may after all realize the utopian dream, White suggests. It is here that neighborliness and brotherly love still make themselves felt, that the Golden Rule and the precepts of the Sermon on the Mount are most often observed. The nineteenth-century struggle with the tycoons was a struggle for the survival of the democratic process. "That struggle between the over-acquisitive and the meek was in the hearts of the American people who were settling the West, building up a democratic civilization." That fight, White declared, had been won. It remained only to bring about economic justice by distributing (primarily to the farmers) the increment that has accrued to our society from its mechanization. This, sweetened with brotherly love, will mark the beginning of a new and better age. In White the hopes and the special claims of the town are once more revived.[5]

Philosopher Josiah Royce was himself a small-town boy and it is possible to read in his plans for the "Great Community" a projection of the town's best experience, an extension of the covenanted community. "Masses of lost individuals," Royce insisted,

> do not become genuine freemen merely because they all have votes. The suffrage can show the way of salvation only to those who are already loyal, who already, according to their lights, live in the spirit, and are directed not to a mere disposition to give good things to everybody, or to give all their goods to feed the poor, or to give their body to be burned, but by a genuinely Pauline charity.[6]

It is, in Royce's view, "only the consciously united community—that which is in essence a Pauline church—

---

[5] Ibid., p. 118.
[6] Josiah Royce: *The Hope of the Great Community* (New York: The Macmillan Company; 1916), pp. 49.

which can offer salvation to distracted humanity and can calm the otherwise insatiable greed and longing of the natural individual man." The salvation of the world "will be found, if at all, through uniting the already existing communities of mankind into higher communities, and not through merely freeing the peoples from their oppressors." Loyalty to the community is mankind's best hope; "the devotion of the self to the interests of the community, is indeed the form which the highest life of humanity must take. . . . Without loyalty, there is no salvation."

In Royce's words, "the 'sign' in which and by which Christianity conquered the world was the sign of an ideal community of all the faithful, which was to become the community of all mankind, and which was to become some day the possessor of all the earth, the exponent of true charity, at once the spirit and ruler of the humanity of the future." [7] This is the ideal of the covenanted community. Royce was brother to John Winthrop.

Baker Brownell is a contemporary champion of the town. For him, as in a sense for Royce, the community becomes God. Only there is salvation to be found. "Language, many customs, myth, religion, and other proud constructions are created only in and by the community of men. Spiritual values too are communal." Urban life, in contrast to that of the small community has no "abiding presentness. It is designed always to subordinate this moment to the next one. . . . It tips and staggers endlessly into postponed values that are never realized." The community, as best expressed in the small town, is "a moral and poetic necessity of life as we value it in western culture." [8]

In Brownell and in Royce we see efforts to reconstitute the community of the covenant. Royce's terms and inspiration are more traditional; Brownell's more marked by the

---

[7] Ibid., pp. 45, 36–7.
[8] Baker Brownell: *The Human Community* (New York: Harper & Brothers; 1950), pp. 201, 269.

spirit of naturalistic rationalism. Both have in their hearts a profound suspicion of the city and of its mass culture. While it is true that they participate in a controversy almost as old as civilization itself, it is equally true that they are conditioned in their thinking by the American experience.

In the same temper, Walter Burr, the son of a United Brethren minister, finds in the small community "the basic unit of all social organization." In his view we need for our salvation

the Creed of the New Christian Community. Its articles of faith attest to faith in humans, and faith in the community which is made up of humans. It presents Jesus as the great divine inspirer of men to live well in human relations in the community. . . . It believes that to the extent that you attempt to live the ideal community life with religious zeal, the social order will move step by step toward the divine pattern. The community movement is a religion. It is the Christian religion—applied.[9]

Brownell and Burr are representatives of a movement for the restoration of community life that has many supporters, most of them to be sure among academics and intellectuals, a movement that is highly idealistic, often colored by Christian idealism as well as by religious zeal, affirming as its goal the establishment of human living groups. Since it runs counter to what are apparently the main currents of American society, it may perhaps be considered atavistic or utopian. In any event it lays no claim to being "scientific."

In the area of the social sciences, however, a considerable part of the work of W. Lloyd Warner and his followers can be read as exaltation of the town robed in the trappings of science. Warner, titling his study of local

[9] Walter Burr: *Small Towns* (New York: The Macmillan Company; 1929), p. 256.

communities *American Life, Dream and Reality*, undertook to argue that the small community is "a laboratory for research on contemporary American life," and a "representative microcosm." "In my research," he says rather pompously, "the local community was made to serve as a microcosmic whole, representing the total American community."

Actually the community is not "a laboratory for research on contemporary American life," it is a laboratory for research on the community which is very far indeed from being synonymous with, or a model of, the greater community, or any large portion of it. What sociologists and anthropologists like Warner miss is the historical perspective. They take the town as a microcosm at the moment when it has been so altered that it is neither representative of the town in its historic role, nor representative of the city and its urgent problems.

Warner attacks the "theoretical system-makers" of a more primitive day. "Illustrations, well-tailored for their purpose, served for evidence, the relaxed comfort of the armchair for the rigor of field study, and philosophical and broad general theories which could not be tested often took the place of sound method." So speak the pedants of every age. Presumably Mr. Warner refers to such "theoretical system-makers" and armchair thinkers as Comte, Sumner, Weber, Durkheim, and Pareto. But the fact is that beneath his apparatus Warner himself is a sentimentalist. His values are to be sure worthy ones—democracy, the opportunity for advancement and success, the absence or the permeability of class barriers, and so on—but when he seizes upon the town as the exemplar of these values and preaches to us that the "opportunity for advancement is available for anyone who wants to try," he is no more "scientific" than Josiah Royce or Baker Brownell. He is but one more perpetuator of the myth, reaffirming the "American Dream" as "real and true" for those with the courage to reach out and grasp it. Warner's work can thus be read as a restatement of the success ethic based on the assumption that "getting ahead" is more important than, let us say, the devoted performance of a "calling." [1]

The image that the town had of itself was an image compounded of the rural version of the Protestant ethic and the Enlightenment ideal of noble yeoman. To this image both town and farm clung with extraordinary tenacity, even after their true expectations had little relation to the myth. The town's dream of the utopian community, defeated by the realities of an industrialized urban society, has found new believers among contemporary intellectuals who call on us to restore the "human community" in order to save the Republic.

What, it might be asked, are the prospects of the American small town? Certainly a process of consolidation is going on whereby many towns are being drained of population. Smaller towns are losing out to county and regional centers—towns that have grown into small cities. Moreover the great metropolitan centers continue to attract large numbers of individuals from small towns. In North Dakota Eric Sevareid found that among the towns he had known in his youth, those favored by industry and business had grown rapidly while neighboring communities withered away or their residents commuted to the nearest city.

On one thing there seems to be general agreement among those who have commented on the present state of the small town. Life in the town is far more pleasant and comfortable than it was a generation or more ago. In Clyde Brion Davis's words, "the internal combustion engine has manumitted the Missouri farmer and consequently brought prosperity to hundreds of communities such as Chillicothe." Davis is certain that "with this prosperity has come wider perspectives, a lessening of provincialism, a sounder sense of fundamental values, better physical and mental

[1] W. Lloyd Warner: *American Life, Dream and Reality* (Chicago: University of Chicago Press; 1953), pp. 31–2, 21.

health, more pleasant living conditions, and, in short, an advancement of culture." [2]

In much the same spirit Sherwood Anderson wrote:

> If some of the color has gone, the towns tending to be more and more of one pattern, the terror that was also part of that intensity, the super-imposing of moral standards often almost viciously, the bullying of the young by the old, the Puritan fear of play, of any expression of joy in life has also, at least partially, been wiped out.[3]

One resident of Main Street argues that today it is

> no different in its outward aspects from the "main stem" of the Big Town except in size. The people do largely the same things the country over. They hear the same programs on the radio, they see the same movies, they read the same news as their city cousins. All that is left of the old time Main Street is its heart and soul, its camaraderie, its community of spirit. . . . Life contains more for the citizen of Main Street and his fellows than it ever contained before. We are more kindly, more tolerant, wiser . . .[4]

The point here that needs emphasizing is the fact that the towns have been drawn into the national community and made a part of it. In the process they have lost many of their traditional characteristics. In some towns, as Granville Hicks observed, "the old controls have disintegrated, and no new controls, whether operating from within the individual or imposed from outside, have been developed." [5]

[2] Clyde Brion Davis: *Age of Indiscretion* (Philadelphia: J. B. Lippincott; 1950), p. 93.

[3] Sherwood Anderson: *Home Town* (New York: Alliance Book Corporation; 1940), p. 142.

[4] Edwin P. Chase: "Forty Years on Main Street," *Iowa Journal of History*, XXXIV (July, 1936), pp. 231, 260.

[5] Granville Hicks: *Small Town* (New York: The Macmillan Company; 1946), p. 125.

The "new controls" are, increasingly, developed outside the community by the vast industry whose business it is to produce in their laboratories synthetic values that are presented as "entertainment" and as "education," and that are in truth as ephemeral as the daily paper. The town has surrendered its version of the ethic to the package deal promoted by the urban hucksters. People in the towns are today better informed, but more formless. They are thus, like the city-dweller, threatened by the "new collectivity," which in its gentle tyranny eats at the old individuality of the community. The town can, like the individual, yield to the ethic of "adjustment"—indeed all that is required is that most of the people of the town succumb to the new ethic and become members of the national collectivity, which, as Martin Buber writes, "is not a warm, friendly gathering, but a great link-up of economic and political forces . . . understandable only in terms of quantity. . . ." [6]

The towns of America have constituted what C. Wright Mills calls "publics," true communities as opposed to the hives of mass urban society. "The growth of the metropolis," Mills writes,

> segregating men and women into narrowed routines and environments causes them to lose any sense of their unity as a public. The members of publics in smaller communities know each other more or less fully, because they meet in the several aspects of the total life routine. The members of masses in a metropolitan society know one another only as fractions in a specialized milieu. . . . Prejudgment and stereotype flourish when people meet in such ways. The human reality of others does not, cannot, come through. [7]

Two things threaten the small community as a "public." First, as has been mentioned, there is a process of consoli-

[6] Will Herberg, ed.: *Writings* (New York: Meridian Books; 1956), p. 130.
[7] C. Wright Mills: *The Power Elite* (New York: Oxford University Press; 1956), p. 320.

dation at work drawing smaller communities into larger ones. Second, as community isolation breaks down and class stratification grows, members of the community begin to conceive of themselves as part of nationwide groups—members of associations of teachers, businessmen, hairdressers, etc.—and loyalty to these vague but powerful national bodies replaces loyalty to the community.

The town is thus losing, if it has not already lost, its psychological, economic, and even its geographical isolation. It is becoming an adjunct of the city instead of remaining a coherent "public." If it is true as history suggests that the preservation of the sense of a viable and open future is dependent upon the preservation of such "publics," communities in which human encounters dominate the encounters of people with "things," or of people with fictionalized personalities, or with individuals abstracted into a single function in a large collective society, the destruction of the town has serious implications for the future of our country. Buber has said that "a nation is a community to the degree that it is a community of communities." Certainly the great society of America has been built up of various societies, societies in which men lived and worked, competed with one another and helped one another; "and in each of the big and little societies composing it, in each of these communities, the individual human being, despite all difficulties and conflicts, felt himself at home as once he felt in the clan, felt himself approved and affirmed in his functional independence and responsibility." [8]

There is at this moment a deep yearning for the community experience of the town and a revulsion against life in the metropolis. The town will not be saved however by the exurbanites who indeed pose new perils for it. Faced with the invasion of the exurbanites, the members of local society can "withdraw and try to debunk the immoral

[8] Herberg, ed.: *Writings,* pp. 130, 125.

ways of the newcomers, or they can attempt to join them, in which case they will come to focus their social ways of life upon the metropolitan area." [9] Whichever course they choose, "they will come to know, often with bitterness, that the new upper class as well as the local upper-middle class, among whom they once cashed in their claims for status, are watching them with close attention and sometimes with amusement." [1] Moreover the townspeople come into the exurbanite sub-society, if they elect to do so, not on their own terms but on the almost inevitably patronizing terms of the urban émigrés, who accept them because of their ability to be almost like urbanites, or conversely because they seem like, in contradistinction to other city refugees, "real people." Both attitudes are equally condescending and, for the small-town resident, equally corrosive.

In many such communities "the natives" become hardly more than retainers in the satrapy of the business tycoons who have chosen to live among them and anoint them with their largesse. But the town does not question; it is grateful to be at last caught up, however humbly, in the complex network of national power, to feel the impulses of that enormous current flowing through it. The town therefore is not apt ever again to create values for the larger society as it has in the past. The town will not be reconstituted by liberal planners, by devoted advocates of "community living," or through establishment of industrial communities by big business. It is also difficult to have much faith in the values created by the manipulators of our mass media. Honest values can only grow out of the shared experience of true communities.

As the towns have absorbed the vague generalized humanitarian mass values of our urban culture, they have produced a smaller proportion of creative individuals. Eric Sevareid has spoken eloquently of the towns as "seedbeds,

[9] Burr: *Small Towns*, p. 256.
[1] Mills: *The Power Elite*, p. 41.

ceaselessly renewing themselves, their seeds constantly renewing the nation." [2] And so they have been, but it is very doubtful if they will be again. If the town accepts its role in the larger collectivity which is the nation, it will doubtless continue to send its young men and women to the cities, but these young people are not likely to come charged with the sense of purpose, the desire for service, the sure confidence that would make them as enterprising and creative as their predecessors.

Yet the city needs the renewal given it by the acquisition of inner-directed youth, for the city is perhaps powerless to create its own values. It may have its fashions and fads and indeed its style, but it is too inchoate for it ever to be said of the city with much confidence that it stands for this or that; that it specifically honors integrity, skill, industry, or that it regards highly the self-effacing wisdom and human warmth that at best have counted for much in the life of the town. The most that we can say for the city is that it is tolerant, and we can seldom say that.[3]

[2] Eric Sevareid: "You Can Go Home Again," *Collier's* (May 11, 1956), p. 67.

[3] In connection with the problem of community it is perhaps worth noting that during the University of California student demonstrations which took place in the fall of 1964, one of the principal complaints of the Free Speech Movement leaders was that there was no contact between students and professors at Berkeley and they wrote glowingly of their movement as having created "a community of love."

The fact is that in the absence of "organic" communities we get the classic problem of "alienation." Individuals so alienated express their despair and frustration in many ways—delinquent behavior, alcoholism, and drug addiction are among the more familiar responses. In recent years we have seen the development of several types of "pseudo-communities," groups of individuals who share some critical problem of social adjustment or personal malaise. The first and best known of these is Alcoholics Anonymous. While AA is very largely middle class, it is a kind of covenanted group whose therapy is based on the sense of solidarity its members feel as part

The small town is symbol and image as well as reality. So deeply do its roots reach into the American experience,

---

of a community of suffering and tribulation. Public confession and exculpation is a central part of its group ritual.

A newer and much smaller pseudo-community is Synanon, a group of drug addicts founded by a former AA who have banded together to kick the habit with apparently remarkable success. The group purports to take its name from its synanons, or group therapy sessions, characterized by ruthless mutual criticism reminiscent of utopian communities. One of the most interesting aspects of Synanon is the fact that it encourages the participation of outsiders in its synanons and lively social gatherings. The warmth and intimacy of its communal living clearly have great attraction for many deracinated middle-class intellectuals in Los Angeles and other cities where it has established "houses."

Synanon has a strong measure of utopianism in addition to (or as a complement of) its primary task of drug rehabilitation. The members take great pride in its interracial character. While they scrupulously avoid blaming society for their addiction and insist that personal weakness is the essential cause, they nonetheless believe their group to be free of the hypocrisy, self-seeking, and false values which disfigure the society "outside."

It may be that in a mass society, the creation of pseudo-communities of various kinds is the best hope for protecting the individual against the demoralizing effects of alienation. Yet it is difficult to see how enough such communities can be formed to seriously affect the sense of anomie that characterizes our culture. Pseudo-communities need a bond of common suffering to tie them together. The well-fed acedia of our society is poor material out of which to fashion communities of any kind.

The Civil Rights movement has, of course, created a very important but hopefully transitory kind of pseudo-community. In it, however, as in the Berkeley demonstrations which were its offspring, one is aware of the danger that mass action, involving as it does an exhilarating sense of human solidarity, may become an end in itself. It is easy to become an inebriate of such activity and to find in it an end rather than the explosive, if sometimes necessary, means to achieve particular social and political reforms. It is certainly clear that pseudo-communities are more problematical and unstable than the type of community experience represented by the American small town.

Conclusion

so entwined are they with the fabric of our national life, that they are not to be readily disentangled, traced, and labeled. The covenanted community was a unique form of social organization. Able to reproduce itself without loss of inner unity, it showed a remarkable capacity to preserve traditional forms and values in the face of socially disruptive conditions. Its core was the congregation of saints bound by the covenant, and when the covenant fragmented, the core became a congeries of Protestant congregations.

The builders of the town were obsessed by the dream of "the good community" where greed, factionalism, poverty, and inequality were to be banished. Their values were oriented toward the community rather than toward the individual. The dreams failed of fulfillment and there was much bitterness in that failure. Making it more bitter was the fact that the town from having been the microcosm, the measure, of the larger society, the asserter of its values and the shaper of its ideals, came to lust after city ways and manners, after the city's success. The city's version of the Protestant ethic at last came to be universally accepted, and was, as a final irony, attributed to the small town.

It is not the time to try to say with final authority what the town has meant in American life. Its meanings are profound and various. But of its importance there can be no question.

Bibliography

I. Town and County Histories

Andreas, A. T.: *History of Cook County*. Chicago: A. T. Andreas; 1884.

Ball, T. H.: *Lake County, Indiana, 1834 to 1872*. Chicago: J. W. Goodspeed; 1873.

Barber, Edward W.: "The Vermontville Colony: Its Genesis and History," *Michigan Pioneer and Historical Collections*, XXVIII (1900), pp. 197–8, 237, 244–5, 248–50, 254, 256, 258.

Beckwith, H. W.: *History of Vigo and Parke Counties*. Chicago: H. H. Hill and N. Iddings; 1880.

Bell, Charles Henry: *History of the Town of Exeter, New Hampshire*. Exeter, N.H.; 1888.

"A Bibliography of Town and County Histories of Kansas," *Kansas Historical Quarterly* (autumn, 1955).

Bingham, H. M.: *History of Green County*. Milwaukee; 1877.

Bisbee, J. H.: *History of the Town of Huntington*. Springfield, Mass.: C. W. Bryan and Company, Printers; 1876.

Bogart, Earnest L.: *Peacham, The Story of a Vermont Hill Town*. Montpelier, Vt.: Vermont Historical Society; 1948.

Boies, H. L.: *History of De Kalb County*. Chicago: O. P. Bassett; 1868.

Bowen, C. W.: *Woodstock*. New York and London: G. P. Putnam's Sons; 1886.

Brown, Warren: *History of the Town of Hampton Falls, New Hampshire*. Concord, N.H.: Rumford Printing Company; 1900–18.

Bushnell, Henry: *History of Granville, Licking County, Ohio*. Columbus, Ohio: Press of Hann and Adair; 1889.

Bushnell, Horace: *Litchfield County, Connecticut*. Hartford, Conn.: E. Hunt; 1851.

Butterfield, C. W.: *History of Racine and Kenosha Counties*. Chicago; 1879.

Caulkins, F. M.: *History of Norwich*. Hartford, Conn.: published by the author; 1866.

Caverly. A. M.: *History of . . . Pittsford, Vermont*. Rutland, Vt.: Tuttle and Company, Printers; 1872.

Chafee, Zechariah, Jr., ed.: *Records of the Suffolk County Court, 1671–1680*, Part 1 (Colonial Society of Massachusetts Collections), XXVII, XXIX, XXX.

Church, Charles A.: *History of Rockford, Illinois, and Winnebago County*. Rockford, Ill.: W. P. Lamb; 1900.

Copeland, Alfred: *A History of the Town of Murraysfield*. Springfield, Ill.: C. W. Bryan and Company, Printers; 1892.

Crowder, Etta May: "Pioneer Life in Palo Alto County," *Iowa Journal of History and Politics*, XLVI (April, 1948), pp. 156–98.

Dana, H. S.: *History of Woodstock*. Boston: Houghton Mifflin Company; 1889.

Davis, George: *A Historical Sketch of Sturbridge and Southbridge*. West Brookfield, Mass.: Press of O. S. Cook and Company; 1856.

Durant, S. W.: *History of Ingham and Eaton Counties*. Philadelphia: D. W. Ensign and Company; 1880.

Emerson, William A.: *History of the Town of Douglas, Massachusetts*. Boston: F. W. Bird; 1879.

Bibliography

Fairchild, James H.: *Oberlin, the Colony and the College, 1833–1883*. Oberlin, Ohio: E. J. Goodrich; 1883.

Farmer, Silas: *History of Detroit and Michigan*. Detroit: S. Farmer and Company; 1884.

Ford, Andrew E.: *History of the Origin of the Town of Clinton, Massachusetts, 1653–1865*. Clinton, Mass.: Press of W. J. Coulter, Courant Office; 1896.

Fowler, W. C.: *History of Durham, Connecticut*. Hartford, Conn.: Press of Wiley, Waterman and Eaton; 1866.

Goodwin, H. C.: *Pioneer History; or Cortland County*. New York: A. B. Burdick; 1859.

Goodykoontz, Colin B., and Willard, James F., eds.: *Union Colony at Greeley*. Boulder, Colo.: University of Colorado; 1918.

Gould, Jay: *The History of Delaware County*. Roxbury, N.Y.: Keeny and Gould; 1856.

Green, Constance M.: *Holyoke, Massachusetts, A Case History in the Industrial Revolution in America*. New Haven, Conn.: Yale University Press; 1939.

Green, Mason: *Springfield, 1636–1886*. Springfield, Mass.: C. A. Nichols and Company; 1888.

Gridley, A. D.: *History of Kirkland, New York*. New York: Hurd and Houghton; 1874.

Hair, James T.: *Gazetteer of Madison County*. Alton, Ill.; 1866.

Hatfield, E. F.: *History of Elizabeth*. New York: Carlton and Lanahan; 1868.

Helm, T. B.: *History of Cass County, Indiana*. Chicago: Kingman Brothers; 1878.

Heywood, William S.: *History of Westminister, Massachusetts, 1728–1893*. Lowell, Mass.: S. W. Huse and Company; 1893.

Hibbard, Benjamin H.: *History of Agriculture in Dana County, Wisconsin*. Wisconsin University Bulletin 101, Economic and Political Science series I, no. 2.

Howell, George R.: *Early History of Southampton, Long Island*. New York: J. N. Hallock; 1866.

Hyde, Ezra: *History of the Town Winchendon, 1735 to Present*. Worcester, Mass.: printed by H. J Howland; 1849.

Jones, Pomroy: *Annals and Recollections of Oneida County*. Rome, N.Y.: published by the author; 1851.

Lamson, Darius F.: *History of the Town of Manchester, Essex County, Massachusetts, 1645–1895.* Published by the town of Manchester, 1895.

Lang, William: *The History of Seneca County.* Springfield, Ohio: Transcript Printing Company; 1880.

Larned, Ellen D.: *History of Windham County, Connecticut.* Worcester: published by the author, printed by C. Hamilton; 1874.

Lucas, Henry S.: "A Document Relating to the Founding of Zeeland, Michigan, in 1847," *Michigan History Magazine,* XII (1928).

McIntyre, A. J. and J. J.: *Country Towns of Victoria.* Melbourne: Melbourne University Press, in association with Oxford University Press; 1944.

McKeen, Silas: *History of Bradford.* Montpelier, Vt.: J. D. Clark and Son; 1875. Northrop, N. B.: *Pioneer History of Medina County.* Medina, Ohio: O. G. Redway, Printer; 1861.

Nourse, Henry S.: *History of Harvard, Massachusetts.* Harvard, Mass.: W. Hapgood; 1894.

Orcutt, Samuel: *History of Tarrington, Connecticut.* Albany, N.Y.: J. Munsell, Printer; 1878.

Orlans, Harold: *Stevenage.* London: Routledge & Paul; 1952.

Paige, L. R.: *History of Hartwich, Massachusetts.* Boston and New York: Houghton Mifflin Company; 1883.

Perrin, W. H., ed.: *History of Alexander, Union and Pulaski Counties.* Chicago: O. L. Baskin and Company; 1883.

————: *History of Cass County.* Chicago: O. L. Baskin and Company; 1882.

Pettibone, John: "History of Manchester," *Proceedings of the Vermont Historical Society* (December, 1930), p. 156.

Phelps, Noah Amherst: *History of Simsbury, Granby, and Canton.* Hartford, Conn.: Press of Case, Tiffany and Burnham; 1845.

Pierce, Frederick C.: *History of Grafton, Massachusetts, From its Early Settlement.* Worcester, Mass.: Press of C. Hamilton; 1879.

Poor, William G.: *Upton, Massachusetts.* Milford, Mass.; 1935.

Records of Charles County, Maryland, Archives of Maryland.

Reed, Jonas: *A History of Rutland, Massachusetts; With a Biography of its First Settlers.* Worcester, Mass.: Mirick and Bartlett printers: 1836.

Bibliography

Richmond, C. W. and Valletti, H. F.: *History of DuPage County*. Chicago: Steam Presses of Scripps, Bross and Spears; 1857.

Sedgwick, Sarah C.: *Stockbridge, 1739–1939, A Chronicle*. Great Barrington, Mass.: printed by the Berkshire Courier; 1939.

Sheldon, George: *A History of Deerfield, Massachusetts*, 2 vols. Greenfield, Mass.: Press of E. A. Hall and Company; 1895–96.

Steiner, B. C.: *A History of the Plantation of Menunkatuck and of the Original Town of Guilford, Connecticut*. Baltimore: published by the author; 1897.

Stiles, H. R.: *History and Genealogies of Ancient Windsor, Connecticut*. Windsor, Conn.; 1891.

Swan, Henry Dana: *History of Woodstock, Vermont*. New York; 1886.

Temple, J. H.: *History of North Brookfield, Massachusetts*. Boston; 1887.

———: *History of the Town of Palmer, Massachusetts*. Palmer, Mass.; 1889.

Town Records of Dudley, Massachusetts, 2 vols. Pawtucket, R.I.; 1894.

Trumbull, J. R.: *History of Northampton, Massachusetts*, 2 vols. Northampton, Mass.: Press of Gazette Printing Company; 1898–1902.

Tucker, William Howard: *History of Hartford, Vermont*. Burlington, Vt.: Free Press Association; 1889.

Weimer, Arthur: "Determining Factors in the Economic Development of Alma," *Michigan History Magazine* (autumn, 1955), pp. 1405–10.

———: "Economic History of Alma Since 1900," *Michigan History Magazine*, XIX (winter, 1935), p. 289.

———: "Outline of the Economic History of Alma, Michigan Prior to 1900," *Michigan History Magazine*, XIX (winter, 1935), pp. 129–38.

Wells, Daniel White: *History of Hatfield, Massachusetts*. Springfield, Mass.; 1910.

Whitaker, Epher: *History of Southold, Long Island*. Southold, L.I.; printed for the author; 1881.

Willard, F. C.: *A Classical Town; The Story of Evanston*. Chicago: Woman's Temperance Publishing Association; 1892.

Wilson, Warren: *Quaker Hill in the Nineteenth Century.* New York: published by the Quaker Hill Conference Association; 1907.

Wright, H. B.: *Historical Sketches of Plymouth.* Philadelphia: T. B. Peterson and Brothers; 1873.

Young, A. W.: *History of Wayne County, Indiana.* Cincinnati: R. Clarke and Company, Printers; 1872.

II. General Accounts

Adams, Charles Francis: *Three Episodes of Massachusetts History*, 3 vols. Boston and New York: Houghton; 1892.

———: "Some Phases of Sexual Morality and Church Discipline in Colonial Massachusetts," *Proceedings* of the Massachusetts Historical Society, Series II, VI, pp. 477–516.

Adams, Phillo: *Diaries of Two Journeys.* Chicago: Chicago Historical Society; n.d.

Akagi, Roy: *The Town Proprietors of the New England Colonies.* Philadelphia: Press of the University of Pennsylvania; 1924.

Allen, Nathan: *Changes in New England Population.* Lowell, Mass.; 1877.

"Analyst Lubell Picks Ike as Winner in California," Los Angeles *Mirror News*, October 15, 1956.

Anderson, Sherwood: *Home Town.* New York: Alliance Book Corporation; 1940.

———: *Marching Men.* New York: B. W. Huebsch, Inc.; 1921.

———: *Poor White.* New York: Modern Library, 1926.

———: *A Story Teller's Story.* New York: B. W. Huebsch; 1924.

———: *Tar; A Midwest Childhood.* New York: Boni and Liveright; 1924.

———: *Windy McPherson's Son.* New York: B. W. Huebsch; 1922.

Andreas, A. T.: *A History of the State of Nebraska*, 2 vols. Chicago; 1882.

Atherton, Lewis: *Main Street on the Middle Border.* Bloomington, Ind.: Indiana University Press; 1954.

Baier, Elsi: "How a Small Town Educates Its Youth," *Survey*, LIV (April 15, 1925), pp. 90–2.

Bibliography

Baltzell, E. Digby: " 'Who's Who in America' and 'The Social
    Register,' Elite and Upper Class Indexes in Metropolitan
    America," in Reinhardt Bendix and Seymour Lipset, eds.:
    Class, Status and Power. Glencoe, Ill.: The Free Press;
    1953.
Barber, John Warner: *Historical Collections of Massachusetts*.
    Worcester, Mass.: Door, Howland and Company; 1839
    and 1844.
Barnes, Gilbert H.: *The Anti-slavery Impulse, 1830–1844*.
    New York and London: D. Appleton-Century Company,
    Inc.; 1933.
Barns, Cass G.: *The Sod House*. Lincoln, Neb.: Cass G. Barns;
    1930.
Beals, Alan: *A Village in Gopalpur*. New York: Holt, Rine-
    hart and Winston; n.d.
Beardsley, Frank B.: *A History of American Revivals*. New
    York: American Tract Society; 1904.
Becker, Carl: *The Heavenly City of the Eighteenth Century
    Philosophers*. New Haven, Conn.: Yale University Press;
    1948.
Belknap Papers, *Massachusetts Historical Society*, III, 440.
Bestor, Alfred: *Backwoods Utopias*. Philadelphia: University
    of Pennsylvania Press; 1950.
Bidwell, P. W.: *Rural Economy in New England at the
    Beginning of the 19th Century*. New Haven, Conn.; 1916.
Biesele, Rudolph Leopold: *The History of German Settle-
    ments in Texas, 1831–1861*. Austin, Tex.: von Boeckmann-
    Jones Press; 1930.
Birkbeck, Morris: *Notes on a Journey in America*. London:
    printed by Severn & Redington, for Ridgway & Sons;
    1818.
Blackmar, F. W.: "Social Degeneration in Towns and Rural
    Districts." *Proceedings* of the National Conference of
    Charities and Correction, XXVII (1900).
Blanchard, Rufus: *History of Illinois*. Chicago: National
    School Furnishing Company; 1883.
Blegen, Theodore C.: "The Competition of the Northwestern
    States for Immigrants," *Wisconsin Magazine of History*,
    III (1919), pp. 3–29.
Bloch, Marc L. B.: *The Historian's Craft*, Peter Putnam, trans.
    New York: Alfred A. Knopf; 1953.

Blumenthal, Albert: *A Sociological Study of a Small Town.* Chicago: University of Chicago Press; 1932.

Bode, Carl: *The American Lyceum, Town Meeting of the Mind.* New York: Oxford University Press; 1956.

Boisen, Anton T.: *Religion in Crisis and Custom.* New York: Harper & Brothers; 1955.

Boynton, Percy: *Literature and American Life.* Boston and New York: Ginn and Company; 1936.

Bradley, Glenn Danford: *The Story of the Santa Fe.* Boston: R. G. Badger; 1920.

Bridenbaugh, Carl: "The New England Town: A Way of Living," American Antiquarian Society *Proceedings,* LVI (April, 1946), p. 33.

Briggs, Harold E.: "The Great Dakota Boom, 1879–1886," *North Dakota Historical Quarterly,* IV (January, 1930), pp. 78–108.

Bristol, Sherlock: *The Pioneer Preacher.* Chicago and New York: Fleming Revell Company; 1887.

Brooks, Van Wyck: *The Ordeal of Mark Twain.* New York: E. P. Dutton & Company; 1933.

Brown, Alice. *Children of Earth: A Play of New England.* New York: The Macmillan Company; 1915.

———: *Meadow Grass.* Boston and New York: Houghton Mifflin Company; 1895.

———: *Tiverton Tales.* Boston and New York: Houghton Mifflin Company; c. 1899.

Brown, Leonard: *Iowa, The Promised of the Prophets.* Des Moines, Iowa: Central Printing and Publishing Company; 1884.

Brown, Norman O.: *Life Against Death.* New York: Vintage Books; 1961.

Brownell, Baker: *The Human Community.* New York: Harper & Brothers; 1950.

Buckingham, Clyde E.: "Early Settlers of the Rock River Valley," *Journal of the Illinois State Historical Society,* XXXV (September, 1942), pp. 241–2.

Buckingham, Joseph T.: *Specimens of Newspaper Literature with Personal Memoirs, Anecdotes* . . . , 2 vols. Boston: C. C. Little and J. Brown; 1850.

Burlend, Rebecca: *A True Picture of Emigration,* Milo M. Quaife, ed. Chicago: R. R. Donnelley & Sons; 1936.

Burr, Walter: *Small Towns*. New York: The Macmillan Company; 1929.

Bury, J. B.: *The Idea of Progress*. New York: Dover Publications; 1955.

Calkins, Earnest E.: *They Broke the Prairie*. New York: Charles Scribner's Sons; 1937.

Callahan, Ellen H.: *A Study of the Political Development of a Typical New England Town from the Official Records, 1659–1930*. Northampton: Smith College Studies in History, XVI, nos. 1 and 2 (October, 1930, and January, 1931).

Calverton, V. F.: *Where Angels Dared to Tread*. Indianapolis and New York: The Bobbs-Merrill Company; 1941.

Capers, Gerald M., Jr.: *The Biography of a River Town*. Chapel Hill, N.C.: University of North Carolina Press; 1939.

Caplow, Theodore: *The Sociology of Work*. Minneapolis, Minn.: University of Minnesota Press; 1954.

Cather, Willa: *My Ántonia*. Boston and New York: Houghton Mifflin Company; 1926.

———:*O Pioneers!* Boston and New York: Houghton Mifflin Company; 1913.

———: *Youth and the Bright Medusa*. New York: Alfred A. Knopf; 1923.

Chase, Edwin P.: "Forty Years on Main Street," *Iowa Journal of History*, XXXIV (July, 1936), pp. 227–61.

Chase, Mary Ellen: *Jonathan Fisher, Maine Parson, 1768–1847*. New York: The Macmillan Company; 1948.

Chickering, Jesse: *Statistical View of the Population of Massachusetts from 1715 to 1840*. Boston: C. C. Little and J. Brown; 1846.

Clark, G. F.: *History of the Temperance Reformation in Massachusetts*. Boston: Clarke and Carruth; 1888.

Clarke, E. L.: *American Men of Letters*, LXXII. New York: Columbia University Studies; 1916, pp. 74–6.

Clement, Ernest W.: "Jesse Clement: A Yankee Westernized," *Iowa Journal of History*, XXXVIII (July, 1940), p. 280.

Codd, Mathew: *Diary of a Journey in America*. Buffalo, N.Y.: Buffalo Historical Society; n.d.

Coffin, Levi: *Reminiscences of Levi Coffin*. Cincinnati: Western Tract Society; 1876.

Coffman, L. D.: *The Social Composition of the Teaching Population*. New York: Columbia University Teachers College; 1911.

Comfort, Alexander: *Sexual Behavior in Society*. London: Gerald Duckworth & Co., Ltd.; 1950.

Cook, James H.: *Fifty Years on the Old Frontier*. New Haven, Conn.: Yale University Press; 1923.

Cooke, Rose Terry: *Root-bound and Other Sketches*. Boston: Congregational Sunday-school and Publishing Society; 1885.

————: *Somebody's Neighbors*. Boston and New York: Houghton Mifflin Company; 1892.

————: *The Sphinx's Children and Other People*. Boston: Ticknor and Company; 1886.

Corey, Paul: *County Seat*. Indianapolis and New York: The Bobbs-Merrill Company; 1941.

Cruikshank, C. W.: "Denmark Academy As I Knew It," *Iowa Journal of History*, XXXVIII (April, 1940), pp. 183, 189–90.

Davies, John D.: *Phrenology, Fad and Science*. New Haven, Conn.: Yale University Press; 1955.

Davis, Clyde Brion: *Age of Indiscretion*. Philadelphia: J. B. Lippincott Company; 1950.

Day, Clive Hart: "Capitalistic and Socialistic Tendencies in the Puritan Colonies," *Annual Report of American Historical Association . . . 1920*. Washington; 1925, pp. 225–35.

Debo, Angie: *Prairie City*. New York: Alfred A. Knopf; 1944.

Dell, Floyd: *The Briary-Bush*. New York: Alfred A. Knopf; 1921.

Deming, Dorothy: *The Settlement of the Connecticut Towns*. New Haven, Conn.: Published for the Tercentenary Commission by Yale University Press; 1933.

Destler, Chester McArthur: "Western Radicalism, 1865–1901: Concepts and Origins," *Mississippi Valley Historical Review*, XXXI (December, 1944), pp. 335–68.

de Tocqueville, Alexis: *Democracy in America*. London: Saunders & Otley; 1835.

De Voto, Bernard: *Mark Twain's America*. Boston: Little, Brown & Company; 1932.

Dexter, Franklin: *Sketch of Yale University*. New York: Henry Holt & Company; 1887.

Doane, A. A.: *The Doane Family*. Boston: A. A. Doane; 1902.

Dondore, Dorothy Anne: *The Prairie and the Making of Middle America: Four Centuries of Description*. Cedar Rapids, Mich.: The Torch Press; 1926.

Dwight, Timothy: *Sermons*. New Haven, Conn.: H. Howe; 1828.

———: *Travels in New England*, 2 vols. New Haven, Conn.: 1821–2.

East, Robert A.: "Puritanism and New England Settlement," *New England Quarterly*, XVII (June, 1944), pp. 255–7, 263.

Eggleston, Edward: *The Circuit Rider*. New York: Charles Scribner's Sons; 1891.

Egle, William H.: *An Illustrated History of the Commonwealth of Pennsylvania*. Harrisburg, Penn.: De W. C. Goodrich and Company; 1876.

Engstrand, Sophia Belzer: *Miss Munday*. New York: The Dial Press; 1940.

Erikson, Erik: *Childhood and Society*. New York: W. W. Norton; 1950.

Estabrook, A. H.: "The Merrills: An Aristogenic Family," *Eugenica*, I, no. 3 (December, 1928).

Farnham, Eliza W.: *Life in Prairie Land*. New York: Harper & Brothers; 1846.

Farnsworth, Benjamin Stow: *Diary 1820–1840*. Detroit: Burton Historical Collection, Detroit Public Library.

Fei, Hsiao-t'ung: "Peasantry and Gentry: An Interpretation of Chinese Social Structure and Its Changes," in R. Bendix and S. Lipset, eds.: *Class, Status and Power*. Glencoe, Ill.: The Free Press; 1963.

Fiedler, Leslie: *An End to Innocence*. Boston: Beacon Press; 1955, p. 142.

Finley, James Bradley: *Autobiography of Reverend James Bradley Finley, or Pioneer Life in the West*, W. P. Strickland, ed. Cincinnati; 1858.

Fisher, Dorothy Canfield: *The Squirrel Cage*. New York: Henry Holt & Company; 1912.

Fisher, Hugh D.: *The Gun and the Gospel*. Chicago: Kenwood Press; 1896.

Fitch, Asa: *Diary*. Manuscript in Yale University Library, New Haven, Conn.

Fletcher, Henry J.: "The Doom of the Small Town," *The Forum*, XIX (April, 1895), pp. 214–23.

Flint, Timothy: *Geography and History of the Western States*, 2 vols. Cincinnati: E. H. Flint; 1828.

Folsom, W. H. C.: *Fifty Years in the Northwest*. St. Paul, Minn.: Pioneer Press Company; 1888.

Ford, Thomas: *A History of Illinois*. New York: Iverson & Phinney; 1854.

Fowler, Orson S.: *Religion, Natural and Revealed*. New York: O. S. Fowler; 1844.

Frank, Waldo: *Rediscovery of America*. New York: Charles Scribner's Sons; 1929.

Franklin, Benjamin: *Works*, 8 vols. London: printed for G. G. J. and J. Robinson; 1793.

Frenay, A. D: *The Suicide Problem in the U.S.; Mortality Statistics*. Boston: R. G. Badger; 1927.

Friedel, Earnestine: *A Village in Modern Greece*. New York: Holt, Rinehart and Winston; 1962.

Fuller, G. N.: *Economic and Social Beginnings of Michigan*. Lansing, Mich.: Wynkoop Hallenback Crawford Company, State Printers; 1916.

Gale, Zona: *Friendship Village Love Stories*. New York: The Macmillan Company; 1909.

————: *Miss Lulu Betts*. New York and London: D. Appleton and Company; 1920.

Galer, Roger B.: "Recollections of Busy Years," *Iowa Journal of History and Politics*, XLII (January, 1944).

Garland, Hamlin: *Afternoon Neighbors*. New York: The Macmillan Company; 1934.

————: *Back Trailers from the Middle Border*. New York: The Macmillan Company; 1928.

————: *Boy Life on the Prairie*. New York and London: Harper & Brothers; 1923.

————: *A Daughter of the Middle Border*. New York: The Macmillan Company; 1922.

————: *Main-Travelled Roads*. New York: The Macmillan Company; 1899.

————: *A Son of the Middle Border*. New York: The Macmillan Company; 1928.

Gates, Paul Wallace: *Illinois Central Railroad and its Colonization Work*. Cambridge, Mass.: Harvard University Press; 1934.

Goodykoontz, Colin B., and Willard, James F., eds.: *Experi-*

ments in Colorado Colonization, *1869–1872*. Boulder, Colo.: University of Colorado; 1926.

———: *Union Colony at Greeley*. Boulder, Colo.: University of Colorado; 1918.

Gregg, Dorothy: "John Stevens, General Entrepreneur, 1749–1830," in William Miller, ed.: *Men in Business*. Cambridge, Mass.: Harvard University Press; 1952.

Gregory, Francis W., and Neu, Irene D.: "Industrial Elite in 1870's," in William Miller, ed.: *Men in Business*. Cambridge, Mass.: Harvard University Press; 1952.

Grey, Lewis Cecil and Lloyd, O. G.: "Farm Land Values in Iowa," *U.S. Department of Agriculture Bulletin No. 874*.

Griswold, A. Whitney: "Three Puritans on Prosperity," *New England Quarterly*, VII (September, 1934), pp. 478–9, 483.

Hadfield, Joseph: *An Englishman in America, 1785*, Douglas S. Robertson, ed. Toronto: The Hunter-Rose Company, Ltd.; 1933.

Hall, B. H.: *History of Eastern Vermont*. New York: D. Appleton and Company; 1858.

Handlin, Oscar: "Laissez-faire Thought in Massachusetts, 1790–1880," *Journal of Economic History*, III (December, 1943).

Hansen, Marcus L.: "Remarks," in Dixon Ryan Fox, ed.: *Sources of Culture in the Middle West*. New York and London: D. Appleton-Century Company, Inc.; 1934.

Hart, Hornell N.: *Selective Migration* Vol. i, No. 7. Iowa City, Iowa: The University of Iowa; 1921, p. 56.

Hartz, Louis: "Laissez-faire Thought in Pennsylvania, 1776–1860," *Journal of Economic History*, III (December, 1943).

Hedges, James B.: "The Colonization Work of the Northern Pacific Railroad," *Mississippi Valley Historical Review*, XIII (December, 1926), p. 321.

Heinrich, Frederick K.: "The Development of American Laissez-faire in the Age of Washington," *Journal of Economic History*, III (December, 1943).

Herberg, Will, ed.: *The Writings of Martin Buber*. New York: Meridian Books; 1956.

Hicks, Granville: *The Great Tradition*. New York: The Macmillan Company; 1935.

Hicks, Granville: *Small Town.* New York: The Macmillan Company; 1946.

Hildreth, S. P.: *Pioneer Settlers of the Ohio.* Cincinnati: H. W. Derby and Company; 1852.

Hinds, William Alfred: *American Communities and Co-operative Colonies.* Chicago: C. H. Kerr & Company; 1908.

Hofstadter, Richard: *The Age of Reform.* New York: Alfred A. Knopf; 1955.

Holliday, F. C.: *Indiana Methodism.* Cincinnati: Hitchcock and Walden; 1873.

Hollingshead, August: *Elmtown's Youth.* New York: John Wiley & Sons; 1949.

――――: "Selected Characteristics of Classes in a Middle Western Community," in William Miller, ed.: *Class, Status and Power.* Cambridge, Mass.: Harvard University Press; 1952.

Holmes, Fred L.: *Side Road Excursions into Wisconsin's Past.* Madison: State Historical Society of Wisconsin; 1949.

Holmes, J. H.: Tape-recorded interview.

Holmes, Roy H.: "A Study in the Origins of Distinguished Living Americans," *American Journal of Sociology,* XXXIV (January, 1929), pp. 670–86.

Hopkins, Samuel Miles: *Autobiography,* unpublished manuscript. Rochester Historical Society.

Howard, G. E.: *History of Matrimonial Institutions.* Chicago: University of Chicago Press, Callaghan and Company; 1904.

Howe, Edgar Watson: *Palin People.* New York: Dodd, Mead & Company; 1929.

――――: *Story of a Country Town.* Boston and New York: Houghton Mifflin Company; 1927.

Howe, Henry: *Historical Collections of Ohio.* Cincinnati: Derby, Bradley & Company; 1848.

Howells, William Dean: "A Boy's Town," in Henry Steele Commager, ed.: *Selected Writings of William Dean Howells.* New York: Random House; 1950.

――――: *Rise of Silas Lapham.* Boston and New York: Houghton Mifflin Company; 1912.

Hudson, Winthrop S.: "Puritanism and the Spirit of Capitalism," *Church History,* XVIII (March, 1949), p. 9.

Hughes, Thomas: *Journal,* E. A. Bentani, ed. Cambridge, England: Cambridge University Press; 1947.

Bibliography

Huntington, Ellsworth: *The Pulse of Progress*. New York and London: Charles Scribner's Sons; 1926.

Jefferson, Thomas: *Notes on the State of Virginia*. Chapel Hill, N.C.: University of North Carolina Press; 1954.

Jeffrey, W. H.: *Successful Vermonters*. East Burke, Vt. The Historical Publishing Company; 1904.

Jewett, Sarah Orne: *Deephaven*. Boston and New York: Houghton Mifflin Company; 1905.

Johnston, Paul H.: "Old Ideals Versus New Ideas in Farm Life." *U.S. Department of Agriculture Yearbook*. Washington, D.C.; 1940, pp. 18–19, 156–7.

Jones, A. D.: *Illinois and the West*. Boston: Weeks, Jordan and Company; Philadelphia: W. Marshall and Company; 1838.

Kardiner, Abram, ed.: *Psychological Frontiers of Society*. New York: Columbia University Press; 1945.

Kinneman, John A.: *The Community in American Society*. New York: Appleton-Century-Crofts; 1947.

Knapp, R. H. and Goodrich, H. B.: *Origins of American Scientists*. Chicago: University of Chicago Press; 1952.

Kolb, John H. and Brunner, Edmund de S.: *A Study of Rural Sociology*. Boston and New York: Houghton Mifflin Company; 1940.

Kollmorgen, Walter Martin: *Culture of a Contemporary Rural Community*. Washington, D.C.: U.S. Department of Agriculture; 1942.

Kramer, Dale: "What Price a Factory," *Survey Graphic*, XXIX (August, 1940), p. 441.

Krout, John Allen: *The Origins of Prohibition*. New York: Alfred A. Knopf; 1925.

Kutak, Robert Ingersoll: *Story of a Bohemian-American Village*. Louisville, Ky.: Standard Printing Company; 1933.

Laird, Charles Kendall: *Autobiography, 1813–1859*. Indiana Historical Society, unpublished manuscript.

Lamb, Robert K.: "The Entrepreneur and the Community," in William Miller, ed.: *Men in Business*. Cambridge, Mass.: Harvard University Press; 1952.

Lane, Rose Wilder: *Old Home Town*. New York and Toronto: Longmans, Green & Company; 1935.

Lawrence, D. H.: *Studies in Classic American Literature*. London: M. Secker; 1933.

Laylander, O. J.: *The Chronicles of a Contented Man.* Chicago: A. Kroch; 1920.

Lewis, Grace Heiddeger: *With Love from Gracie; Sinclair Lewis: 1912–1925.* New York: Harcourt, Brace & Company; 1955.

Lewis, Oscar: "Peasant Culture in India and Mexico: A Comparative Analysis," in McKim Merriott, ed.: *Village India.* Chicago: University of Chicago Press; 1955.

Lewis, Sinclair: *Babbitt.* New York: Harcourt, Brace & Company; 1922.

————: *Main Street.* New York: Harcourt, Brace & Company; 1921.

————: *Work of Art.* Garden City, N.Y.: Doubleday, Doran and Company, Inc.; 1935.

————: *World So Wide.* New York: Random House; 1951.

Lindsay, Vachel: *Collected Poems.* New York: The Macmillan Company; 1925.

Lockridge, Ross: *Raintree County.* Boston: Houghton Mifflin Company; 1948.

Lockwood, George B.: *The New Harmony Movement.* New York: D. Appleton and Company; 1905.

Ludlum, David M.: *Social Ferment in Vermont, 1791–1850.* New York: Columbia University Press; 1939.

Lynd, Robert Staughton, and Lynd, Helen Merrell: *Middletown.* New York: Harcourt, Brace & Company; 1929.

————: *Middletown in Transition.* New York: Harcourt, Brace & Company; 1937.

Lynn, Kenneth: *The Dream of Success.* Boston: Little, Brown & Company; 1955.

McClure, Russel S.: "The Natural Gas Era in Northwestern Ohio," *Quarterly Bulletin of the Historical Society of Northwestern Ohio,* XIV (1942).

McGuffey's Fourth Reader, Eclectic Series. Cincinnati and New York: Van Antwerp, Bragg and Company; 1879.

McLaren, Gay: *Morally We Roll Along.* Boston: Little, Brown & Company; 1938.

Makal, Mahmut: *A Village in Anatolia.* London: Vallentine, Mitchell; 1954.

Manning, William: *The Key of Libberty.* Billerica, Mass.: The Manning Association; 1922.

Marden, Orison S.: *Pushing to the Front.* New York: Thomas Y. Crowell Company; 1894.

Bibliography

Marquis, Don: *Sons of the Puritans*. New York: Doubleday, Doran and Company; 1939.

Masters, Edgar Lee: *Domesday Book*. New York: The Macmillan Company; 1920.

————: *Mitch Miller*. New York: The Macmillan Company; 1920.

————: *Spoon River Anthology*. New York: The Macmillan Company; 1915.

Mather, Cotton: *Diary*. Massachusetts Historical Society *Collections*, LXVII, Part 1.

Mathews, Lois Kimball: *The Expansion of New England, The Spread of New England Settlement and Institutions to the Mississippi River, 1620–1865*. Boston: Houghton Mifflin Company; 1909.

————: "Migrations from Connecticut after 1800." *Tercentenary Commission of the State of Connecticut*, LIV. New Haven, Conn.: Yale University Press; 1936.

Mathews, William: *Getting On in the World*. Chicago: S. C. Griggs & Company; 1873.

Maurer, Heinrich H.: "Studies in the Sociology of Religion," *American Journal of Sociology*, XXX (November, 1924), p. 276.

Maxwell, William: *Time Will Darken It*. New York: Harper & Brothers; 1948.

Men Who Have Risen, Book for Boys. Anonymous New York: Miller; 1859.

Miller, Arthur: "The Family in Modern Drama," *Atlantic Monthly* (April, 1956), pp. 35–41.

Miller, Elva: *Town and Country*. Chapel Hill, N.C.: University of North Carolina Press; 1928.

Miller, Perry E. G.: *Errand Into the Wilderness*. Cambridge, Mass.: Harvard University Press; 1956.

————, and Johnson, Thomas H.: *The Puritans*. New York and Cincinnati: American Book Company; 1938.

Miller, William: "American Historians and the Business Elite," *Journal of Economic History*, IX, no. 2 (November, 1949).

————: *Essays in the History of Entrepreneurship*. Cambridge, Mass.: Harvard University Press; 1952.

————, ed.: *Men in Business*. Cambridge, Mass.: Harvard University Press; 1952.

Mills, C. Wright: "The American Business Elite: A Collective

Portrait," in "The Tasks of Economic History," *Journal of Economic History*, Supplement V (December, 1945), p. 44.

———: *The Power Elite*. New York: Oxford University Press; 1956.

———: *The Sociological Imagination*. New York: Oxford University Press; 1959.

Mitchell, Edwin V.: *American Village*. New York: Stackpole Sons; 1938.

Mitchell, Mary H.: "The Great Awakening and Other Revivals in the Religious Life of Connecticut," *Tercentenary Commission of the State of Connecticut*, pamphlet no. 26. New Haven, Conn.: Yale University Press; 1934.

Morris, Richard B.: "Labor and Mercantilism," in Richard B. Morris, ed.: *Era of the American Revolution*. New York: Columbia University Press; 1939.

———: "Price-fixing in Colonial America," in *Era of the American Revolution*.

Mosier, Richard D.: *Making the American Mind*. New York: King's Crown Press; 1947.

Mott, David C.: "Abandoned Towns, Villages and Post Offices of Iowa," *Annals of Iowa*, XVII (October, 1930), pp. 434–65; (January, 1931), pp. 513–43; (April, 1931), pp. 578–99; XVIII (July, 1931), pp. 42–69; (January, 1932), pp. 189–220.

Munger, Theodore: *On the Threshold*. Boston: Houghton Mifflin Company; 1885.

Murray, Orson S.: *Vermont Telegraph* (June 2, 1836), quoted by D. M. Ludlam in *Social Ferment in Vermont, 1791–1850*. New York: Columbia University Press; 1939.

Nelson, Lowry: "The Mormon Village: A Study in Society Origins," *Proceedings* of the Utah Academy of Sciences, VII (1930).

Newcomber, Mabel: "The Chief Executives of Large Business Corporations," *Explorations in Entrepreneurial History*, V. Cambridge, Mass.: Harvard University Press; 1952.

Niebuhr, Richard: *The Social Sources of Denominationalism*. New York: Henry Holt and Company; 1929.

Nordhoff, Charles: *The Communistic Societies of the United States*. New York: Harper & Brothers; 1875.

Bibliography

Norton, J. M.: "Early Schools and Pioneer Life," *Michigan Pioneer and Historical Collections*, XXVIII (1900).

Oberholtzer, Emil, Jr.: *Delinquent Saints*. New York: Columbia University Press; 1956.

Pareto, Vilfredo: *Mind and Society*, 4 vols. New York: Harcourt, Brace & Company; 1935.

Parker, Joel: "The Origin, Organization and Influence of the Towns of New England," Massachusetts Historical Society *Proceedings*, IX (first series: 1866–7).

Parker, Robert A.: *A Yankee Saint: John Humphrey Noyes*. New York: G. P. Putnam's Sons; 1935.

Parsons, Herbert C.: *A Puritan Outpost*. New York: The Macmillan Company; 1937.

Parsons, Talcott: "A Revised Analytical Approach to the Theory of Social Stratifications," in R. Bendix and S. Lipset, eds.: *Class, Status and Power*. Glencoe, Ill.: The Free Press; 1953.

Patten, Mathew: *Diary of Mathew Patten, 1754 to 1788*. Concord, N.H.: Rumford Printing Company; 1903.

Patton, Julia. *The English Village*. New York: The Macmillan Company; 1919.

Pease, Theodore Calvin: *The Frontier State, 1818–1848*. Springfield, Ill.: Illinois Centennial Commission; 1918.

Peck, J. M.: *Gazetteer of Illinois*. Jacksonville, Ill.: R. Goudy; 1834.

———: Papers, unpublished material. Shurtleff College Library, Upper Alton, Ill.

Pomeroy, Earl: "Towards a Reorientation of Western History." *Mississippi Valley Historical Review*, XLI (March, 1955), pp. 593, 597.

Pooley, William V.: "The Settlement of Illinois from 1830 to 1850, *Bulletin* of the University of Wisconsin, no. 220 (1908).

Pope, Liston: "Religion and the Class Structure," in R. Bendix and S. Lipset, eds.: *Class, Status and Power*. Glencoe, Ill.: The Free Press; 1953.

Porter, Jeremiah: *Journals*, 18 booklets, Chicago Historical Society.

Porter, Noah: *New England Meeting House*. New Haven, Conn.: published for the Tercentenary Commission by the Yale University Press; 1933.

Poston, Richard W.: *Small Town Renaissance*. New York: Harper & Brothers; 1950.

Potter, David M.: *People of Plenty*. Chicago: University of Chicago Press; 1954.

Quick, Herbert: *One Man's Life*. Indianapolis, Ind.: The Bobbs-Merrill Company; 1925.

Redfield, Robert: *The Little Community*. Chicago: University of Chicago Press; 1955.

Richardson, Anna S.: "The Call of the Old Home Town," *The Forum*, CXI (March, 1934).

Roberts, George S.: *Historic Towns of the Connecticut River Valley*. Schenectady, N.Y.: Robson and Adee; 1906.

Roche, John: "We've Never Had More Freedom," *The New Republic* (January 23, 1956), p. 12.

Rosenberry, Lois Kimball Mathews: "Migrations from Connecticut after 1800," *Tercentary Commission of the State of Connecticut*, LIV. New Haven, Conn.: Yale University Press; 1936.

Rossiter, Clinton: *Conservatism in America*. New York: Alfred A. Knopf; 1955 (2nd edition, 1962).

Royce, Josiah: *The Hope of the Great Community*. New York: The Macmillan Company; 1916.

Sandoz, Mari: *Old Jules*. Boston: Little, Brown & Company; 1935.

Sawyer, John E.: "Social Structure and Economic Progress: The European Inheritance," *American Economic Review Proceedings*, XLI (May, 1951).

Schorer, Mark: *Sinclair Lewis*. New York: McGraw-Hill Book Company; 1961.

Sevareid, Eric: "You Can Go Home Again," *Collier's* (May 11, 1956), pp. 58, 61–4, 67.

Severance, Henry O.: "The Folk of Our Town," *Michigan History Magazine*, XII (January, 1928), p. 62.

Shambaugh, Berta Maud: *Amana That Was and Amana That Is*. Iowa City, Iowa: State Historical Society of Iowa; 1932.

Shaw, Albert: *Local Government in Illinois*. Baltimore, Md.: Johns Hopkins University; 1883.

Shipton, Clifford K.: "The New England Clergy of the 'Glacial Age,'" *Publications* of the Colonial Society of Massachusetts, XXXII.

Sims, Newell L.: *A Hoosier Village*. New York: Columbia University Press; 1912.

Sinclair, Harold: *American Years*. New York: Doubleday, Doran and Company, Inc.; 1938.

Smith, Mapheus: "University Student Intelligence and Occupation of Father," *American Sociological Review*, VII (December, 1942).

Smith, T. Lynn: *The Sociology of Rural Life*. New York and London: Harper & Brothers; 1940.

Snyder, Margaret: *The Chosen Valley: The Study of a Pioneer Town*. New York: W. W. Norton; 1948.

Sorokin, Pitrim, and Zimmerman, Carle: *Principles of Rural-Urban Sociology*. New York: Henry Holt and Company; 1929.

Spillman, W. J.: "Country Boy," *Science*, XXX (September 24, 1909), pp. 405–7.

Srinivas, M. N.: "The Social System of a Mysoke Village," in McKim Marriott, ed.: *Village India, Studies in the Little Community*. Chicago: University of Chicago Press; 1955.

Stearns, Alfred E.: *An Amherst Boyhood*. Amherst, Mass.: Amherst College; 1946.

Stein, Maurice: *The Eclipse of Community*. New York: (Harper Torchbooks) Harper & Row; 1964.

Stephenson, George M.: *The Religious Aspects of Swedish Immigration*. Minneapolis, Minn.: University of Minnesota Press; 1932.

Stevens, J. Harold: "The Influence of New England in Michigan," *Michigan Historical Magazine*, XIX (autumn, 1935), pp. 321–53.

Stilwell, Lewis D.: *Migration from Vermont*. Montpelier, Vt.: Vermont Historical Society; 1948.

Stong, Philip D.: *State Fair*. New York: The Century Press; 1932.

Stow, Horace: *Diary*, in Indiana Historical Society.

Stowe, Harriet Beecher: *Oldtown Folks*. Boston: Fields, Osgood & Co.; 1869.

Suckow, Ruth: *The Folks*. New York: Farrar and Rinehart, Inc.; 1934.

Sweet, Olney: "An Iowa County Seat," *Iowa Journal of History*, XXXVIII (October, 1940), pp. 339–408.

Tarkington, Booth: *The Gentleman from Indiana.* New York: Doubleday and McClure Company; 1899.

Taussig, F. W., and Joslyn, C. S.: *American Business Leaders: A Study in Social Origins and Social Stratification.* New York: The Macmillan Company; 1932.

Taylor, Walter F.: *Economic Novel in America.* Chapel Hill, N.C.: University of North Carolina Press; 1942.

Terman, Lewis M.: *Genetic Studies of Genius.* Palo Alto, Calif.: Stanford University Press; 1926.

Thorndike, Edward L., and others: *Prediction of Vocational Success.* New York: The Commonwealth Fund; 1934.

Thrasher, Max B.: "A New England Emigration," *New England Magazine,* XVI (May, 1897).

Turner, Frederick Jackson: *The Frontier in American History.* New York: Henry Holt & Company; 1958.

Twain, Mark: *Autobiography,* 2 vols. New York: Harper & Brothers; 1924.

———: *The Man That Corrupted Hadleyburg.* New York: Harper & Brothers; 1900.

Tyler, Alice: *Freedom's Ferment.* Minneapolis. Minn.: University of Minnesota Press; 1927.

Usher, E. B.: "Puritan Influence in Wisconsin," *Proceedings of the Wisconsin Historical Society* (1898).

Vaile, Roland S.: *The Small City and Town.* Minneapolis, Minn.: University of Minnesota Press; 1930.

Van Der Zee, trans.: "An Eminent Foreigner's Visit to the Dutch Colonies of Iowa in 1873," *Iowa Journal of History and Politics,* XI (April, 1913).

Veblen, Thorstein: "The Country Town," *Freeman,* VII (July 11, 18, 1923), pp. 417–20, 440–3.

Visher, Stephen S.: *American Men of Science.* Baltimore, Md.: Johns Hopkins Press; 1947.

———: *Indiana Scientists.* Indianapolis, Ind.: Indiana Academy of Science; 1951.

———: "A Study of the Type of the Place and Birth and of the Occupation of Fathers of Subjects of Sketches in 'Who's Who in America,'" *American Journal of Sociology,* XXX (March 25, 1925), pp. 551–7.

Vold, George B.: "Crime in City and County Areas," *Annals of the American Academy of Political and Social Science,* CCXVII (September, 1941).

Walker, D. C.: "Evolution of Religion, Morals and Legislation in this Country During the Past Century." *Michigan Pioneer and Historical Collections*, XXVIII (1900), pp. 460–1.

Warner, W. Lloyd: *American Life, Dream and Reality*. Chicago: University of Chicago Press; 1953.

———, and James C. Abegglen: *Big Business Leaders in America*. New York: Harper & Brothers; 1955.

———: *Occupational Mobility in American Business and Industry, 1928–1952*. Minneapolis, Minn.: University of Minnesota Press; 1955.

Warren, Charles: *A History of the American Bar*. Boston: Little, Brown & Company; 1911.

Watkins, Albert: *Outline of Nebraska History*. Lincoln, Neb.: Nebraska State Historical Society; 1910.

Wells, Charles W.: *A Frontier Life*. Cincinnati: Press of Jennings and Pye; 1902.

West, James: "Plainville, U.S.A.," in Abram Kardiner, ed.: *Psychological Frontiers of Society*, New York: Columbia University Press; 1945.

Wescott, Glenway: *Good-bye Wisconsin*. New York and London: Harper & Brothers; 1928.

Wheeler, J. H.: *Historical Sketches of North Carolina; 1584 to 1851*. Philadelphia: Lippincott, Grambo and Company; 1851.

White, William Allen: *The Autobiography of William Allen White*. New York: The Macmillan Company; 1946.

———: *The Changing West: An Economic Theory About Our Golden Age*. New York: The Macmillan Company; 1939.

———: *Forty Years on Main Street*. New York and Toronto: Farrar and Rinehart, Inc.; 1937.

———: "It Is All Over," editorial in the *Emporia Gazette* (November 3, 1896), reprinted in *Forty Years on Main Street*.

———: "What's the Matter with Kansas," *Emporia Gazette* (August 15, 1896), reprinted in *Forty Years on Main Street*.

———: *In the Heart of a Fool*. New York: The Macmillan Company; 1919.

Wilder, Thornton: *Our Town*. New York: Coward McCann, Inc.; 1938.

Wilkinson, Asbury: *Diary*, in Indiana Historical Society.

Williams, James M.: *An American Town*. New York: The J. Kempster Printing Company; 1906.

Wilson, Harold: "Population Trends in North-Western New England, 1790–1930," *New England Quarterly*, VII (June, 1934).

Wohl, Richard: "Henry Day," in William Miller, ed.: *Men in Business*. Cambridge, Mass.: Harvard University Press; 1952.

Wolfe, Thomas: *Of Time and the River*. New York: Charles Scribner's Sons; 1935.

———: *Look Homeward, Angel*. New York: Modern Library edition.

———: *The Web and the Rock*. New York: Harper & Brothers; 1939.

———: *You Can't Go Home Again*. New York: Harper & Brothers; 1941.

Wood, L. S.: "The Town in Literature; A Bibliography of Town and County Histories of Kansas," *Kansas Historical Quarterly* (autumn, 1955).

Woods, Frederick A.: "Birthplaces of Leading Americans; The Question of Heredity," *Science*, vol. 30, pp. 17–21.

———: "City Boys Versus Country Boys," *Science*, XXIX (1909), pp. 577–9.

Woolen, W. W.: *Biographical and Historical Sketches of Early Indiana*. Indianapolis; 1883.

Working-Man's Gazette (September 23, 1830).

Wright, Louis B.: *Culture on a Moving Frontier*. Bloomington, Ind.: University of Indiana; 1955.

Wright, Luella M.: "The Cedar Falls Parlor Reading Circle," *Iowa Journal of History and Politics*, XXXIV (October, 1936), pp. 343–4, 352, 369.

———: "Culture Through Lectures," *Iowa Journal of History and Politics*, XXXVIII (April, 1940), pp. 118, 123.

Wylie, Laurence: *Village in the Vaucluse*. New York: (Harper Colophon Books) Harper & Row; 1964.

Wyllie, Irwin G.: *The Self-Made Man in America, The Myth of Rags to Riches*. New Brunswick, N.J.: Rutgers University Press; 1954.

Zimmerman, Carle C.: *The Changing Community*. New York and London: Harper & Brothers; 1938.

Index

Index

Index

Index

Index

Index

[*xvii*]